When Everyone Knows
That Everyone Knows . . .

By the Same Author

When Everyone Knows
That Everyone Knows . . .

Common Knowledge and the Science of
Harmony, Hypocrisy and Outrage

STEVEN PINKER

ALLEN LANE
an imprint of
PENGUIN BOOKS

ALLEN LANE

UK | USA | Canada | Ireland | Australia
India | New Zealand | South Africa

Allen Lane is part of the Penguin Random House group of companies
whose addresses can be found at global.penguinrandomhouse.com.

Penguin Random House UK
One Embassy Gardens, 8 Viaduct Gardens, London SW11 7BW

penguin.co.uk

Penguin
Random House
UK

First published in the United States of America by Scribner,
an imprint of Simon & Schuster, LLC 2025
First published in Great Britain by Allen Lane 2025

001

Printed and bound in India by Replika Press Pvt. Ltd.

The authorized representative in the EEA is Penguin Random House Ireland,
Morrison Chambers, 32 Nassau Street, Dublin D02 YH68

A CIP catalogue record for this book is available from the British Library

Hardback ISBN: 978-0-241-61882-0
Trade Paperback ISBN: 978-0-241-61883-7

Penguin Random House is committed to a sustainable future
for our business, our readers and our planet. This book is made from
Forest Stewardship Council® certified paper.

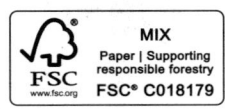

MIX
Paper | Supporting
responsible forestry
FSC
www.fsc.org
FSC® C018179

TO MY STUDENTS

CONTENTS

PREFACE

As a cognitive scientist, I have spent my life thinking about how people think. So the ultimate subject of my fascination would have to be how people think about what other people think, and how they think about what other people think they think, and how they think about what other people think they think they think. As dizzying as this cogitation may seem, we engage in it every day, at least tacitly, and in the limit this state of awareness has a technical name, *common knowledge.*

Originating in game theory and philosophy, the theory of common knowledge can illuminate a vast range of puzzles about human social life. I first came across it through my interest in language when writing *The Stuff of Thought.* I had long wondered why people often don't say what they mean in so many words but veil their intentions in innuendo and doublespeak, counting on their listeners to read between the lines. The answer, I suggested, was that barefaced statements generate common knowledge but genteel euphemisms do not, and common knowledge is what ratifies or annuls social relationships.

In this book I'll expand on that theory and show how common knowledge also explains fundamental features of societal organization, such as political power and financial markets; some of the design specs of human nature, such as laughter and tears; and countless curiosities of private and public life, such as bubbles and crashes, road rage, anonymous donations, long goodbyes, revolutions that come out of nowhere, social media shaming mobs, and academic cancel culture. By the time you finish the book I hope you'll be equipped to understand phenomena I never got around to explaining, such as gaslighting, Kardashian celebrity (being famous for being famous), mock outrage ("I'm shocked, shocked to find that gambling is going on in here"), "red lines" in international relations, and the psychological difference between "cc" and "bcc" in email etiquette.

This oceanic scope, I hope to convince you, is not a sign of explanatory megalomania. Common knowledge really is that powerful a concept. It is the mental feat that explains one of the hallmarks of the human condition: individual minds can coordinate their choices for mutual benefit, allowing our species to thrive in collectives ranging from couples to societies. Many of our harmonies and discords, I hope to show, fall out of our struggles to achieve, sustain, or prevent common knowledge.

This is the second of my popular books to feature my own research, and as with *Word and Rules* I dedicate it to the graduate and post-doctoral students who collaborated with me on the studies. Every professor knows that the best part of the job is learning from students, and while pursuing this research I was fortunate to have learned from Julian De Freitas, Peter DeScioli, Omar Sultan Haque, Moshe Hoffman, Yuhui Huang, James Lee, Miriam Lindner, Maxim Massenkoff, Jason Nemirow, Laura Niemi, Lawrence Ian Reed, Kyle Thomas, and Dylan Tweed. Special thanks to Peter DeScioli for his sharp and deep comments on the first draft.

Several people provided patient guidance in their areas of expertise:

Scott Aaronson, Robert John Aumann, Herbert Clark, Peter DeScioli, Rebecca Goldstein, Dacher Keltner, Eric Maskin, Dov Samet, and Jeannie Suk Gersen. Others commented on drafts of chapters: Charleen Adams, Cory Clark, Tyler Cowen, Alan Fiske, Komi Frey, Robin Hanson, Moshe Hoffman, Greg Lukianoff, Michael Macy, Jason Nemirow, Bruce Schneier, Dan Sznycer, and Jessica Tracy. Still others answered questions or offered suggestions: Paul Bloom, Yi-Chia Chen, Eve Clark, Jeffry Frieden, Bill Gates, Andrew Gelman, Joshua Goldstein, Marc Hauser, Coleman Hughes, Jillian Jordan, Peter Kinderman, Gary King, Sarah Kious, Louis Liebenberg, Lucy Matthew, Dani Passow, Dan Schacter, Fred Shapiro, Richard Shweder, Lawrence Summers, Philip Tetlock, Jeffrey Watumull, David Wolpe, and Hirschy Zarchi. Bob Woods provided skilled assistance with bibliographic and research materials. Ilavenil Subbiah designed the elegant graphics. I thank all of them.

I am grateful to my editor at Scribner, Rick Horgan, for his encouragement and guidance, and to my friend and literary agent John Brockman. Special appreciation goes to Katya Rice for copyediting the manuscript, our tenth collaboration over forty years.

Three of the dedicatees of my previous books died as I wrote this one. This is my first trade book not to have been read in draft by my mother and primary imagined reader, Roslyn Wiesenfeld Pinker. Gone too are my dear friends and intellectual inspirations John Tooby and Donald Symons. They all left a stamp on the book in their examples, ideas, and voices. Also deeply missed are two other influences, Daniel Dennett and Daniel Kahneman.

My greatest intellectual inspiration is also my life partner, and I thank Rebecca Newberger Goldstein for continually showing me what matters, intellectually and personally. It's a pleasure to acknowledge the rest of my loving family: Yael, Solly, Danielle, Kai, Susan, Martin, Eva, Carl, Eric, Rob, Kris, Jack, and David.

1

The Emperor, the Elephant, and the Matzo Ball

What common knowledge is, and why it matters

When the little boy said the emperor was naked, he wasn't telling anyone anything they didn't already know. But he added to their knowledge nonetheless. By blurting out what every onlooker could see within earshot of the others, he ensured that they now knew that everyone *else* knew what they knew, that everyone knew that everyone knew that, and so on. And that changed their relationship to the emperor, from obsequious deference to ridicule and scorn.[1]

Hans Christian Andersen's immortal story draws on a momentous logical distinction. With *private knowledge*, person A knows something, and person B knows it. With *common knowledge*, A knows something, and B knows it, but in addition, A *knows* that B knows it, and B knows that A knows it. On top of that, A knows that B knows that A knows it, and B knows that A knows that B knows it, and so on, ad infinitum.[2]

"The Emperor's New Clothes" dramatizes two features of common knowledge that make it not just a mind-blowing logical concept but a key to understanding human social life. One is that common knowledge need not be deduced from an infinite chain of musings about other people's mental states ("I know that you know that I know that you know . . ."), which no mortal could ever think. It can be instantly imparted by a conspicuous event, like a plain sentence uttered in public. The other is that the difference between private knowledge, even when widely shared, and common knowledge is not a mere logical nicety but can unify knowers in coordinated action and sometimes explode a social status quo.

To help distinguish the different kinds of knowledge, let's visualize them in little cartoons that depict knowing as seeing. The first is a picture of private knowledge. Each observer sees something, but neither sees the other seeing it:

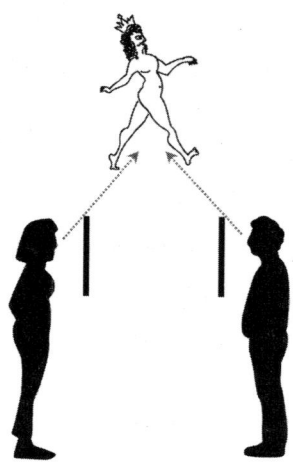

Next we have a state we will call reciprocal knowledge, in which each observer sees the event and sees the other seeing it. But because each espies the other through the anonymity of a keyhole, their awareness falls short of common knowledge; neither one knows that they have been seen seeing it:

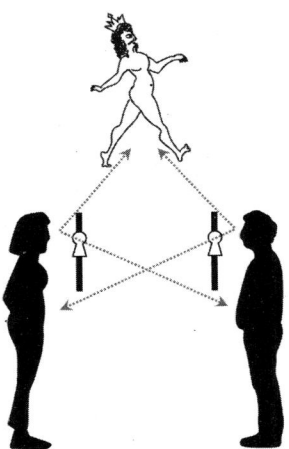

The last cartoon shows common knowledge. Each sees the other seeing the event, and sees the other seeing them seeing it, from which they can infer that each can see as many seeings of seeings as they care to ponder:

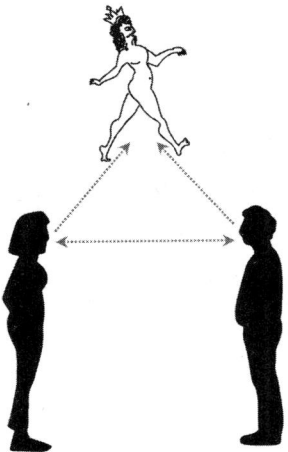

What is going on in the observers' minds when they are in a situation that provides common knowledge? It needn't be a hall of mirrors with "He knows that she knows that he knows that she knows . . . ":

Our heads start to spin with just two layers of thoughts within thoughts, and common knowledge requires an infinite number of them, which can't fit inside a finite skull. Most likely it's the simple intuition that the event is "public" or "out there" or "there for all to see":

My goal in this book is to explain the obscure but momentous research on common knowledge, together with some ideas of my own, and show how the concept illuminates many enigmas of our public affairs and personal lives. The scholars I know who have worked on the concept—mathematicians, economists, philosophers, linguists, computer scientists—agree that it is a keystone in understanding the social world. But they have struggled to spread the news to a wide readership, and they often wonder how human minds handle what seems like an impossibly abstruse state of knowing. This book, written from the vantage point of psychology and cognitive science, aims to bridge these gaps.[3]

Here are the main ideas. First, common knowledge (in the technical sense) is logically different from private knowledge: learning about something in public, even if everyone already knows it, can change everything. Second, the main thing that common knowledge changes is the ability to *coordinate*: two or more people with common knowledge can benefit each other with complementary choices that they would have no confidence making with private knowledge. Third, because common knowledge is so potent, humans are intuitively sensitive to it, almost as if we had a sense organ for this logical concept. Fourth, this awareness is what has empowered our species to coordinate our behavior in social networks like communities, economies, and nations. For this reason, many peculiarities of public life—its mindless rituals, conventions, and norms—become intelligible as solutions to coordination problems. So do some of the pathologies of public life, including fads, mobs, panics, bubbles, and spirals of silence. Fifth, personal relationships—our bonds with family, friends, lovers, authorities, subordinates, neighbors, colleagues, and transactional partners—are also coordination games, and they, too, must be cemented by common knowledge. Sixth, because all of these coordination equilibria come with perquisites and obligations, we often find ways to work around them by *preventing* ourselves from knowing what everyone knows, giving rise to rituals of benign hypocrisy, pretending not to know, catching someone's drift, and not going there. In other words, many of our tensions, personal and political, arise from the desire to propagate or suppress common knowledge.

⚶

Because common knowledge is the book's touchstone, I must begin with a word about the term itself, which I will be using in a different sense from its everyday meaning. In ordinary English, the expression *common knowledge* refers to something that many or most people know, especially open secrets, as in "It's common knowledge that the police around here can be bribed." This is almost the opposite of the meaning of the technical term from game theory and philosophy that we will explore in this book. Just as confusingly, *common knowledge* in the technical sense does not correspond to the literal meaning of its words, namely "knowledge that people have in common," since that could pertain to identical private knowledge, where everyone knows the same thing without necessarily knowing that the others know it.

A more transparent term would be *mutual knowledge,* with its implication of people deliberately mirroring or pooling their knowledge. Linguists sometime use that term when referring to the common knowledge between a pair of conversational partners, and that's what I called it in *The Stuff of Thought.*[4] But in most of the technical literature mutual knowledge has drifted into a different meaning, either widespread private knowledge (like the first diagram) or layers of reciprocal knowledge (like the second).[5] Other terms for common knowledge include *open knowledge, conspicuous knowledge, public knowledge, interactive knowledge, shared reality, shared awareness, collective consciousness*, and *common ground*. But the term *common knowledge*, however misleading, has become entrenched among the experts, and that's the one I will stick with.

Happily, this concession provides an opportunity to introduce the power of common knowledge in human affairs, starting with language itself. When it comes to established vocabulary, logic and grammar are beside the point. No one cares that *awful* no longer means "filled with awe," or that *bathroom* needn't mean "a room with a bath." And as Voltaire quipped, the Holy Roman Empire was neither holy nor Roman nor an empire. A word or fixed phrase conveys a meaning not because people deduce it from the word's parts but simply because they expect everyone else to interpret it the way they do.[6]

The purpose of language is to *coordinate* our behavior—you pass me the pepper when I want pepper and the salt when I want salt. Language allows us to do this because it is a *convention*, a tacit agreement among the members of a language community to use words to refer to certain concepts, in this case that the sound [ˈpɛpɹ] will be used to indicate pepper and [sɔlt] to indicate salt, though it could have been the other way around if English speakers long ago had agreed on the opposite pairing. I can request the salt with confidence because I know you interpret the word as I do, and crucially, you know that I know this—if you knew that *salt* meant "salt" but thought that I thought *salt* meant "pepper," you'd pass the pepper instead. And I know that you know that I know this, ad infinitum.

Ever since the linguist Noam Chomsky called attention to the intricacies of syntax, human language has inspired awe because of the vast number of meanings we can express by combining words into sentences.[7] But the power of a single word to coordinate minds is just as awesome. As the poet Craig Morgan Teicher writes, "To speak is an incomparable act of faith. What proof do we have that when I say *mouse*, you do not think of a stop sign? The obvious response to such a question is that whoever asks it is thinking too hard about a soft thought."[8] The less obvious response is that the meaning of a word is common knowledge among the speakers of the language. Children tacitly make this assumption from the start; it's hard to see how they could master language if they had to worry that *mouse* meant "mouse" to them but "stop sign" to someone else and still other things to other people.[9] Experiments by the psychologists Gil Diesendruck and Lori Markson showed that indeed children don't worry. They taught three-year-olds words for unfamiliar objects, like *mef* for a dumpling press, and found that the children immediately assumed that a stranger knew what the word meant. It's not because children indiscriminately blur their own knowledge with everyone else's: when the three-year-olds were taught a new *fact* about an object (such as that "my cat likes to play with it"), they didn't assume that a stranger knew the fact.[10] Words are the earliest and most omnipresent exercise of common knowledge in our lives.

The idiom "to be on speaking terms" reminds us that language is the quintessential social activity, and the logic of linguistic conventions opens the door to questions about the rest of our sociality. The most basic is why we are social in the first place. Humans chat, work, play, build, and learn in ensembles, whether they are related or not, a rarity among animals, who are mainly held together by ties of blood. What are the evolutionary advantages of hanging out together so that one person can benefit another?

Evolutionary biologists think about this question by distinguishing the two possibilities for what's in it for the helper. When one organism benefits the other at a cost to itself, that's called *altruism*. Readers of Richard Dawkins's 1976 classic *The Selfish Gene* or the dozens of books on cooperation that have appeared in its wake know that altruism is a major puzzle in biology because at first glance it seems that it could never have evolved by natural selection. Why do monkeys groom each other, each sacrificing time to pick parasites off the other, when a selfish monkey could enjoy being groomed without grooming in turn, outcompeting its generous troopmates and flooding descendant generations with its selfish genes, eventually driving grooming to extinction?

The common solution to this puzzle is reciprocal altruism, the strategy of starting out by cooperating (in this case, grooming another upon request), and thereafter doing unto others as they have done unto you: cooperate with those who cooperated, and defect (in this case, refuse to groom) against those who defected.[11] The problem can be modeled in game theory as a Prisoners' Dilemma, the hypothetical scenario in which two incommunicado partners in crime have no choice but to betray each other out of fear of being betrayed, leaving them both worse off than if they had cooperated. (More on this in chapter 3.) When the partners are placed in the dilemma repeatedly, strategies of reciprocal altruism (playing "Tit for Tat") can outcompete the exploitative ones, since cheaters will eventually be excluded from beneficial cooperation.[12]

Psychologists have pointed out that several of our mental faculties—our memory for other people and what they did to us, our sense of fairness, and our moral sentiments such as sympathy, gratitude, and anger—seem uncannily designed to implement a strategy of reciprocity, and presumably evolved as adaptations to the problem of altruistic cooperation. Not, in our case, grooming, but the myriad ways in which we trade goods, services, and favors, like bartering, carpooling, and babysitting. Sympathy impels us to cooperate on the first move, gratitude to repay cooperation with cooperation, anger to repay defection with defection.

By now this is a familiar story; I myself have told it in five books.[13] It absorbs our attention because it resolves an evolutionary paradox and because it shines a light on a major theater of the human condition: our dramas of fairness, debt, obligation, exchange, guilt, appreciation, and treachery. Only recently have I come to appreciate that the story of cooperation makes up just one side of the problem of what makes humans social. The other side is *coordination*.[14]

When one organism benefits another, it doesn't necessarily incur a cost to itself; it may enjoy a benefit. Biologists call this second kind of helping *mutualism*, as when an oxpecker bird eats ticks off the back of a willing zebra. The oxpecker gets a meal, the zebra is tormented by fewer pests, and everyone wins (except the ticks). Reciprocity is unnecessary: the oxpecker doesn't demand that the zebra nibble ticks out of its feathers in repayment. For this reason mutualism would not seem to carry the frisson of altruism. Each party clearly gets something out of the relationship, so each has an incentive to allow the arrangement to evolve. It's not "If you scratch my back, I'll scratch yours"; it's "One hand washes the other."

But the evolution of mutualistic coordination is by no means boring. It raises another daunting evolutionary puzzle, with a different but equally fecund explanation.

Life is filled with opportunities to coordinate with other people for mutual gain. We agree on a time and place to meet, bring complementary fare to a potluck dinner, divide responsibilities on a project, dub a meeting room with a nickname, and carry opposite ends of a heavy couch up the stairs. As with the oxpecker and the zebra, there's no incentive for anyone to cheat or to fear being cheated: when coordination works, everyone wins. This doesn't mean that it's easy to bring it about. Coordination can fail if people are not on the same page, even when they want the same thing. Schedules clash, signals get crossed, and shared goals fall through the cracks or are spoiled by too many cooks.

Consider a game that boils coordination down to its bare logic the way the Prisoners' Dilemma does for cooperation.[15] In Rendezvous, two people, James and Charlotte, enjoy each other's company and have agreed to meet for coffee, but James's cell phone goes dead before they have settled on a place. They both know that James tends to frequent the Java Joint and Charlotte usually patronizes the Coffee Connection, but neither has a real preference; they just want to end up at the same place. James predicts that Charlotte will gravitate to the Connection, so he heads there, but then realizes that she will predict that he will gravitate to the Joint, so he changes course and heads there, until he realizes that she will anticipate that he will guess that she will opt for the Connection, so he does another about-face, only for it to dawn on him that it will occur to her that he knows she is aware that he haunts the Joint, so he pirouettes once again. Meanwhile, she is whipsawed by the same futile empathy.

Note that in the game of Rendezvous there is no conflict of interest: the two friends want the same thing. Trust and mistrust, generosity and selfishness, honesty and deception, good deeds enjoyed and repaid, simply don't arise. James and Charlotte's problem is not motivational but cognitive. What they long for is common knowledge. It's not enough for one of them to know the other's likely intention. Each must know that the other knows what the first one knows, ad infinitum.

The easiest bestower of common knowledge, direct speech, is unavailable to them. But all is not lost. The next-best thing is *common salience,* also known as a *focal point.* Suppose that the Java

Joint is running a promotion and has plastered the local kiosks with ads, or the café has come up in their previous conversation, or it was recently in the news, or it's situated at the busiest intersection of the town. None of these is inherently a "good reason" to meet at the Joint, but the mere fact that a location is likely to intrude into the consciousness of each is reason enough, and they both can break their empathic impasse by heading there.

Whatever the source, when a coordination dilemma recurs in life, the parties will yearn for a focal point, any focal point, and are apt to stick with whichever solution is known to be a solution. These commonly known solutions are called *conventions*.[16] James and Charlotte, for instance, might adopt a personal convention to rescue them should they ever find themselves incommunicado again, such as going with the tiebreaker "Ladies first" and meeting at the Connection, or taking turns and going wherever they hadn't met the last time.

Among society-wide conventions, an obvious one we've seen is the vocabulary of a language. Other examples include closing businesses on Sunday, accepting paper currency in exchange for goods and services, using appliances that run on 110 volts, and driving on the right side of the road (or the left; it doesn't matter, as long as everyone sticks to the same side). It's irrelevant that this last convention is enforced by the police. As with many conventions, people have an incentive to conform to it as long as others do.

A sweeping narrative of the past and future of our species by the historian Yuval Noah Harari, told in his books *Sapiens*, *Homo Deus*, and *21 Lessons for the 21st Century*, is animated by a big idea, which he summarizes as follows: "Our world is built on fictions. They're all around us: nations, corporations and religion were invented in the human imagination. And if it weren't for the fictional stories we collectively tell, we might not be the dominant species on the planet."[17] He explains:

Ever since the stone age, self-reinforcing myths have served to unite human collectives. Indeed, *Homo sapiens* conquered this planet thanks above all to the unique human ability to create and spread fictions. We are the only mammals that can cooperate with numerous strangers because only we can invent fictional stories, spread them around, and convince millions of others to believe in them. As long as everybody believes in the same fictions, we all obey the same laws, and can thereby cooperate effectively.[18]

It's a worthy insight, though I would put it differently. Our world is built on *conventions* that allow us to *coordinate* effectively and are self-reinforcing because they are *common knowledge.* Conventions like the English language, Christianity, the United States of America, the euro, and Microsoft are not exactly "fictions." They are very real, even if they are not made out of physical stuff. Common knowledge creates nonphysical realities.[19]

While the dilemma of cooperation sets the stage for the human drama of beneficence, exploitation, and fairness, the dilemma of coordination sets the stage for its own operas, with storylines driven by privacy, publicity, precedent, fame, fads, norms, panics, rituals, piety, and outrage. The rest of this chapter will try to convince you of this ambitious claim, visiting four examples from the news that are best understood with the logic of common knowledge. I'll conclude with a peek at how the logic is experienced in our consciousness and conversation.

⚜

We have become used to social media proliferating posts about celebrity indignities, cats riding Roombas, and blue and black dresses that some people see as gold and white.[20] But rarely does a viral meme originate in a math problem. That happened in 2015, when Kenneth Kong, a Singaporean television host, posted a photo of an exam question for the country's fifth-grade students on his Facebook page. The brainteaser soon took the internet by storm, attracting coverage by the *New York Times*, the *Guardian*, and the BBC, and soon getting its own Wikipedia entry.[21] Here it is verbatim, questionable tenses and all:

Albert and Bernard just become friends with Cheryl, and they want to know when her birthday is. Cheryl gives them a list of 10 possible dates:

> May 15, May 16, May 19
>
> June 17, June 18
>
> July 14, July 16
>
> August 14, August 15, August 17

Cheryl then tells Albert and Bernard separately the month and the day of her birthday respectively.

> ALBERT: I don't know when Cheryl's birthday is, but I know that Bernard doesn't know too.
>
> BERNARD: At first I don't know when Cheryl's birthday is, but I know now.
>
> ALBERT: Then I also know when Cheryl's birthday is.

So when is Cheryl's birthday?

Try it—it's a small mental workout, but solvable without math. It helps to arrange the possibilities in a grid and work by a process of elimination.

		Day (Bernard knows)				
	May	15	16		19	
Month	**June**			17	18	
(Albert	**July**	14		16		
knows)	**August**	14	15		17	

Bernard, recall, has been told the day but not the month—that is, he knows which column Cheryl's birthday is in but not which row. Now, if he had been told her birthday was "the 18th," he'd know it was *June* 18, since that's the only 18 among the possibilities (it's the only date in its column). Similarly, if he had been told it was the 19th, he'd know it was May 19. Albert says he knows that Bernard doesn't know the answer, so he must know that Bernard wasn't told it was the 18th or 19th, the two sure things. But how could Albert have figured that out just by knowing the correct row, namely the birth month? He'd know only if he had been told it was July or August, which lack those easy solutions.

Now, if you and I can figure this much out, so can Bernard. And Bernard has announced that he now knows when Cheryl's birthday is. How could he know this? Well, the day couldn't have been the 14th, because that would not have allowed him to decide between July 14 and August 14. And if it had been the 15th or the 17th, then Albert would have no way of knowing which it was.

But Albert announces that he does know. That means it could only have been the month with a single day left among the possibilities, July, and that day is the 16th. Cheryl's birthday is July 16.

What does the Cheryl problem tell us? For one thing, it bears the hallmark of viral social media posts: moralization about a story which turns out to be false. Commenters moaned either about the draconian workouts inflicted on Asian schoolchildren or about the intellectual flabbiness of their Western counterparts. But in reality the problem did not come from a fifth-grade curriculum; it was drawn from an Olympiad for the nation's math-savviest teenagers.

The real reason I bring up Cheryl is to show how knowledge about knowledge is logically different from mere knowledge, and how it can be used to infer facts about the world. It also shows that people are capable—with some effort when it comes to unfamiliar situations—of thinking about other people's thoughts about still other people's thoughts. It's a talent that goes beyond the thought process that cognitive scientists call mentalizing, mind reading, intuitive psychology, or theory of mind (the "theory" here referring to an ordinary person's intuitions, not to the scientist's own theorizing). This talent can be called *recursive* mentalizing: thinking about thoughts about thoughts; reading the mind of a mind reader. The Cheryl problem calls upon us to think about Albert and Bernard's private knowledge of the birth month and day, their reciprocal knowledge of each other's private knowledge, and the common knowledge conveyed by their pronouncements.

Later in the book we'll ask how good people really are at thinking about thinking about thinking. Before that we'll exercise the ability to use states of knowledge to whittle down states of the world and will come to an astonishing conclusion: that rational, honest people cannot agree to disagree.

Those of us who have lived through the steady democratization of computers, from room-filling mainframes to refrigerator-sized minicomputers to desktop PCs to laptops to smartphones, recall that the sharpest turning point came in 1984. That's when Apple introduced an affordable personal computer with a graphical user interface (GUI), the Macintosh. Before that time, home computers were difficult and tedious to use. Their monitors displayed twenty-four rows of eighty characters each, and their operating systems required textual commands like "rmdir c:\foobar" whose syntax had to be memorized and which could fail with an errant keystroke. Early adopters of Apple's alternative were dazzled by the windows, icons, menus, and mouse which today we take for granted. Richard Dawkins marveled at the time: "I have been an intensive programmer and user of a wide variety of digital computers for twenty-five years, and I can testify that using the Macintosh (and its imitators) is a qualitatively different experience from using any earlier type of computer. There is an effortless, natural feel to it, almost as if the virtual machine were an extension of one's own body."[22]

Yet the takeover by the GUI computers was not a foregone conclusion. They had been invented a decade earlier at Xerox Palo Alto Research Center—according to legend, Steve Jobs stole the idea after a visit in 1979—and Apple itself had introduced a version in 1983, the Lisa, which flopped. The problem was how to jump-start the mass acceptance of an exotic new computing platform. Enough people had to buy one that the price could come down, communities of users could share software and expertise, and a market could develop for third-party peripherals, apps, and consumables like floppy disks. Until they materialized, few consumers would take a chance at buying a computer, however "insanely great," that might leave them as oddballs and orphans. But how could Apple sell enough units to create those "network externalities," as economists call them, if no one was willing to buy one until it did?

Apple cut the knot with an ad that ran only once, during the third quarter of Super Bowl XVIII.[23] Directed by Ridley Scott of *Alien* and *Blade Runner* fame, it said nothing about windows, icons, menus, or mice; nothing about an effortless natural feel or an extension of one's own body; nothing about the product at all. A line of sackcloth-clad drones, prodded by riot police, trudges into a cavernous hall where a projected face intones corporate drivel about "information purification directives." The blue-gray monochrome is intercut with shots of a lithe blond woman in red shorts and a tank top sprinting into the hall with a large mallet. She hammer-throws it into the screen, which explodes in a white fireball, leaving the drones gaping. A voice-over reads the message scrolling up the screen: "On January 24th, Apple Computer will introduce Macintosh. And you'll see why 1984 won't be like '1984.'"[24]

The contrast between corporate conformity and youthful iconoclasm, though certainly an image Apple was happy to convey, was not the real point of the ad. The real point was that it captured people's attention during the Super Bowl, which is an American national rite, standing out in the calendar like a religious holiday. Not only were a lot of people watching, but everyone knew that a lot of people were watching, and knew that everyone knew it. A Super Bowl ad generates common knowledge. And common knowledge is necessary to entrench a convention, like the hardware and software specs of the Macintosh computer. The tens of millions of people who saw the ad knew that tens of millions of people might be intrigued by this upstart technology.

The special role of the Super Bowl ad as an instant common-knowledge creator was explained by the political scientist Michael Chwe in his 2001 book *Rational Ritual*. Chwe noted that other start-ups that depended on network externalities also advertised heavily on the Super Bowl, especially during the dot-com era when creating those network effects was the key to success. Monster.com, for example, was one of the first job sites that took advantage of the vast reach of the Web, but it needed job seekers expecting employers to post ads there and employers expecting job seekers to seek jobs there. The Discover card boasted high credit limits, no annual fees, and cashback bonuses, but it was unappealing without a network of merchants who accepted it, which they would do only if there were a network of cardholders who used it.

Chwe argued that the Super Bowl also attracts a second kind of company: those selling products that depend on their brand image. American beer is American beer, and running shoes are running shoes, but it matters to consumers that they be seen as Budweiser or Miller drinkers, Nike or Adidas wearers, and certainly not as buyers of no-name generics. Also, some products are enjoyed communally, like restaurants, plays, movies, and books; it's more fun to see a movie if you can join a conversation about it with friends later. These social products are like technology standards or credit card networks: the more people adopt it, the more people want to adopt it. Chwe confirmed that goods like these which are consumed in public, like cars, beer, sodas, movies, clothing, and shoes, are more heavily advertised on the Super Bowl than goods consumed in private, like batteries, motor oil, and breakfast cereal.

Of course, the Super Bowl (and other heavily hyped happenings) have massive audiences, so maybe it's sheer numbers rather than common knowledge that appeal to advertisers. Using statistical regression techniques, Chwe did his best to control for this and other confounding factors. He confirmed that companies that sold products consumed in public were more willing to advertise, were more willing to advertise on popular shows than on niche ones, and were willing to pay more *per viewer* than companies that sold products consumed privately.

In the decades since the "1984" ad, Super Bowl ads have become a cultural spectacle, attracting almost as much attention as the game itself. This has made the ads all the more appealing for hawkers of products whose value depends on common knowledge. The climax may have been Super Bowl LVI in 2022, sometimes called the Crypto Bowl because of its plethora of high-concept ads featuring cryptocurrency exchanges, the sites or apps on which people could buy and sell cryptocurrencies like Bitcoin.

It's not that cryptocurrencies themselves depend on common knowledge manufactured by advertising. They do depend on one kind of common knowledge, to be sure; all currencies do. I accept a green piece of paper in exchange for an old couch because I know that Stop & Shop will take that paper in exchange for some groceries, which they do because they expect that their wholesalers will accept it, and so on. At one time the common knowledge that currencies had value was reinforced by a promise that the government would exchange a dollar for a fixed amount of gold, which, according to the popular understanding, was stored in Fort Knox. Nowadays that knowledge is backstopped by government fiat, particularly the law that legal tender must be accepted to settle debts. When a government is monetarily stable, that common knowledge can become self-sustaining. People trust the American dollar because they know that everyone else does, and that the US Federal Reserve works hard to keep it that way. But when a government is unstable, the common knowledge can unravel and lead to hyperinflation, in which people furiously raise prices and wages because they see and anticipate others doing so, quickly rendering the currency worthless.

With cryptocurrency, the common knowledge is provided by a public ledger, the blockchain. In a blockchain, all transactions are indelibly recorded and protected from embezzlement or forgery by complex cryptographic algorithms, which are transparent but impossible to hack. Everyone can see the blockchain and how it works, so there's no need for gimmicks to get people to expect others to expect that the cryptocurrency has value.

Where common knowledge has to be artificially ginned up is in cryptocurrency *speculation*. Like all currencies, the supply of crypto can grow only at a limited rate so as to prevent hyperinflation. This is accomplished by allowing people to "mine" it by solving math problems that require substantial computing time and power. If speculators anticipate that the demand will outrun this supply, fueled by the perception that crypto is the wave of the future, they might buy crypto now in hopes that they can sell it at a profit later. And that can work only if there are buyers out there who plausibly expect that *they* can sell it at a profit to still *other* buyers—"greater fools," as investment analysts call them. What inflates a speculative bubble isn't exactly common knowledge, since there's nothing objectively to "know." But it is a common *expectation*, which uses recursive mentalizing in a similar way: everyone expects that everyone expects something—in this case, that the asset price will rise, which does make it rise (at least for a while). Meanwhile, the exchanges skim a profit on each transaction.

A conspicuous public event like a Super Bowl ad can prop up the common expectation, and that is what the crypto exchanges were paying for in 2022. None of the exorbitant ads praised or even mentioned the virtues of cryptocurrency, such as confidentiality and protection against hyperinflation or government confiscation. Instead they paid celebrities to generate a common expectation that other people were investing in crypto, so they should too.

In one of the ads, Matt Damon, backdropped by mountain climbers, aviators, and astronauts, intoned, "In these moments of truth, these men and women—these mere mortals, just like you and me—as they peer over the edge, they calm their minds and steel their nerves with four simple words that have been whispered by the intrepid since the time of the Romans: Fortune favors the brave." In another, Larry David played incarnations of his cranky self at various turning points in history dismissing innovations like the wheel ("What does it do?" "It rolls." "So does a bagel, OK? A bagel you can eat!"), the fork, the toilet, the vote, the lightbulb, and the moon program. It ended with his dismissing a representative of the FTX crypto exchange: "Ehhhh, I don't think so. And I'm never wrong about this stuff—never!" The end tag reads, "Don't be like Larry. Don't miss out on crypto . . . on the next big thing."[25]

Of course, it's only so long that an asset can levitate in midair suspended by nothing but common expectation. Bubbles pop when a market starts running out of the greater fools who don't want to miss out on the next big thing, or when a reason for doubt itself becomes common knowledge. That can upend the common expectation and send investors running for the exits, each desperate to sell the asset out of fear that others are selling it out of fear that still others are selling it.

That's what happened a few months after the Crypto Bowl, when the value of Bitcoin sank by 75 percent and two trillion dollars of cryptocurrency value swiftly evaporated. Worse was to come. In November, a leaked balance sheet revealed that FTX had invested customer deposits in its own hedge fund, whose reserves were mostly held in a conjured-out-of-thin-air cryptocurrency, FTT. That led the CEO of Binance (a rival exchange that had also advertised on the Super Bowl) to sow doubt about the value of FTT and sell its own holdings, which FTX could not easily redeem, setting off a self-fulfilling common expectation of plunging value, that is, a bank run. Within weeks, FTX declared bankruptcy, its founder and CEO, Sam Bankman-Fried, was arrested and charged with wire fraud and money laundering, and blockchain investments were said to have entered a Crypto Winter (a short winter, as it turned out; many cryptocurrencies recovered).

The FTX implosion of 2022 had a bit of dark humor linked to the common-knowledge generator that had helped set it up: Larry David, it turned out, was right. "Ehhhh, I don't think so" joined "1984 won't be like '1984'" as one of the most prescient ad lines in history.

⚓

One of the best jokes from the vein of subversive humor in the Soviet Union has a man standing in the Moscow train station handing out leaflets to passersby. Soon enough the KGB arrest him, only to discover that the leaflets are blank sheets of paper. "What is the meaning of this?" they demand. The man replies, "What is there to write? It's so obvious!"

The point of the joke is that the pamphleteer was generating common knowledge.[26] Everyone knew that the Communist regime was inefficient and oppressive, but they could not have been sure that everyone else had come to that conclusion. A man in a public place calling attention to the existence of reasons for discontent was making that discontent known, and the awareness of it known, even if he didn't need to make the reasons themselves known.

The man's arrest—and more generally, the repression of speech, the press, and assembly in autocracies—raises the question of why dictators find the expression of opinions so terrifying. After all, one could imagine that dictators would allow their powerless subjects to bitch and moan all they wanted. Political power, wrote Mao Zedong, "grows out of the barrel of a gun."

In reality there is an excellent reason why dictators brook no dissent. The immiserated subjects of a tyrannical regime are not deluded into thinking that they are happy. And if tens of millions of disaffected citizens act together, no regime on earth has the brute force to resist them. The reason that citizens don't resist their overlords en masse is that they lack the prerequisite to coordinating their behavior for mutual benefit, namely common knowledge.[27] Most citizens may be concealing their political opinions to avoid being punished, with the result that no one knows that a majority of their compatriots share their disgruntlement. They might even mistakenly think that everyone else is loyal to the regime—a combination of private knowledge and common misconception known as pluralistic ignorance, or a spiral of silence.[28] And even if they did suspect their discontent was shared, they would have no reason to believe that others would express that discontent at the same time as they did, overwhelming the regime rather than exposing themselves to being picked off or locked up one at a time.

A demonstration in a public place, though, can generate the common knowledge needed to coordinate resistance. Each protester in a throng can not only see the others but see that the others are seeing the others. As the pluralistic ignorance unravels, the protest can snowball and take in a growing number of defectors who had been falsifying their loyalty. This allows all the protesters to coordinate their actions, whether by literally storming the palace or by bringing the state machinery to a halt through work stoppages and boycotts. As Gandhi told a British general in the eponymous 1982 movie, "In the end you will walk out. Because one hundred thousand Englishmen simply cannot control three hundred fifty million Indians if the Indians refuse to cooperate."[29]

Walk out they did. By the same dynamic, 150 other regimes in the twentieth and twenty-first centuries walked, ran, or scrambled in a panic from nonviolent but coordinated protesters.[30] In the decades flanking the turn of the twenty-first century, these revolutions, often named after colors, plants, or soft fabrics, transformed the world.[31] According to figures from the political scientist Erica Chenoweth, in the second half of the twentieth century nonviolent resistance movements overtook violent ones in number and enjoyed double their success rate (51 versus 25 percent), even when pitted against brutal dictatorships. (The trend is part of the long-term decline of violence I documented in *The Better Angels of Our Nature*.) An important accelerant has been the use of media that generate ever-wider networks of common knowledge, namely the photocopier, fax, internet, Web, and social media.

Chenoweth has found that in the past two decades the success rate of nonviolent civil resistance campaigns has started to decline (though they still outperform the violent ones). One reason is "the dictator's learning curve": autocrats have become cleverer at disrupting civil resistance campaigns, often by throttling social media.[32] The most sophisticated is the government of China, which employs tens of thousands of censors to read every social media submission and take down the ones it deems dangerous. Tellingly, the dangerous posts are not ones criticizing the government. On the contrary, the government shrewdly uses this feedback to replace officials who are failing at their mandate of mollifying the masses. What the censors squelch is posts that might coordinate action: notices of protests, rallies, and grassroots movements, even if the author was criticizing them.[33]

Dictators' attempts to quash common knowledge have in turn inspired activists to think up ever more creative means of generating it, often by baiting the government to criminalize innocuous activities. The stunts include clapping hands, singing songs, opening umbrellas, wearing buckets on their heads, baring their breasts, setting their cell phones to ring simultaneously, tying flags to the tails of stray cats, performing sword fights, or frying eggs and sausages on the eternal flame of a war monument.[34] (A satirical notice in Belarus reported, "A kindergarten teacher has been found guilty of fomenting disorder for teaching her charges how to play pattycake."[35]) And in a case of life imitating a joke, in 2022 Russian police arrested a woman for, yes, holding a blank sign.

A common saying in the Soviet era, sometimes attributed to Aleksandr Solzhenitsyn, was "We know they are lying. They know they are lying. They know that we know they are lying. We know that they know that we know they are lying. And still they continue to lie."[36] Perhaps they continued to lie because even three levels of mutual knowledge stopped short of the common knowledge that would have allowed the people to coordinate a challenge to the lies.

On December 20, 2013, Justine Sacco, a young director of communications at the media and internet company IAC, achieved an odd kind of fame.[37] During a layover on a plane trip from New York to South Africa to attend a family gathering, she tweeted a series of wisecracks about her surroundings and fellow passengers. The last one she posted before boarding the plane was: "Going to Africa. Hope I don't get AIDS. Just kidding. I'm white!" Given the context, anyone could have inferred that Sacco was not denying that white people can get HIV/AIDS, nor callously dismissing the tragedy of the epidemic in sub-Saharan Africa. On the contrary, by impersonating an oblivious white tourist she was sardonically commenting on the injustice of the racial disparity in the incidence of the disease and of the world's failure to respond to it. Tasteless, perhaps, but not racist.

A *New York Times* editor once explained to me the Second Law of Journalism: Never use irony, because many readers won't get it.[38] Sacco, it would seem, had little to fear from the Second Law. She was not a journalist, and the paltry 170 followers of her Twitter account presumably knew her well enough to get the irony. But Twitter's "Retweet" and "Trends" features were fairly new, and users were only vaguely aware of the power of those features to launch a tweet into escape velocity. (The expression *viral tweet* had gone viral only a year before.[39]) One of Sacco's followers snitched to the editor of a tech industry blog, who posted the joke and retweeted it to his fifteen thousand followers, many of whom retweeted it in turn. Between the time Sacco boarded her flight and the time she landed, her wisecrack had become the number one trend on Twitter.

Given the Second Law, it was perhaps not surprising that the main response to the joke among the tens of thousands of tweets was not groans but outrage:

> In light of @JustineSacco disgusting racist tweet, I'm donating to @care today

> How did @JustineSacco get a PR job?! Her level of racist igno-rance belongs on Fox News. #AIDS can affect anyone!

> I'm an IAC employee and I don't want @JustineSacco doing any communications on our behalf ever again. Ever.

> [From her employer:] This is an outrageous, offensive comment. Employee in question currently unreachable on an intl flight

More surprising was the schadenfreude, bordering on ecstasy, in the anticipation that Sacco's life was in the process of being ruined:

> All I want for Christmas is to see @JustineSacco's face when her plane lands and she checks her inbox/voicemail

Oh man, @JustineSacco is going to have the most painful phone-turning-on moment ever when her plane lands

We are about to watch this @JustineSacco bitch get fired. In REAL time. Before she even KNOWS she's getting fired.

Seriously. I just want to go home to go to bed, but everyone at the bar is SO into #HasJustineLandedYet. Can't look away. Can't leave

Right, is there no one in Cape Town going to the airport to tweet her arrival? Come on, Twitter! I'd like pictures #HasJustineLandedYet.

Despite her public apology, Sacco was sacked. Friends and family turned on her. Workers at hotels threatened to strike if she showed up. Paparazzi followed her; men refused to date her. News sites trawled her Twitter feed for more embarrassing jokes, and ridiculed her as she tried to rehabilitate her reputation and career. She described the emotional toll to a journalist: "I cried out my body weight."

The Justine Sacco affair is said to have inaugurated twenty-first-century cancel culture, in which a person's career and reputation are destroyed for legally protected and often innocuous speech that someone managed to find offensive. The crimes include quotations, dad jokes, social media likes, ironic remarks, historical accounts of racism, denials of accusations of racism, devil's-advocate teaching exercises, compliments taken the wrong way, well-sourced factual assertions, and, in a Kafkaesque trap, reasoned criticism of the very policies that would be used to punish the critic. A database on the site "canceledpeople.org" lists more than two hundred examples and their punishments, usually being suspended or fired. Another database, focused on academia, lists several hundred more (a topic I'll take up in chapter 8).[40] Though most of the cancellations involved an insinuation of bigotry, in virtually no case could a reasonable person interpret the offender as intending to express prejudice or malice toward a marginalized group. A literature professor who was suspended for quoting a racial slur from a novel by James Baldwin in a classroom discussion of racial slurs is patently not a racist. Nor is the truck driver who was fired for making an "okay" gesture, unaware that it had been appropriated by some members of the American alt-right as a symbol for white power. And to state the obvious, ruining their lives did not improve the well-being of a single African American or member of another marginalized group.

In 2022, an exasperated social psychologist, Jonathan Haidt, wrote an essay for *The Atlantic* called "Why the Past 10 Years of American Life Have Been Uniquely Stupid."[41] Haidt identified an obvious cause. Almost half of the cancellations in the database were for postings on social media, and many others were responses to a barrage of indignant social media posts declaring the situation unacceptable. Haidt did not blame the social media platforms themselves but rather the virality generators they implemented in 2009: the Like, Share, and Retweet buttons. He compared this innovation to handing out a billion dart guns. The snipers can signal their moral superiority and tribal loyalty at low cost to themselves by shooting an unpopular target. The attacks are launched in the privacy of a keyboard and screen rather than in person, so they aren't stifled by our ordinary inhibitions against vilifying a person to the person's face. The ignoramuses have a means to take down the erudite, and the trolls can indulge their pastime in anonymity.[42] The snipers can in turn intimidate the leaders of organizations into cowardly concessions to make the dartings stop, because while a single attack can be blown off, hundreds or thousands are harder to ignore.

This explanation seems right, but I think it can be taken further. Haidt called attention to the sheer number of viewers that the sharing options can generate, with each share leading to more shares, leading to still more shares. But virality does not just exponentiate the number of viewers. It also creates a sense of common knowledge. Now, social media platforms don't literally generate the nationwide common knowledge that television did in the three-network era, because their posts are not broadcasted across the country but delivered in a personalized feed. But now that the platforms are known to have hundreds of millions of users, that they interconnect virtual communities with similar interests and politics, and that the sharing buttons allow any post to end up in anyone's feed, the messages *feel like* common knowledge, at least among the people who matter to you. When you see a post that has been retweeted or shared, you know that many other recipients are seeing it, and know that the other recipients know that, with no limit in sight. And often virality really does generate common knowledge. When a viral post is listed in a "What's happening" or "Trending" or "Explore" column, it could become as commonly known as a Super Bowl ad, especially now that the mainstream media themselves often reproduce viral social media posts. This is the reason why challengers to the big social media platforms that claim some political or technological advantage, like Truth Social, Mastodon, and Threads, have made only minor inroads. They cannot claim to be a "town square" where the users know they will see what everyone else is seeing, and will be seen by everyone else.

The biggest difference between social and traditional media is that billions of people can now *generate* common knowledge rather than just perceive it. And that can feed into a pernicious ritual: when it's common knowledge that someone has breached a norm, people feel it must become common knowledge that they are punished. Let me expand on how this feature of human sociality can incite a social media shaming mob.

As we have seen, people can benefit from coordinating their actions through commonly known norms.[43] The norms holding together a community don't just consist of practical conventions like words, traffic lights, or days of rest; they also embrace commonly held beliefs and values. Religious communities are called "faiths" for just this reason. Unverifiable beliefs are the best signals of commitment to the coalition's norms: anyone can say that the sun rises in the east, but only a stalwart would affirm that Jesus is the son of God or that America is the greatest country on earth.[44] Common dogmas can ratify who is a party to a set of conventions and thereby entitled to benefit from the coordination.

Twenty-first-century America has become polarized into political sects, each functioning as a quasi-religious community united by its own commonly held but not easily verified beliefs.[45] A prominent coalition-signaling belief among the American right is that the 2020 presidential election was stolen from Donald Trump. Prominent belief signals among the young educated left are that being a man or a woman has nothing to do with biology and that America is saturated with racism.

Norms exist only insofar as everyone knows they exist and knows that everyone else knows it. This makes them vulnerable to unraveling if they are publicly flouted, and that can have harmful consequences. To take a simple example, if someone believes it's OK to drive through red lights, they are a danger to others, and an even worse danger if still other drivers inferred it was OK. To take a more complicated one, faith-based communities and other informal coalitions may punish heretics and infidels who cast doubt on the common dogmas that bind them in a pact of coordination. And to take a contemporary example, Sacco (and many other cancelees), by treating racism with less than the appropriate awe and dread, were undermining the belief that racism is insidious, unconscious, and ubiquitous, and thus were seen as threats to the relentless vigilance necessary to extirpate it.

Communities thus have an incentive to enforce their norms by punishing flouters—and crucially, the punishment must be common knowledge as well, so the community is assured that the norms still hold. For eons, punishments were made common knowledge by being meted out in a public space where onlookers could see one another seeing the spectacle, such as on crosses, pillories, stakes, gallows, and guillotines. With the rise of humanitarian sentiments and of the mass media, the common knowledge (minus the gory details) is generated instead by media coverage of trials and sentences.[46]

The need to punish violators of collective norms in informal communities raises the question of who will do the punishing, since there is no single victim who is motivated to seek revenge.[47] Norm enforcement raises a version of the puzzle of altruism: an enforcer incurs costs in time and risk, but the benefit accrues to the entire community, so why would anyone step up to do the punishing? A common suggestion is that community-minded punishers are repaid in esteem. Recent studies by a team of psychologists and game theorists (Jillian Jordan, Moshe Hoffman, Paul Bloom, and David Rand) bear this out. In experimental games, players who altruistically forfeit money to punish an exploitative player tend to earn the trust of other players, who in turn grant them opportunities for profitable cooperation.

This still leaves the problem of who esteems the esteemers. How do informal communities avoid the fate of Dr. Seuss's village of Hawtch-Hawtch, which hired a Bee-Watcher to ensure that the town bee worked hard enough, but *he* did not watch the *bee* hard enough, so they had to hire a Bee-Watcher-Watcher, and then a

Bee-Watcher-Watcher-Watcher, and so on, until "all the Hawtchers who live in Hawtch-Hawtch" were "watching on Watch-Watch-er-Watchering-Watch"?[48] The solution in the real world is that the punishment and the esteem are public: everyone is both watcher and watched.

And this gets us back to the dart guns. Social media have equipped a billion people to step into the role of common-knowledge norm enforcers, meting out punishment at a low cost to themselves and the possible benefit of kudos from a vast audience. Like Haidt, I think this explains a good part of why the last decade of American life has been uniquely stupid.

But not all. Why are so many innocent people singled out for vilification despite the obvious lack of racist intent? Why do the mobbers seem not so much altruistic as malicious, even sadistic? And why do the denunciations sometimes snowball into an ecstatic frenzy, long past the point where the norm violator has been chastened? I think an additional feature of our psychology comes into play, our coalitional instincts. And they, too, are driven by common knowledge.

The psychologists Peter DeScioli and Robert Kurzban argue that moral condemnation is not just a strategy to signal one's virtue but a strategy for aligning oneself with a dominant faction.[49] People thrive in groups, but they have to choose their group with care. While joining a group promises advantages, such as spreading risks and dividing spoils, it also brings dangers, such as finding oneself exploited by dominant members, or entangled in someone else's fight, or on the losing side of a dispute, or embroiled in a destructive conflict between evenly matched factions. To avoid these costs, people can try to join the majority coalition as a conflict breaks out, which requires aligning themselves on the same side, whichever side that is.

Public condemnation of a recognizable offense offers a solution. If a faction designates a certain act as wicked, it can grow by recruiting bystanders to join them in condemning the offender. To enjoy this coordination, the choice of the designated offender must be common knowledge. A blatant harm, like violence or theft, can serve as a focal point, but in its absence, coalition builders can devise victimless offenses like blasphemy, sacrilege, witchcraft, or eating beef, whose main function may be to single out a target for coordinated condemnation. Like cowardly children in a schoolyard who join a group of bullies tormenting a weaker kid lest they become the one bullied, each denouncer may join the mob to avoid becoming the one denounced.[50] Social media can set off these moral panics by swiftly generating common knowledge of a norm breaker among hundreds of thousands of right-thinking people.

The requirement that coalitional denunciation find a common-knowledge target explains why the shaming mobs are not just enforcers of moral norms. In two ways the mobbing flouts the logic of moral reasoning but fits with the logic of common-knowledge generation.

A bedrock of moral reasoning is that intentions matter. We make different judgments of the driver who loses control of a car with a hidden defect and tragically strikes a pedestrian and of a driver who takes aim at a pedestrian, floors the accelerator, and mows him down. Blaming people for outcomes they never intended is a mindset that children outgrow by the age of eight, and it's a major difference between archaic and modern regimes of justice.[51] The rationale is that people can be deterred only from acts they intend, so punishing innocent mistakes is pointless cruelty.

Another bedrock is that consequences matter. If no one is hurt, it can't be wrong (or at least you need a strong argument for why it is). That's why homosexuality, heresy, contraception, premarital sex, and other victimless practices have been decriminalized, even if they offend some bluenoses and busybodies.

Yet the database of cancelees is filled with jokesters and opinion sharers who neither meant nor caused any obvious harm. But their infractions *are* well-suited as focal points for coordinated condemnation. DeScioli and Hoffman both point out that to serve this role, an infraction must be public, observable, and undeniable.[52] Mobbable infractions can't be defined only by intentions, which are hidden in the heart of the actor, nor by outcomes, which may lie far in the unforeseeable future. So people's offense-detectors tend to ignore these intangibles and instead scan the social horizon for easily shareable affronts.

Fiction writers often bring to life the unsettling ways in which game-theoretic predicaments play out in human affairs. Several haunting works of mid-twentieth-century literature dramatize the game of punitive mobbing. They emphasize the dubious nature of the transgression, and the way in which the denunciation and punishment are displayed in public to create common knowledge. And each of them found ways to distance the events from the times and places in which they are set so as to suggest that the dynamic of punitive mobbing is a recurring vulnerability of human societies.

Arthur Koestler's 1940 novel *Darkness at Noon* tells the story of an old Bolshevik who is imprisoned for treason during the era of "show trials" (the term is telling), in which the activists who founded the revolutionary state are successively denounced and punished by their erstwhile comrades. Though transparently about Stalin's purges, the novel does not identify the Soviet Union, the Communist Party, or Stalin by name but refers to them in generic terms like "the Party" and "Number One."

Arthur Miller's 1953 play *The Crucible* enacts the 1692 Salem witch trials, in which accusations of witchcraft, threats to punish the accused if they did not confess, and threats to punish those who refused to accuse others culminate in a series of public tortures and hangings. The play was a thinly veiled dramatization of the persecution of alleged Communists during the American Red Scare. But as Miller wrote in retrospect, "The Salem interrogations turn out to be eerily exact models of those yet to come in Stalin's Russia, Pinochet's Chile, Mao's China, and other regimes. . . . The play seems to present the same primeval structure of human sacrifice to the furies of fanaticism and paranoia that goes on repeating itself forever as though imbedded in the brain of social man."[53]

In George Orwell's 1949 novel *Nineteen Eighty-Four*, daily life in Oceania is punctuated by the Two Minutes Hate, a moment at which party members turn to their telescreens and watch a film that vilifies the enemies of the state, in particular Emmanuel Goldstein. Within thirty seconds, "a hideous ecstasy of fear and vindictiveness, a desire to kill, to torture, to smash faces in with a sledge-hammer, seemed to flow through the whole group of people like an electric current, turning one even against one's will into a grimacing, screaming lunatic. And yet the rage that one felt was an abstract, undirected emotion which could be switched from one object to another like the flame of a blowlamp."

The ultimate tale of arbitrary collective punishment was told in a short story that has engaged, enraged, and baffled readers ever since it was published in the *New Yorker* in 1948. In Shirley Jackson's "The Lottery," the townsfolk of a bucolic American village carry out an annual ritual. They gather in the town square and draw lots from a box. This year the ticket with a black spot is drawn by a mother of three. The prize is revealed to the reader in the story's famous ending:

Tessie Hutchinson was in the center of a cleared space by now, and she held her hands out desperately as the villagers moved in on her. "It isn't fair," she said. A stone hit her on the side of the head. . . .

"It isn't fair, it isn't right," Mrs. Hutchinson screamed, and then they were upon her.

⽈

We have seen how common knowledge can matter in logic, economics, politics, and public morals. I will return to these domains throughout the book, but another major theme is that common knowledge matters in everyday life.

The key idea is that *social relationships are coordination games*, a bit like Rendezvous.[54] Two or more people can benefit if they have a common understanding of their relationship, be it kinship, friendship, romance, sexual intimacy, authority, or a transactional arrangement. Each relationship comes with tacit norms of how the two parties may lay claim to particular goods, and they both benefit if they adhere to them. If we're friends or family or lovers, I can ask you in a pinch for a lift to the airport, and vice versa. I might also politely ask my administrative assistant or a graduate student, though probably not vice versa. And if I were to ask a taxi driver, he would demand payment in return. This works well for everyone, but only if they are on the same page. It would be awkward if I offered to pay my best friend for a ride or if I asked a taxi driver to take me to the airport as a personal favor.

As with all the norms that enable coordination, a social relationship is ratified by common knowledge. You and I are friends (or lovers, or supervisor and employee, or seller and customer) only if we both know that we are, and if we both know that the other knows, ad infinitum. The common knowledge between us may be generated by any of a variety of public signals: a ritual, like a wedding; direct speech, like "I love you"; a legal arrangement, as in a signed contract; or any of the countless symbols that competent members of a culture know how to interpret.

And this works both ways: sometimes people want to *avoid* the common knowledge that would thrust them into a certain kind of relationship, with all its perks and obligations, or which would bounce them out of a relationship they are currently enjoying. This might happen, say, when one person explores whether the other is open to a new arrangement, as in courtship or a sexual come-on. Or it might happen when one of them violates the tacit terms of the relationship but neither wants to end it, as with a minor insult or a selfish act that a friend may choose to let pass for the sake of the friendship. These benign hypocrisies supply material for the comedy of manners that is human social life—privacy, confidentiality, politeness, euphemism, tact, innuendo, gentility—and the topics of the second half of the book.

If common knowledge is as big a deal as I've been making it out to be—nothing less than the guarantor of social coordination—why do so few people, aside from a few mathematicians, economists, and philosophers, know or talk about it? Why isn't common knowledge common knowledge?

The answer is that we do talk about common knowledge, but not in the language of logic or game theory. We use the language of conceptual metaphor.[55] In their classic little book *Metaphors We Live By,* the linguist George Lakoff and the philosopher Mark Johnson showed how languages provide the means to speak about abstract concepts with families of idioms that each refer to a single image.

Their first example was ARGUMENT IS WAR:

> His position is indefensible.
> She attacked every one of his claims.
> I demolished that argument.

Another one was LOVE IS A JOURNEY:

> Our relationship isn't going anywhere.
> Look how far we've come.
> We may have to go our separate ways.

Is there a conceptual metaphor for common knowledge? Yes, its quintessential generator: COMMON KNOWLEDGE IS A CONSPICUOUS SIGHT OR SOUND. An example may be found in this snatch of dialogue from the romantic comedy *When Harry Met Sally*. Shortly after the titular event, Harry compliments Sally's looks a bit too insistently, and she accuses him of coming on to her:

> HARRY: All right, all right, let's just say just for the sake of
>   argument that it was a come-on. What do you want me
>   to do about it? I take it back, OK? I take it back.
> SALLY: You can't take it back.
> HARRY: Why not?
> SALLY: Because it's already out there.
> HARRY: Oh jeez, what are we supposed to do, call the cops? It's
>   already out there.[56]

"It's out there" and "You can't take it back" are two of many idioms for common knowledge that refer to something in plain sight or public earshot. Here are some others:

The cat is out of the bag.
It's on the record.
The insult was in his face.
She spilled the beans.
It's best if we bring this into the open.
For years he was in the closet, but he finally came out.
Let's put this on the table.
The bell can't be unrung.

When people wish to *avoid* common knowledge, the conceptual metaphor can be adapted to refer to efforts to avoid seeing things that are in plain sight:

The emperor has no clothes.
She chose to look the other way.
He buried his head in the sand.
Don't go there.
That's the elephant in the room.

This includes awkward moments when one person enters a fact into common knowledge and the other may prefer to keep it out. Here is a well-known exchange from the situation comedy *Seinfeld* in which George Costanza discusses an upcoming date, and Jerry suggests a new metaphor for common knowledge:

GEORGE: I'm thinking of making a big move.
JERRY: What?
GEORGE: I might tell her that I love her.
JERRY: Oh, my!
GEORGE: I came this close last night and I just . . . chickened
   out.

JERRY: Well, that's a big move, Georgie boy. Are you confident in the "I love you" return?

GEORGE: Fifty-fifty.

JERRY: 'Cause if you don't get that return . . . that's a pretty big matzo ball hanging out there.[57]

2
Common Knowledge and Common Sense

Why it's hard to say goodbye, how to tell if you have spinach in your teeth, and why we shouldn't agree to disagree

Isn't common knowledge common knowledge? Doesn't everyone know (and know that they know) that people care about who knows what? In this chapter we'll see that in fact the logic of common knowledge is often an insult to common sense. Logicians have uncovered implications of that special state of knowing which have astonished everyone who becomes aware of them. I'll try to explain three.

The first is that you can deduce facts about the world from what people don't know. The second is that two people really do need to think an infinite vortex of "I know that he knows that I know that he knows . . . " thoughts to be sure they will coordinate their plans; two or three, or any finite number, aren't enough. The third is that rational agents with the same understanding of the world, after examining evidence and sharing their assessments, must arrive at the same conclusion: they cannot agree to disagree.

These conclusions may sound preposterous, and to be sure, the proofs depend on idealizations of reasoners which are less than fully realistic. Scientists joke about the theoretical physicist hired by a farmer to increase milk yields who tells him, "First, assume a spherical cow . . ." I will suggest that while these findings about common knowledge may not literally apply to particular situations in everyday life, they are not spherical cows: each offers insight into the human condition.

✂

Connoisseurs of common knowledge love to challenge their readers with a brainteaser that has been called "one of the greatest logic puzzles ever invented."[1] I prepped you for it in chapter 1 with a similar but easier problem, "When Is Cheryl's Birthday?" Here's another warmup, "Three Logicians Walk into a Bar":

Source: Spiked Math Comics, #445. Licensed under a Creative Commons License; https://www.beingamathematician.org/Jokes/LogiciansJoke.html.

"Everyone wants beer" means that each of the three logicians wants it; it's false if at least one does not. If the first logician didn't want beer, that would be enough to know that not everyone wanted beer. The fact that she *doesn't* know implies that she must want beer. Same for the second. The third, having deduced that the first two want beer, and knowing that she wants it herself, can conclude that everyone among the three wants beer. The Cheryl and Logicians-in-a-Bar problems require recursive mentalizing—the reader thinks about what one of the characters knows about what the other characters know—though not common knowledge in all its infinite glory.

The more devilish problem has been presented in several books of recreational mathematics, including ones by the revered Isaac Asimov, George Gamow, and Martin Gardner. It has also appeared in the academic literature in variants with different characters and clues but the same logical structure (what cognitive psychologists call problem isomorphs).[2]

The original version was published in the politically innocent early 1950s and has, by today's standards, something to offend almost everyone. A sultan challenged the men in his city to figure out which of their wives were unfaithful so they could kill them. The story's Orientalism, Islamophobia, slut-shaming, and normalization of violence against women did not survive the changing sensibilities of subsequent decades, and by the 1980s the Puzzle of the Cheating Wives had become the Puzzle of the Cheating Husbands, the sultan having given way to an equally punitive queen of Atlantis. Unfortunately, this perpetuated a negative stereotype of female leadership, and another sex-reversed isomorph, the Castrati of Womensa, was no less problematic. Only marginally better was a version with an island whose inhabitants, upon deducing they had blue eyes, had to kill themselves, since it violated best practices for reporting on suicide.

Subsequent safer-for-work isomorphs featured muddy children, messy-faced logicians, and the excruciatingly inoffensive girls wearing red or white hats. Here's my version.

A dozen psychologists, proud of both their social and cognitive skills, are seated at a dinner party where they are served halibut with rice and sautéed spinach. Three of the psychologists get an unsightly morsel of spinach lodged in their teeth, but there are no mirrors around, so they're unaware of the faux pas, nor can the others be sure that their own teeth are clean. Psychologists are garrulous, and as they keep up their conversations each of them can see that some of the others have spinach in their teeth. But no one wants to embarrass them by telling them that, nor does anyone want to pick their own teeth if they're clean. The department chair can't stand it any longer and announces, "At least one of you has spinach in your teeth. When I clink my glass, that would be a good time to remove it." She clinks the glass, but no one moves. She clinks it a second time, and still everyone is tight-lipped. After a third clink, the three psychologists with spinach in their teeth pick them clean. Everyone returns to the meal.

How did they figure it out? When the chair made her announcement, she wasn't telling anyone anything they didn't already know, because they could already see that at least one person had spinach in their teeth. But as with the small child and the emperor, the fact that she uttered those words in the presence of the other diners changed their knowledge. It informed each of them that everyone else knew what they knew: it generated common knowledge. But how did the common knowledge allow the three spinach-toothed diners to know it was them?

Imagine a simpler version of the puzzle in which only one psychologist's smile is marred. When the chair says that at least one diner has spinach in their teeth, the bespinached diner looks around, sees that everyone else's teeth are clean, and concludes that he must be the one. When she clinks her glass, he cleans his teeth. So far, so easy.

Now suppose there are *two* psychologists with besmirched grins, Xavier and Yolande. When the chair makes her announcement, Xavier sees that Yolande's teeth are blemished, but he has no idea about his own teeth, so he does nothing. Yolande thinks the same thing. But after the glass has been clinked and no one has stirred, Xavier realizes that his own smile must be disfigured, because if Yolande were the only one, she would have known to clean her teeth, as we saw in the one-marred-smile scenario. The fact that she didn't means that she must have seen another spinach-flecked set of choppers, and since all the other teeth visible to him are clean, Xavier concludes that they must be his. When the chair clinks her glass a second time, he cleans his teeth. So does Yolande, because she has worked through the same inference.

The same logic applies in our example with three sloppy chewers: each one deduces from the lack of activity after two clinks, together with their seeing two spinachful smiles, that they must have spinach in their own teeth. This mathematical induction can be extended to any number of sloppy chewers, who will simultaneously clean their teeth after the glass has been clinked a corresponding number of times.

Crucially, the telltale announcement could not be private knowledge. Suppose the chair had walked around the table whispering into each psychologist's ear that at least one of them had spinach in their teeth. Suppose as well that each one thought he or she was the only one being vouchsafed that fact and assumed that the others were privy to different gossip. Then one messy chewer could still infer he was the one, simply by seeing everyone else's clean smile. But in the case of two, each would still be in the dark, because as far as Xavier is concerned, the lack of activity by Yolande after a few seconds could just mean that she was unaware that *anyone* had spinach in their teeth. Likewise with Yolande pondering Xavier's awareness.

What if we up the level of knowledge by one mind while still falling short of common knowledge? In this scenario, in addition to telling each psychologist that at least one of them had spinach in their teeth, the chair divulged that she was telling the others the same thing but that she was leaving the others to think they were the only ones who knew that. That is, as far as Xavier is concerned, he is the only one who knows that they are *all* being told about the spinach; he knows that Yolande has been told, but he thinks she thinks she's the only one who has been told. When it's just Xavier and Yolande, they can still deduce that they have spinach in their teeth, because each knows that the other knows that one or more is bespinached, and Yolande's inactivity after the first clink betrays to Xavier that she has no way of knowing she's one of them, so therefore he must be one of them (and vice versa). But the induction stops there—three bespinached diners would still be in the dark. As before, when Yolande does nothing, Xavier can't conclude that she's seen his messy teeth, because she could have been looking at Zeke's. But this time Zeke can't know that—he doesn't know that Xavier knows that Yolande knows that there's someone with messy teeth. Common knowledge, in a single stroke, would have set any number of them on the path to figuring out it's them, given enough rounds of inactivity.

You will not be surprised to learn that this has also been called "the *hardest* logic puzzle in the world."[3] But the cognitive process that powers the puzzle, namely drawing conclusions about the state of the world from what someone does or doesn't know, is not as exotic as the head-spinning example would suggest. We do it all the time when we "connect the dots" or "read between the lines," not least in situations with some of the naughtiness of the original puzzle. In David Lodge's novel *Thinks . . .* , a creative writing instructor reads a draft of her student's novel and comes across a description of a unique intimate practice that she and her husband had liked to indulge in. She infers that the student must have had an affair with him. (The cheating husband was dead, so there was no question of her reacting like the wives of Womensa.)

An entire genre of fiction, the mystery, is a workout of the mental muscles for learning about the world by thinking about other people's thoughts. An early example is Edgar Allan Poe's 1844 story "The Purloined Letter." The brilliant, pipe-puffing amateur sleuth C. Auguste Dupin (an inspiration for Sherlock Holmes) is approached by a hapless police officer for help with an unsolved case. An unscrupulous government official has stolen a compromising letter addressed to an "exalted royal personage" (presumably the queen). The minister snatched it from under her nose because he knew that if she protested, it would arouse the suspicions of another exalted royal personage in the room, presumably the king. The minister *wanted* the queen to know he had stolen the letter, because his power over her depended on "the robber's knowledge of the loser's knowledge of the robber." The police, for their part, know that the minister still has the letter by the very fact that no royal scandal has yet erupted: "It is this possession, and not any employment of the letter, which bestows the power. With the employment the power departs." They know, too, that he is keeping the letter close at hand, because he is embroiled in ongoing court intrigues and must be able to produce or destroy it at a moment's notice.

The police ransack the minister's apartment but fail to find the purloined letter. Dupin thinks back to a schoolyard game in which one child concealed some marbles in his hand and they bet a marble on whether the other could guess whether the number was odd or even. A clever schoolboy won all the marbles in the schoolyard by empathizing with his counterpart and anticipating his next choice—"an identification of the reasoner's intellect with that of his opponent." Dupin reasons that the clever minister anticipated that the police would think he would conceal the letter from them in a secret hidey-hole, so instead he left it in plain sight. Dupin pays him a visit, and, his gaze concealed by sunglasses, spots the letter in a rack on the wall. He returns the next day, having arranged for a commotion outside the window, and when the minister is distracted, replaces the letter with a facsimile. Far better than having the minister arrested, Dupin has set him up to incriminate himself when the queen defies his blackmail and the letter he produces contains only a taunt from Dupin.

This game of out-psyching-out, with the reader, narrator, protagonist, and antagonist drawing inferences about the state of the world (in this case the letter's location) from what each of the others knows and doesn't know, is endlessly engaging. We exercise it in several kinds of cognitive play: logic puzzles, mystery stories, and most commonly jokes. The classic example is an old Jewish joke analyzed by Sigmund Freud in *Jokes and Their Relation to the Unconscious*. A businessman meets a rival at a train station and asks him where he's going. He replies that he's going to Minsk. The first businessman says, "The only reason you're telling me you're going to Minsk is that you want me to think you're going to Pinsk. But I happen to know that you *are* going to Minsk. So why are you lying to me?" My own favorite comes from *Plato and a Platypus Walk into a Bar*:

A defendant was on trial for murder. There was strong evidence indicating his guilt, but there was no corpse. In his closing statement, the defense attorney resorted to a trick. "Ladies and gentlemen of the jury," he said. "I have a surprise for you all—within one minute, the person presumed dead will walk into this courtroom."

He looked toward the courtroom door. The jurors, stunned, all looked eagerly. A minute passed. Nothing happened. Finally the lawyer said, "Actually, I made up the business about the dead man walking in. But you all looked at the door with anticipation. I therefore put it to you that there is reasonable doubt in this case as to whether anyone was killed, and I must insist that you return a verdict of 'not guilty.'"

The jury retired to deliberate. A few minutes later, they returned and pronounced a verdict of "guilty."

"But how could you do that?" bellowed the lawyer. "You must have had some doubt. I saw all of you stare at the door."

The jury foreman replied, "Oh, we looked, but your client didn't."[4]

When we left James and Charlotte in the preceding chapter, they were lost in thought, struggling to coordinate a rendezvous without the common knowledge of a face-to-face conversation or a phone call. In the end, James chivalrously went to Charlotte's favorite, the Coffee Connection, and Charlotte considerately chose James's favorite, the Java Joint, to their mutual frustration, because the cafés are miles apart.

This time they want to be certain that they will end up at the same place. They decide to leave nothing to the imagination and settle on the Joint, each with a strong preference not to end up alone at the Connection, though they'd be happy to be there together if there was a reason to switch. They agree to resolve any last-minute changes by exchanging text messages and confirming that each message was received. James gets there early and discovers that there *is* a reason to switch:

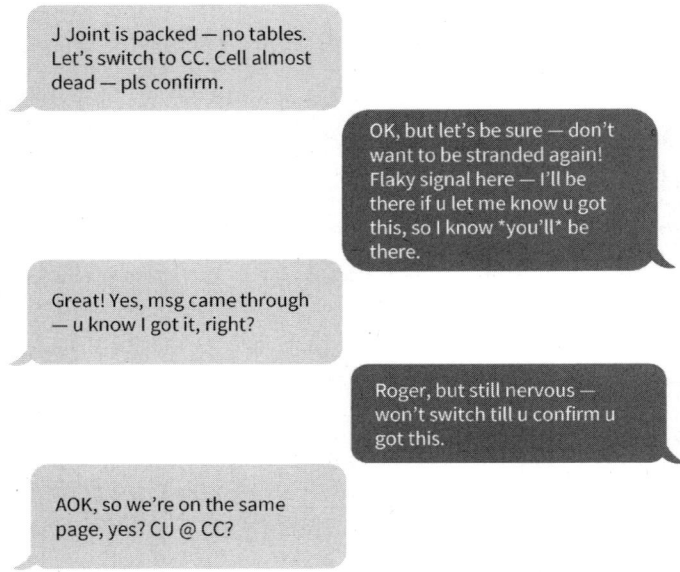

> J Joint is packed — no tables. Let's switch to CC. Cell almost dead — pls confirm.

> OK, but let's be sure — don't want to be stranded again! Flaky signal here — I'll be there if u let me know u got this, so I know *you'll* be there.

> Great! Yes, msg came through — u know I got it, right?

> Roger, but still nervous — won't switch till u confirm u got this.

> AOK, so we're on the same page, yes? CU @ CC?

And then nothing—an eerie white space at the bottom of the screen. James doesn't know whether Charlotte didn't get his last text or if she got it and sent a confirmation that never arrived. And she can't tell from her own frozen screen whether her confirmation never arrived or if it did arrive and *his* confirmation got lost. In each case, it's likelier that a message never arrived (one iffy event) than that it did arrive and the confirmation didn't arrive (two iffy events). The two chums figure that standing with each other in a noisy café would still be better than ending up miles apart, so each plays it safe and sticks with the Java Joint, even though both know that the Coffee Connection would be more pleasant, and each knows that the other knows it. They end up with the second-worst option, the same as if they had never bothered to communicate in the first place!

This is true regardless of how many messages they send and confirm: since no channel is perfect, it's only a matter of time before one of the messages fails to arrive. They knew this, of course, but figured—incorrectly—that several confirmations would be better than none. Paradoxically, their desire for an open-ended exchange of confirmations left them *less* likely to coordinate on their top choice rather than more likely. Without common knowledge—each of them perceiving that the other one got the message while knowing that the other knew they knew, and so on—*no* number of message volleys would give them the confidence they need to rule out the chance of a miscoordination.

This dilemma, called the Electronic Mail game (after the original parable by the economist Ariel Rubinstein in 1989), is the most widely known paradox about common knowledge after the spinach-in-teeth puzzle.[5] It's another affront to our common sense about common knowledge. A frequently asked question about common knowledge is: "So you're saying it has to be 'He knows that she knows that he knows that she knows' . . . *ad infinitum*? Really? Isn't a whole bunch of 'He knows that she knows' enough to ensure coordination between them?" The answer from the Electronic Mail game is: "Yes, really. A whole bunch—the state called 'almost common knowledge'—*isn't* enough."

The conclusion is surprising enough that a couple of other examples may be needed to help it sink in. Consider the commanders of two army divisions, each camped on a hilltop overlooking a valley occupied by an invading force. They know that if they attack simultaneously they can drive out the invaders, but if only one division attacks, it would be outnumbered and slaughtered. The enemy has cyber-sabotaged the electronic channels, so the generals communicate with couriers, some of whom, unfortunately, are bound to get lost or captured. Suppose the first general sends the message "Let's attack at dawn." Will the attack go through? No, because the first general doesn't know whether the second one got the message, and is reluctant to take a chance on sending his troops into the valley of death.

The second general anticipates this reticence and keeps his troops on his own hilltop. What if he sends back a message acknowledging that he got the order to attack; now will the first general attack? No, because he worries that the second general doesn't know that he got the message, and thus may also be reluctant to attack, which would render his troops sitting ducks. So he sends a message back to the second general confirming that the acknowledgment was received. Of course this is not enough either. No number of messages back and forth is enough to cement coordination—even if in fact the courier got the message through every time.

Now let's look at the actual probabilities. The math is simple, and we can make it personal by replacing each army in the example with a fighter pilot, like in *Top Gun*. If they can agree upon a target over a noisy radio channel, they can fly in together and one pilot can take out the target under the protection of the other, but if one of them flies in alone, he will be shot down. Suppose there's a 10 percent chance that a message won't get through (the exact number doesn't matter). Start with the case in which one pilot radios the coordinates of the target to the second and they just attack without either expecting an acknowledgment. There's a 90 percent chance that the coordinated attack succeeds and a 10 percent chance that the first pilot will be shot down. What happens if the first pilot requests an acknowledgment? If it comes in, both pilots know where to attack, and each one knows that the other knows—but the second one doesn't know that the first one knows that he knows, so he might still hold back. How should the first one prepare for this uncertainty? If he decides that he'll attack regardless of whether he receives an acknowledgment, then he's in the same position as if he hadn't asked for an acknowledgment at all. He certainly should not attack if he *doesn't* receive an acknowledgment, because in that case it's likelier that his original message got lost (10 percent) than that it was received and the acknowledgment got lost (90 percent × 10 percent, or 9 percent). So his strategy should be "Attack only if you get an acknowledgment." Suppose the second pilot's strategy is "Attack only if you get the coordinates." The probability of a successful attack is 81 percent: the 90 percent chance that the coordinates were received multiplied by the 90 percent chance that the acknowledgment was received. The probability that the second pilot will disastrously attack on his own is 9 percent: the 90 percent chance that he received the coordinates multiplied by the 10 percent chance that his acknowledgment was lost. The probability that neither attacks is 10 percent, which is just the chance that the original message with the coordinates was lost.

The surprising result is that the demand for an acknowledgment has left the mission no better off than if the first pilot had just sent his command and left it at that. Indeed, it's left it worse off: there's now an 81 percent chance of a successful attack, as opposed to a 90 percent chance. The only difference is in which pilot is left vulnerable. With an attack after two messages, each with a 90 percent chance of getting through, the second pilot assumes the risk; with an attack after one message, it's the first pilot.

The economist John Geanakoplos, who laid out this version of the puzzle, concludes, "The upshot is that when coordinating actions, there is no advantage in sending acknowledgements unless one side feels more vulnerable, or unless the acknowledgement has a higher probability of successful transmission than the previous message." He notes that in real life, when one pilot issues a command the other acknowledges him just once with the word *roger*, presumably because a one-word message has a higher chance of being transmitted than an echo of the command, and also because the acknowledgment puts the commanding officer in the less vulnerable position. He also offers a civilian example: tourists who contact hotels for reservations demand confirmation before going.[6]

❧

Now, even with these links back to reality, you may find the analysis far-fetched. In the real world, people often do coordinate while communicating with less than perfect certainty, and they don't have to be in each other's faces to do so. You're not alone—mathematicians have found loopholes in Rubinstein's draconian scenario in which only common knowledge, with its infinity of levels, can guarantee that people will end up on the same page.[7]

The most prominent solution is to weaken the very idea of common *knowledge*. "Knowledge" is an onerous burden. According to the philosophers' standard definition, it requires "justified true belief," which means that the knowers' belief has to be *correct* by the lights of an ideal understanding of reality, not just an excellent guess or a deeply held conviction.[8] This definition explains why it would be peculiar to say, "Felix knows the Earth is flat," even if he believes it in his bones, because the Earth is not, in fact, flat. It's also why we smile at the quip attributed to Mark Twain, "The trouble with the world is not that people know too little, but that they know so many things that aren't so."[9] So in a sense none of us fallible mortals can ever say with certainty that other fallible mortals have any "knowledge" at all, common or not. We can, though, say they have *beliefs* held with varying degrees of confidence, like 30 percent (logicians call it ".3-belief"), or 99 percent (".99-belief"), and so on.

And that opens the door to their having something called "common *p*-belief," common belief for short.[10] James and Charlotte can relax their demand for certain knowledge and just entertain fallible beliefs. For them to have "common .9-belief" that the Coffee Connection is the better venue, for instance, James has to believe with at least 90 percent confidence that Charlotte believes with at least

90 percent confidence that James believes with at least 90 percent confidence that . . . and so on. Strictly speaking, whenever in the rest of this book I refer to "common knowledge" in a real-life context, what I'm really referring to is highly confident common belief.

And crucially, in a coordination game (like Rendezvous or Coordinated Attack), there's a certain minimum level of confidence, whose value depends on the relative payoffs of coordinating and acting alone, for which it is rational for agents with mere common belief to choose to coordinate.[11] If the costs of miscoordinating are high, as with the pilots who are putting their lives on the line, the confidence level (the p in their common p-belief) must be high. With James and Charlotte, ending up at the noisier café or at different cafés would be annoying but not the end of the world, so one or both could take the leap with a lower degree of common belief. They could do this by deciding beforehand to cap the number of acknowledgments they exchange, or by one of them just writing at some point "No need to reply" or "I'll be there" and taking their chances.

Though the exact conditions of the Electronic Mail game seldom apply in real life, its overall logic can help us make sense of dilemmas in which two agents without common knowledge struggle to coordinate with iterated exchanges of fallible messages. The situation in which the game was originally applied didn't even involve human communicators.[12] In the early decades of computing, an IBM System/360 or other mainframe was enshrined in a Holy of Holies in a campus or corporate computing center, and a bouquet of cables fanned out that connected it to terminals, printers, and disk drives. The mainframe was a repository of common knowledge among all the users and computational resources. This hub-and-spoke arrangement was superseded in the 1980s by "distributed computing," in which a network of processors, servers, peripherals, and modems relayed packets of data every which way—raising the problem of how any pair of them could achieve coordination over noisy wires or airwaves. A set of "handshaking protocols" were implemented in which one device would send a message to the other, wait for a confirmation to come back, send a confirmation of the confirmation, and so on—not ad infinitum, but some number of times which depended on the clarity of the channel and the cost of an error. When the channel was a telephone line, the handshaking was audible as the call-and-response of hisses, howls, and hums that many of us remember from the era of dial-up modems and the movie *You've Got Mail*. Nowadays we see it in the blinking LEDs of a Bluetooth device as we try to pair it with a computer or smartphone.

And the game, with all its possibilities for miscoordination, is often played out in human life, sometimes with electronic mail itself. Many of us have had the experience of getting stood up for an appointment because we never confirmed it with the inviter, who had been waiting for a confirmation while we assumed that it had already been settled and no confirmation was necessary—or even, sometimes, when a confirmation *had* been sent, but one party was waiting for a confirmation of the confirmation.

The messages needn't be verbal. Sometimes when I jog, a courteous driver stops to let me cross an unmarked intersection even though he has the right of way. I'm grateful for the courtesy and would like to cross, but I know he can't wait forever, and I'm reluctant to step off the sidewalk in case he decides the time is up and he's going to hit the gas. For his part he's happy to wait for me to decide it's safe to cross, but if he guesses I've decided to play it safe and let him proceed, he has to move on. I might take a baby step onto the road and then think the better of it and retreat; he may ease off the brake pedal and creep forward, then jam it back down. This nervous back-and-forth can go on for a long time as the cars behind him stack up. Even if I could see him through the tinted windows, should I take his nod as indicating that I should go, or that he thinks I'm telling *him* to go? This is why courtesy is a poor basis for coordination: we're both better off hewing to convention and taking advantage of the common-knowledge generators that were created for just that purpose, namely traffic lights and zebra crossings. With the costs of miscoordination so high, even these may need to be reinforced by yet another common-knowledge generator (chapter 6), as explained by this sign at the San Francisco airport.

At other life junctures, the coordination dilemma consists in affirming a social relationship in the presence of a possible threat to it. When friends or family or lovers are engaged in conversation and one of them has to leave, she is putting an end to a pleasant communal activity. This can mean that the time has come when some other demand can be put off no longer, like sleep or work. Or it could mean that she has had enough of him for the time being and would rather be alone, which is a rebuff to the unspoken understanding that the interest that friends and lovers take in each other is limitless. It could even mean that she is no longer interested in continuing the relationship and wants to break it off, an ambiguity reflected in the two senses of the standard word for terminating a joint activity: *We said our goodbyes* and *This is goodbye.* The obvious generator of common knowledge, direct speech, is inappropriate here, because as we shall see in chapter 5, communal relationships are not the kind of thing that people affirm in so many words: it's awkward to say, "I have to go now, but we're still friends, OK?"[13] More disconcerting still, ending a conversation forecloses any opportunity to clarify why the ender chose to end it.

All this makes goodbyes inherently fraught. As Juliet put it, parting is such sweet sorrow (and she would come to know a thing or two about the costs of miscoordination when messages fail to get through). Hence the phenomenon of the long goodbye.[14] One example is the interminable conversation as the guests leave a dinner party, what my grandmother called *klamke-talk,* from the Yiddish word for doorknob, a conversation with one hand on the doorknob. Another is the agony of young lovers nervously trying to end a phone call. This was enacted in *The Simpsons Movie* in a scene where the National Security Agency surveils ordinary Americans' telephone conversations in all their banality:

> WOMAN ON PHONE: You hang up first.
>
> MAN ON PHONE: No, you hang up first.
>
> WOMAN ON PHONE: Okay.
>
> MAN ON PHONE: She hung up on me![15]

In an era of culture war and toxic polarization, the ideal of "agreeing to disagree" would seem like something devoutly to be wish'd. That makes a famous theorem about common knowledge proved in 1976 by the mathematician and Nobel laureate Robert Aumann a real shocker: rational agents cannot agree to disagree.[16] The theorem states: "If two people have the same priors, and their posteriors for a given event *A* are common knowledge, then these posteriors must be equal. This is so even though they may base their posteriors on quite different information." After announcing the result in the first paragraph of a three-page paper, Aumann noted, "We publish this observation with some diffidence, since once one has the appropriate framework, it is mathematically trivial. Intuitively, though, it is not quite obvious; and it is of some interest in areas in which people's beliefs about each other's beliefs are of importance." The first sentence is too modest and the second an understatement. People who have pondered Aumann's famous Agreement theorem have been rubbing their eyes in incredulity ever since.

The background is Bayes's Rule, a simple formula for calibrating one's beliefs to the strength of the evidence. Advocates of rationality considered it to be indispensable to making sound judgments in the public arena and in private life, and very close to the ideal of rationality itself. In my book *Rationality* I devoted a chapter to it, called "Beliefs and Evidence."[17]

The rule starts from the idea that one's credence in a hypothesis should not be black or white but shades of gray. (We've already encountered this idea in the concept of *p*-belief.) That means that degree of belief can be treated as a probability, a number between 0 (certainty that it's false) and 1 (certainty that it's true), where higher numbers mean greater confidence that the hypothesis is true. Then the degree to which one calibrates one's degree of credence in the hypothesis in light of the strength of the evidence for it can be treated as a *conditional* probability, a "given that" or an "if–then" estimate.[18] The intuition "There's compelling evidence for this hypothesis" means "There's a high probability that the hypothesis is true given that evidence."

From these two assumptions, Bayes's Rule is simple algebra. What we seek is a *posterior* probability: the rational degree of credence in a hypothesis given some new evidence (that is, *after* seeing the evidence, hence "posterior"). To get it, we need just three numbers. First, the *prior* probability, "priors" for short, namely the degree of credence we have in the hypothesis before we even look at the new evidence, based on everything we know about the world so far. In the case of diagnosing a disease based on some symptoms, the prior probability might be the base rate of the disease in the population: what proportion of people at any given time have the disease. Then we multiply the prior by the *likelihood*, the conditional probability that *if* someone has the disease, *then* they have the symptoms. Finally, we divide by the *marginal* probability or prevalence of the evidence, namely how common the data or symptoms are across the board, whether the hypothesis is true or not. In the case of disease diagnosis, this would be the percentage of people who show the symptoms, regardless of the cause.

Though in some circumstances human beings flout Bayes's Rule (a discovery by the psychologists Amos Tversky and Daniel Kahneman, another Nobel laureate), it's pretty much common sense, and almost everyone understands it when it's explained in concrete terms.[19] Does my headache mean that I have a malignant brain tumor? Well, brain cancer is pretty rare, found in about six out of every hundred thousand people, or a prior probability of just .00006. Now, even though the likelihood of having headaches given that you have a brain tumor is high (around six in ten), the overall prevalence of headaches from all causes (blocked sinuses, muscle tension, caffeine withdrawal, and so on), which forms the denominator, is also high: around half of the population periodically gets headaches. So relax, hypochondriacs: according to Bayes's Rule, the posterior probability that you have a brain tumor (hypothesis) given that you have a headache (evidence) is .00006 × .6 / .5, or about .00007. (It may still be worth seeing your doctor, according to another tool of rationality which gets a chapter in *Rationality*, expected utility: the odds may be low, but the consequences are dire.)

We now have the vocabulary to translate Aumann's Agreement theorem into everyday English. If two rational people start out with the same background assumptions about a hypothesis (the same priors), and they each look at different evidence and share their degree of confidence that the hypothesis is true (that is, their posteriors are common knowledge), then they cannot agree to disagree (those posteriors must be the same).

That's right: no leaving it at that, splitting the difference, acknowledging opposing views, allowing for different perspectives, respectfully disagreeing, or letting a thousand flowers bloom. It all sounds intolerant and dogmatic and authoritarian, an insult to the ideal of civility. But as we shall see, the implications of the theorem are rather enlightened, more along the lines of: facts don't care about your feelings, it's bigger than all of us, and it's not about being right, it's about getting it right.[20]

As with the other mathematical demonstrations that challenge common sense, this result may best be understood by warming up with a simpler example, which I have adapted from my correspondence with Aumann. You and I are trying to predict the winner of a prestigious literary prize, and the finalists have been announced: Amy, a 42-year-old American; Andy, a 71-year-old American; Alice, a 65-year-old American; and Barnaby, a 37-year-old Briton. Neither you nor I have reason to believe that any of them has an edge, so our priors are .25 for each of them. The committee's selection—Amy—will be announced at noon. Excitement is running high: in previous years, the winner was always a British man over 50, which won't happen this year. Present is one of the jurors; we beg him to tell us who won, promising to tell no one. He says he's honor-bound not to do so, but agrees to tell me the winner's sex (female) and you the winner's age (under 50), on condition that we not tell each other. Here is a diagram of our knowledge, with the winner (unknown to each of us) circled:

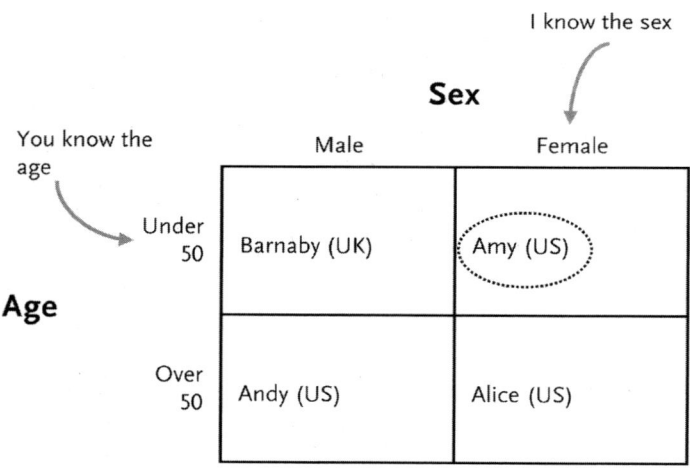

Though we cannot share the exact information vouchsafed to us, we can share our new posteriors. Mine are .5 for Amy, 0 for Andy, .5 for Alice, and 0 for Barnaby. Yours are .5 for Amy, 0 for Andy, 0 for Alice, and .5 for Barnaby. Obviously we should pool our conclusions and strike the finalists off each of our lists that have a 0 probability on the other's. We end up with the same posteriors—1.0 Amy, 0 for the others—and agree that it has to be Amy. Agreeing to disagree—say, if I insisted that Alice still had an even chance—would be perverse. Why throw away perfectly good information just because it wasn't *my* information?

Now, this simple example really *is* common sense, and it doesn't involve common knowledge: we'd reach the same conclusion if we had privately written our estimates in notebooks and then each snooped at the other's. What Aumann proved is that with mere reciprocal knowledge, where each of us knows the other's posterior but can't know that the other knows ours, those two posteriors *can* differ, whereas with common knowledge, they must be the same.

To show how the first state of affairs is possible, let's get back to the literary prize, but change what has been leaked. This time, the judge has divulged to me the winner's sex and to you the winner's *nationality*. We each know what kind of information has been leaked to the other, but not the information itself. For now, let's assume that we don't share our posteriors, and we are speculating on what neither of us has been told, the winner's age. Here is a diagram of our knowledge in the new example, with the winner (again unknown to each of us) circled:

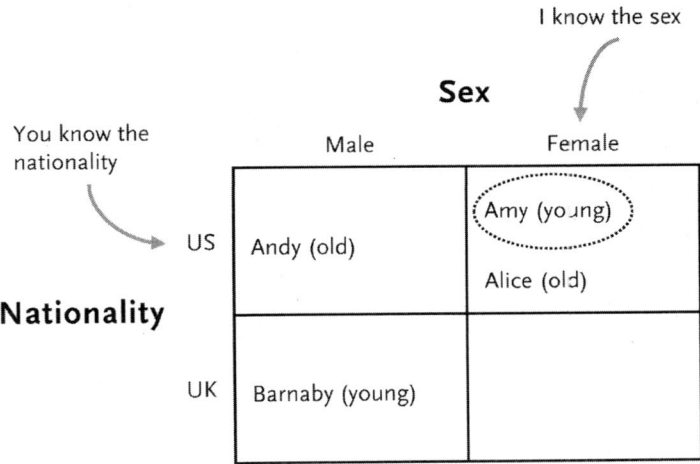

Of the four finalists, two are young and two are old, so our prior probabilities (before the leaks) that the winner is young are both .5. What are our posterior probabilities, after the leaks?

The reasoning is like figuring out Cheryl's birthday in chapter 1. You know that the winner is American, and one of the three Americans (Amy) is young, so your posterior that the winner is young is 1/3. And I can figure that out even if you don't tell me. That's because I know that the winner is female, and both are Americans, so I know that you had to have been told that the winner is American. Only one of the three Americans is young, so I know that your posterior for the winner being young is 1/3. (As you may have gleaned, this entire discussion assumes that everyone is rational, and everyone knows it—in other words, that everyone's rationality is itself common knowledge.)

What about my posterior? I know the winner is female, either young Amy or old Alice, so my posterior estimate that the winner is young is 1/2. And you can figure this out. Suppose I had been told that the winner was male. Well, one of the two men is young, the other old, so either way, my posterior for the winner being young is 1/2, and you know this.

But you do not *know* that I know your posterior. That's because as far as you are concerned, I could have been told that the winner is male. There are two males, one American and one British. If the winner is American, your posterior is 1/3 for the winner being young. If the winner is British, there is only one Briton, and that Briton is young, so your posterior for the winner being young would be 1. So, as far as you know, I can't know whether your posterior for the winner being young is 1 or 1/3. What we have, then, is a situation of *reciprocal* knowledge (we each know the other's posteriors) that falls short of *common* knowledge (you don't know that I know your posterior), *and* our posteriors are different. Therefore, it's possible for two rational agents to have different posteriors, even if each knows the other's, as long as they are not common knowledge.

The wallop in Aumann's theorem is the converse: the posteriors *cannot* differ if they *are* common knowledge. The result is not as easy to show with numbers as in the previous example, but one way to get the idea is to imagine a dialogue. Suppose I were to make my tentative estimate common knowledge with you by telling you what it is. Being rational, you update your estimate to take advantage of the information packed into my estimate, just as in the first scenario, and announce the result. Then I update mine in response, you look at my new estimate and update yours, then I look at your new estimate and update mine again, and so on. Aumann notes that "the process of exchanging information on the posteriors . . . will continue until these posteriors are equal."[21]

Why must they converge in this way? Two rational people with common knowledge are almost like a single mind whose knowledge is the intersection of theirs. It should no more matter who was exposed to which evidence than it matters which of two pieces of evidence I think about first. True, it's not the actual evidence we share, only the updated posteriors, which is why the theorem is so surprising. But those posteriors are a distillation of each of our histories of hard-won knowledge about the same world, there for use by the other. If they differ, one or both of us is wasting perfectly good information, like leaving money on the table. This cannot stand, and so we must keep adjusting our posteriors until they end up the same. And not only do we agree, but since each of us knows that the other has come to that realization, we cannot agree to disagree.

As Aumann dryly remarked, his theorem is "not quite obvious." In addition to the arresting main conclusion, his conception of what it means for rational agents to come to agreement is utterly foreign to our usual understanding of how people exchange ideas. In a paper called "We Can't Disagree Forever," Geanakoplos and Heraklis Polemarchakis spell out how the game of posterior ping-pong actually plays out.[22]

Naively, we might expect that two reasonable people with a bone of contention, say, one on the political left and one on the right, might start off far apart, and gradually each might bring the other closer to his side until they meet somewhere in the middle. But in Aumann's world, a rational dialogue doesn't work that way. Rationality is not like a buyer and seller haggling over a price until they split the difference. After all, why should we expect reality to just happen to lie midway between the convictions of two people who find themselves in an argument?

Instead, rational discourse consists in jointly squeezing as much information about the world as you can from what each of you has learned, always being open to being surprised. As soon as one party learns the other's best guess, he should adjust his own guess exactly as far as the math tells him he should, not partway as a kind of opening offer or grudging concession. Nor is there any reason to expect that on the next round he will move his guess still closer to hers, because, being rational, he should already have moved it as close to hers as the evidence warrants. When he sees her next guess, it might even force him to lurch back toward his first guess, or overshoot hers. None of their moves should go in a predictable direction, because if one did, they would already have known the direction and would thus *already* have shifted their position that way. A rational argument, at least in Aumann's idealization, is a random walk, the two sides neither predictably converging nor predictably zigzagging, but meandering chaotically like in the right-hand diagram below.

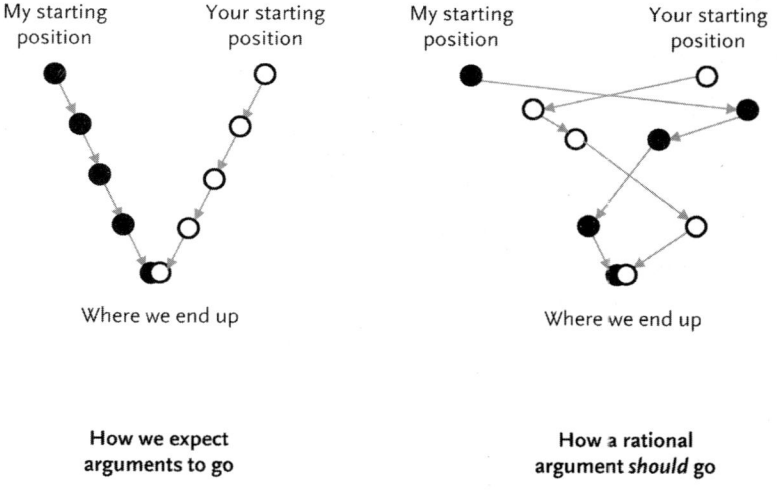

How we expect
arguments to go

How a rational
argument *should* go

That loop-de-loop is just one of the unpredictable trajectories an argument could take on its way to convergence. The parties could even stick to their guns until the very last step, when they suddenly coalesce into agreement, like the three diners who clean the spinach from their teeth upon the third clink of the glass.[23]

The shocker in Aumann's theorem is how different this ideal of rational convergence is from real human discourse. People, even highly rational people, who exchange their best-informed opinions end up disagreeing with each other all the time! (As we used to say in my community, "Ten Jews, eleven opinions.") And not just about subjective values and tastes, but about factual matters like who killed JFK or the origins of SARS-CoV-2 or whether there's life on other planets. And the process is as different from the world of the theorem as the outcome. When people trade opinions, they rarely flipflop from their starting position or leapfrog over each other but stand their ground and relinquish it only when forced to. What do we make of the difference between the ideal and the reality?

Perhaps the Agreement theorem is a spherical cow. Alternatively, the model might serve as a benchmark for rational discourse, and its strangeness should embarrass us into realizing how far we have to go! We already know that humans can be irrational when left to their own devices, not least in how they gather evidence and engage in Bayesian reasoning. Just as we look to logic and probability as yardsticks by which to improve our individual reasoning, perhaps we should use the Agreement theorem as an aspiration for more constructive collective reasoning.[24]

Let's start with the random walk in opinion exchanges. The computer scientist Scott Aaronson has pointed out that as unlikely as it sounds, at least one arena famous for prizing rationality works a bit like the Aumannian ideal. Two mathematicians arguing at a whiteboard often will flip sides as they struggle for clarity, each passionately arguing for the conclusion that they had passionately argued against just moments before. It's a display of an epistemic virtue called active open-mindedness, of treating beliefs as "hypotheses to be tested, not treasures to be guarded." As the economist John Maynard Keynes did not in fact say but often gets credit for saying, "When the facts change, I change my mind. What do you do, sir?"[25]

Consider, too, a jarring implication of the Agreement theorem: that rational agents should not engage in speculative trade.[26] Of course, a trade is rational when the two sides have complementary needs: when I have more milk than I can drink and you have more wool than you can wear, or I'm sitting on a pile of cash and you need to make a down payment on a house, or I'm willing to gamble on a lucrative but risky investment and you'd prefer to sleep at night with a smaller but safer one. But in a speculative trade, the two sides disagree on what they think an asset will be worth to third parties in the future: one thinks the price will go up and wants to buy, the other thinks it will fall and wants to sell.

According to the Agreement theorem, they should never do this. No acting on a hot stock tip, or shorting the yen, or going all in on pork bellies. A price reflects a posterior probability on the present value of the asset. And that price is common knowledge: everyone in the marketplace knows the price, and knows that everyone knows it. Therefore, rational agents with the same understanding of the world (the same priors) should not disagree about its value. As with the zigzagging arguers, if there were a good reason for the price to move up or down, the agents should already have factored that into their bidding or selling prices, each tipping off the others as to its likely value. If the speculative buyer and seller consummate the trade anyway, at least one of them is irrational—as they say, the greater fool. (Of course, the same is true of betting in sports.)

This corollary of the Agreement theorem, it turns out, is not that strange after all. Honest financial experts are unanimous in saying that the soundest advice for everyday investors is not to try to outsmart the market.[27] Don't follow hot tips, don't buy shares of a company with an insanely great gadget, don't prognosticate that in the next few years everyone will buy less detergent or more scotch or more crypto, don't invest in the mutual fund managed by the meticulous research team or the visionary genius. The reason is that any scrap of information that gets you excited is almost certainly common knowledge, and many other traders have already acted on it, bidding the price up or down to incorporate that scrap. If you disagree with a buyer or seller on the price, then one of you is irrational, and as they say in poker, if you look around the table and can't tell who the sucker is, it's you. Rather than forking over an annual management fee which almost certainly will not give you an edge, and which will compound your loss over the years, invest in a low-cost index fund, a mindless basket of assets sampled from the marketplace as a whole, and be content to share in the appreciation of companies as productivity rises. So in this case, a corollary of the Agreement theorem, strange as it sounds, is consistent with—indeed explains—our best understanding.

To be sure, there is a loophole in the Agreement theorem through which one can drive a coach and six horses. That's the assumption of equal priors; without it, the conclusion of common posteriors doesn't follow. Why should we believe that two rational agents come to a problem with the same background assumptions? Where do priors come from, anyway?[28]

On one interpretation, a prior is an inalienable conviction which needs no justification and may not be disputed, like a personal taste or an article of faith. This is how the term is often used in everyday discourse now that it has escaped from the world of statistics, as in "Supreme Court justices are going to decide in ways that are consistent with their ideological priors." People have whatever priors they have, and it's nobody else's business.

The problem with this licentiousness is that it would mean that anyone can believe anything they want! Since a Bayesian posterior is just a prior multiplied by the likelihood of the evidence divided by the commonness of the evidence, if the likelihood of the evidence against your pet belief is embarrassingly high, just say that your priors are low, and you can jigger the posterior to be as low as you'd like! I consider it to be so implausible that Donald Trump would lose an election that even if a mountain of evidence suggests he did lose, it's not enough to overcome my rock-bottom prior. Therefore, I rationally conclude that he probably won. Now, that can't be right. A prior today is just a posterior from yesterday, the fruit of considering all the evidence available up until then. Unless one of us is privy to a secret, why wouldn't it be the same for both of us?

To be sure, someone who still wanted to escape the Agreement theorem by slipping through the identical-priors loophole could raise the same question about yesterday, or the day before, or the day before that. You can't do Bayes without priors. At *some* point we had to start from scratch with no evidence to go on, and who's to say my assumptions on the starting line at Day 1 have to be the same as yours? Maybe I come from a different culture, or belong to a different race or sex, or have had a different lived experience, or am constitutionally optimistic or conservative or oppositional.

The response is: It's not about you. Why should the SARS-CoV-2 virus, or life on Mars, or the gunman of November 1963, care about your melanin or your genitals or your DNA or what you learned at your mother's knee? But for fortune you could have been born into a different culture, or body, or brain chemistry, yet that can't affect what's true or false about the world. And even if it did—if, say, congenital pessimists are always right because the world is a place where whatever can go wrong will go wrong—then everyone ought to adjust their priors to be more pessimistic, ironing out the differences once again. Rational agents reason from the viewpoint of eternity, behind a veil of ignorance of which bodies they are incarnated as—that is, with equal priors. So when they make their conclusions common knowledge, they should not agree to disagree.

Which makes the puzzle of why people *do* disagree all the more acute. The economists Tyler Cowen and Robin Hanson have taken up the puzzle. They start from the observation that disagreements often seem to be rooted in different priors about the relative virtues of the two disputants. Both sides hew to their beliefs, despite commonly known evidence, because each is convinced that they are the more rational, honest, informed, and competent of the two. Of course, common sense should tell them that they can't both be right, so they should give no more weight to their own convictions than to the other guy's. Do people innocently believe that it's OK for the two sides to have these different, self-serving priors? Or do they know it's not OK but dishonestly press ahead because they want to win the argument?

Cowen and Hanson chose to sidestep the metaphysical and admittedly murky line of reasoning about whether people ought to have the same priors because they could have been born into different bodies. Instead, they pondered whether ordinary people *think* that everyone should have the same priors, in particular, that they should set aside the self-serving priors about their own competence and rectitude that make disagreements so common. They observed that people readily condemn self-serving decisions in *others*. They are aghast at the judge who fails to recuse himself from the trial of a relative and rules in his favor, or the politician who awards a contract to a campaign contributor. They just make an exception for themselves. Cowen and Hanson conclude that most disagreements are dishonest: people adopt a stance that makes them come out ahead while knowing, at some level, that they shouldn't. It's not that disputants are consciously lying. Cowen and Hanson cite Robert Trivers's theory that people deceive themselves, the better to deceive others, since the most convincing liar is the one who believes his own lies.[29]

Whether real human disagreements come from dishonesty or incompetence, the idealization of rational deliberation in Aumann's proof is a wake-up call for how we could make our own deliberation more rational. The status quo leaves something to be desired. At the most refined levels of intellectual colloquy, in debating forums named after venerable British universities and periodicals whose names are permutations of *New York, London, Review, Literary, Books,* and *Times,* the customary style of argumentation is gladiatorial combat. The goal is to vanquish one's adversary, and the tactics are the projection of unshakable confidence, the withering caricature, the targeting of unguarded flanks, the self-defense against falsification, the advantage taken in having the last word. It's an entertaining sport, but a dubious way to seek the truth.

An alternative mode of deliberation has recently been advocated by a family of intellectual movements that call themselves forecasters, the rationality community, or simply Bayesians.[30] Guided by Bayes's Rule, and, in the case of Cowen, Hanson, and Aaronson, by Aumann's theorem itself, they advocate norms of debate that are designed to steer the deliberators toward consensus about the hypothesis with the highest posterior probability of being true. The norms include expressing ranges of confidence ("I think there's a .5 to .7 chance that I'm right"), "steel-manning" rather than "straw-manning" one's opponent (stating his position in as strong a form as possible rather than setting up an effigy to knock down), agreeing to adversarial collaborations (where disputants design a study that they agree in advance would settle an issue), and betting on concrete predictions derived from their theories (as the economist Alex Tabarrok has put it, "A bet is a tax on bullshit").

I concluded the previous chapter with George Lakoff and Mark Johnson's observation that language is filled with families of idioms that draw on a common metaphor, like LOVE IS A JOURNEY and KNOW-ING IS SEEING. Lakoff and Johnson invite their readers to interrogate the "metaphors we live by" and see whether they tether us to a way of construing the world that we might transcend. They call special attention to the conceptual metaphor ARGUMENT IS WAR:

> Try to imagine a culture where arguments are not viewed in terms of war, where no one wins or loses, where there is no sense of attacking or defending, gaining or losing ground. Imagine a culture where an argument is viewed as a dance, the participants are seen as performers,

and the goal is to perform in a balanced and aesthetically pleasing way. In such a culture, people would view arguments differently, experience them differently, carry them out differently, and talk about them differently.[31]

For decades after I read Lakoff and Johnson's book, I thought the example was strained. Surely the goal of an argument is to home in on the truth, not put on a performance. But since reading Aumann's explanation of how common knowledge can guide rational discussants toward consensus, and the weaving, twisting path they take to get there, I appreciate Lakoff and Johnson's insight: rational argument really should be more like a dance than a war.

3
Fun and Games

The Stag Hunt, the Battle of the Sexes,
Hawks and Doves, and other coordination games
that explain the need for common knowledge

What good is common knowledge? The surprises in chapter 2 drove home the fact that common knowledge is a special state of awareness. But the scenarios were contrived to throw a spotlight on that specialness and sometimes verged on the fantastical.

In this chapter[1] I'll show how common knowledge is not a trick we occasionally pull out to make a neat logical point but a regular feature of human social life, indeed a prerequisite to social life. I'll lay out a few predicaments in which humans repeatedly find themselves—situations in which rational actors must choose among alternatives whose outcomes depend on the choices of other rational actors. These are the "games" in the branch of mathematics called game theory.[2] Though each is stylized, they capture recurring plot twists that make up the human drama, and show that many apparent oddities of social life can be explained as rational ways out of these predicaments.

The focus will be games of coordination, in which the actors prosper only if they make complementary choices, but face more than one way of doing so, and need common knowledge to align their choices. Often the best way to understand something is to be shown what it is *not*, so I'll set the stage with a game that is game theory's best-known brainchild, but which differs from coordination games in just about every way. As I mentioned in chapter 1, it's called the Prisoners' Dilemma.[3]

A prosecutor detains partners in crime in separate cells, lacks the evidence to convict them, and offers them a deal. If one defects on his partner by testifying against him, he will go free and his partner will go to prison for ten years. If each rats out the other, they both get six years. If they cooperate with their partner and keep mum, the prosecutor can convict them only on a lesser charge and they'll serve six months.

The dilemma is diagrammed below as a matrix in which the possible choices for one player, in this case Choo-choo, are shown as rows, and the choices for the other, Onions, are shown as columns.[4] Each cell displays what happens to them if they make that combination of choices. Choo-choo's outcome is shown in gray in the lower left corner of each cell, Onions's in black in the upper right.

Onions

	Cooperate (mum)	Defect (rat)
Cooperate (mum)	6 months 6 months	Go free 10 years
Defect (rat)	10 years Go free	6 years 6 years

Choo-choo

In making his choice (picking a row), Choo-choo considers what's in it for him (the gray payoff) given each of Onions's choices (the two columns). If Onions chooses to cooperate (left column), Choo-choo's best choice is to defect (bottom row), because going free is better than serving six months. If Onions chooses to defect (right column), Choo-choo's best option is to defect, because six years in the hoosegow is preferable to ten. It's a no-brainer (in jargon, a "dominant strategy"): Choo-choo defects. Now consider it from the point of Onions, who works through his own choices (which column to pick) row by row, looking at the payoffs in black. If Choo-choo cooperates, he's better off defecting. If Choo-choo defects, he's better off defecting. Onions picks his own dominant option, defecting.

A "game" in the game theorist's sense doesn't necessarily have a winner or loser, nor a correct solution. But it may have a Nash equilibrium, named after the mathematician John Nash, the subject of the biography and movie *A Beautiful Mind*. A Nash equilibrium, equilibrium for short, is a set of choices (a cell in the matrix) in which neither player has an incentive to switch given the choice of the other. The Prisoners' Dilemma has one equilibrium: the lower right cell, mutual defection. The partners tragically find themselves sucked into the second-worst outcome for each of them (six years in the pen), whereas if they had stayed true to each other, they could have enjoyed the second-best (six months).

The Prisoners' Dilemma is one of the great ideas in intellectual history, and ought to be understood by every educated person.[5] It shows how individuals acting rationally in their own interests can end up worse off than if they somehow mustered the will to be altruistic. It calls for a higher rationality in which actors submit to a social contract that ties their hands for their own good (in this case, by knowing that if they broke the vow of *omertà* by ratting out their partners they would end up sleeping with the fishes). Alternatively, if the game is repeated, the players can escape the dilemma by evolving a sense of fairness that impels them to reward cooperation and punish defection. In the multiplayer version called the Public Goods Game or Tragedy of the Commons, it explains why, in the absence of externally imposed rewards and punishments, every person, and every nation, has an incentive to overconsume resources and pollute the environment even while knowing that when they all do so they end up worse off. In *The Better Angels of Our Nature,* I argued that an isomorph I called the Pacifists' Dilemma explains why it's so hard to reduce violence, and described the ways in which the game changed over time to bring about the declines that historians have observed.

But the Prisoners' Dilemma is just one out of seventy-eight ways in which the outcomes of two players facing two choices can be ordered.[6] Fans of game theory, including the international relations expert Joshua Goldstein, the legal scholar Richard McAdams, and the philosopher Brian Skyrms, have pointed out that it has become a hammer that leads writers into treating the world like a nail.[7] Many human predicaments are not Prisoners' Dilemmas, with a single equilibrium dictated by the payoffs.

This brings us back to the coffee klatschers of the preceding two chapters, Charlotte and James. Recall that they enjoy badinage over a cup of joe, but neither could care less whether their tête-à-tête takes place at the Coffee Connection or the Java Joint. A dead battery and cellular dead zone force them to make their choices incommunicado.

Though they are in a dilemma, the matrix laying it out is entirely different from the one that faced the unfortunate prisoners. Let's set a number from 0 to 100 on the subjective value that each places on the outcomes, 100 for the enjoyment of a consummated rendezvous, 0 for the annoyance at the missed opportunity.

Rendezvous has *two* equilibria: the top left cell, where Charlotte

James

	Connection	Joint

Connection

Charlotte

	Connection	Joint
Connection	100 / 100	0 / 0
Joint	0 / 0	100 / 100

has no incentive to switch her choice to the Joint given that James has picked the Connection, or vice versa, and the bottom right cell, for the same reason.

And this is where the game leaves off and the fun begins. Game theory tells us that Charlotte and James are best off if they end up in the top left or bottom right squares, and that if they should ever be so fortunate, they'll stay there. But what does it advise about how they should find their way into one or the other blessed equilibrium? The answer is: nothing. The payoffs are the same, and if either of them finds themselves in one of the mismatched cells, they both have an incentive to switch, but that's the problem: if they both switch, they're no better off. As we saw in chapter 1, trying to get into each other's heads won't extricate them from the dilemma, and as we saw in chapter 2, exchanging and confirming messages without assurance they'll get through won't help either.

Of course by now you know what would help. If we gave them back their working cell phones, then a short chat would generate the common knowledge that would solve their problem in a stroke. But the idea that language generates the common knowledge which can resolve a coordination dilemma is not as foolproof as it seems.

Many game theorists are skeptical that language can have this power, because words are cheap. As the movie mogul Sam Goldwyn pointed out, an oral contract isn't worth the paper it's written on.[8] In the Prisoners' Dilemma, even if Choo-choo could tell Onions, "I'll cooperate if you do," why should Onions believe him, given that when the time comes, the temptation to defect will be overwhelming? Worse, if he *could* get Onions to believe him, it would only heighten his temptation, tantalizing him with the opportunity to go free. Similarly, if for some reason it served Charlotte's interests for James to go the Connection, she could hoodwink him into going there by saying *she* was going there, whether or not she was. James wasn't born yesterday, so he would turn a deaf ear, with the result that no one would ever say anything to anyone.

The problem of cheap talk leads to the theory of costly signaling.[9] Communicators can only convey information credibly, given the threat of liars who say the same thing, if in doing so they incur a cost which they can bear more readily than the liars. That's why an antelope sproings into the air to signal to a lioness that she'd be best off chasing another antelope, rather than just flexing his haunches, which slower antelopes could learn to do too. Peacocks grow splendiferous tails to impress peahens with their health, rather than evolving thermometers on their foreheads whose readouts could be mimicked by sicker rivals. And students earn degrees in literary theory or cosmology from elite universities to impress employers with their intelligence and discipline rather than bragging about these qualifications in a personal statement.[10]

But with a pure coordination game like Rendezvous, costly signaling is a solution in search of a problem.[11] Cheap talk works just fine, because the interests of the two players are aligned. Charlotte's announcement "I'll see you at the Coffee Connection" is self-signaling, because she has no reason to lie, and it's self-committing, since once she says it and it's believed, she has every reason to carry it out. For the same reason, the equilibria in other games of pure coordination, like driving on the right or the left, need no costly signaling or enforcement. It's in everyone's interests to respect them, as explained in a joke. A woman calls her husband on his mobile phone while he is driving to work and warns him, "Be careful, honey. The radio says there's a maniac out there driving on the wrong side of the freeway." "*One* maniac?" he replies. "There are hundreds of them!"

Whether cheap talk is credible depends on whether there is a conflict of interest. In this case, there's no cell in the matrix with a higher number for Charlotte than for James, or vice versa. In games that do have a conflict, like those we'll see in the rest of the chapter (and, of course, in the Prisoners' Dilemma), cheap talk may indeed not be worth the paper it's written on. When the conflict is partial, as in a business deal, contracts are bound by the threat of costly lawsuits and penalties. When the conflict is total, as in chess or poker, the players have no use for speech at all.

We can also flip the question. What does the ease of conversation tell us about human social life? Most speech is not costly, of course; we don't talk with marbles in our mouth to prove our sincerity. This suggests that in most of human history, people found themselves in opportunities for symmetrical coordination in which cheap talk was helpful. If we spent most of our time in the presence of our enemies, we'd have evolved to zip our lips and block our ears. This trust is backstopped, of course, by wariness for obvious conflicts of interest or a reputation for duplicity, but conversation would be impossible without a default maxim of honesty.[12] The exception that proves the rule is con artists, who cunningly exploit the default of trust in casual social interactions to bilk the unsuspecting.[13] Indeed, in experiments in which people play out the games from game theory, if they are given the opportunity to exchange cheap talk, they are likelier to cooperate, suggesting that people really do start from a self-fulfilling presumption of common interests.[14]

Coordination games also suggest an answer to the question "Why did language evolve?," which has embroiled cognitive and evolutionary scientists ever since the psychologist Paul Bloom and I whacked that beehive in 1990.[15] Among the hypotheses that have been bruited: language was an accidental by-product of a big brain; it arose all at once from a single lucky mutation; it allowed us to exchange know-how; it enabled us to negotiate reciprocal agreements; it was a means to share gossip; it is a sexually selected costly signal of neurobiological fitness, like the peacock's tail, in which spellbinding orators and silver-tongued seducers were likelier to get laid. Curiously absent from all these debates is what I now think is the simplest explanation of all: language cheaply generates the common knowledge that makes social coordination possible.

Let's go back to the scenario in which direct speech is unavailable, such as when a cell phone goes dead. Game theory is silent on what a rational actor ought to do, because there is nothing to choose between the upper left and lower right cells, with their identical payoffs. But here is a case in which psychology can solve a problem that mathematics cannot. In chapter 1, I introduced a seminal idea from the political scientist Thomas Schelling (another Nobel laureate)—common salience, or a focal point.[16] If one of the options jumps out at Charlotte, for any reason, and she knows that James is cut from the same cloth, she can gravitate to that option, confident that James will lean the same way, because he expects her to tilt that way, ad infinitum. Their expectations are self-fulfilling.

Schelling's classic example was a separated couple who had to reunite somewhere, anywhere, in New York. They'd be wise to get themselves to the big clock in Grand Central Terminal at noon, even if it wasn't particularly close to where they had lost sight of each other, because each can expect it to pop into the other's mind.[17]

The power of focal points to settle coordination dilemmas opens the door for caprices of psychology, history, and culture to become solutions to cut-and-dried problems of rational actors pursuing their interests. As Schelling put it:

> Finding the key, or rather finding a key—any key that is mutually recognized as the key becomes the key—may depend on imagination more than on logic; it may depend on analogy, precedent, accidental arrangement, symmetry, aesthetic or geometric configuration, casuistic reasoning, and who the parties are and what they know about each other. Whimsy may send the man and his wife to the "lost and found"; or logic may lead each to reflect and to expect the other to reflect on where they would have agreed to meet if they had had a prior agreement to cover the contingency. . . . But in the final analysis we are dealing with imagination as much as with logic; and the logic itself is of a fairly casuistic kind. Poets may do better than logicians at this game, which is perhaps more like "puns and anagrams" than like chess.[18]

In an informal study Schelling offered rewards to pairs of people if they both picked either heads or tails. Most picked heads and claimed their prize, presumably because the word comes first in the phrase *heads or tails*. The ordering of the two words is a linguistic phenomenon—in conjunctions, the shorter vowel and less obstruent consonant tend to come first—which is utterly irrelevant to the problem, yet solved it.[19] Focal points depend on the consciousness of the players and can vary with their local culture and recent history. When the anthropologist Lee Cronk tried to replicate Schelling's old demo in his classroom, he was surprised to find that a majority of students picked tails.[20] He learned that in the intervening decades a new expression about coin-flipping had gained currency, "Tails never fails." Now rhyme, equally irrelevant, solves the problem.

Because focal points are hostages to variability in human attention, a culture will often pick one and try to stick with it, at which point we call it a convention.[21] Seven is not a particularly useful number to count out a weekly cycle of days, but once the Babylonians settled on it for their screwball astrological reasons, it was there for every subsequent civilization as a solution to the problem of coordinating days of work and rest. That still left open which of the seven days to set aside as the day of rest. Jews picked the last, because that's when God relaxed after creating heaven and earth; Christians picked the first, because that's when the son of God rose from the dead. However nonsensical, these rationales worked for each community as long as it didn't have to coordinate too often with the other. Members of the minority community could recognize each other by sartorial and tonsorial signals that provided common knowledge of their shared equilibria: their day of rest and their conventions for other coordination challenges such as marriage, law, diet, and conferral of adulthood.

The idea that conventions can be solutions to coordination games can make sense of the phantasmagoria of cultural practices that are the stuff of Anthropology 101. And it can cut through a major debate in that field, namely whether cultural practices have practical rationales (Jews avoid pork because it might harbor trichinosis) or are arbitrary symbolic structures (Jews avoid pork because it falls on the wrong side of the sacred–profane binary). In coordination games, the arbitrary can be eminently practical.[22]

Note how the concerns raised by coordination games are very different from those raised by the Prisoners' Dilemma and other classic games where the payoffs alone determine the rational responses. Coordination dilemmas, even when analyzed with the hardheaded math of game theory, give pride of place to the messy human preoccupations of culture, history, tradition, symbolism, aesthetics, and casual conversation.

All these are reasons, the legal scholar McAdams argues, to avoid seeing a Prisoners' Dilemma behind every tree. Even the dilemmas facing prisoners are seldom Prisoners' Dilemmas. Consider Alibi, an isomorph of Rendezvous. Once again the partners in crime are held in different interrogation rooms, but this time the prosecutor's case is so feeble that the prisoners could win their freedom by giving a credible alibi for their whereabouts at the time of the crime. To make it credible, the alibi has to be corroborated, if only by the partner, but they have not given any thought in advance to getting their stories straight. Each tries to think of what the other would think: Were they at the home of the first partner, or of the second? At a movie theater? In a certain bar? The exact alibi doesn't matter as long as they come up with the same one. Cheap talk, if they could only sneak away for a quick chat, would generate the common knowledge they need; otherwise, they must hope for the best with the common salience of a focal point.

Meeting at Grand Central or Penn Station, driving on the right or the left, sleeping late on Saturday or Sundays, and coming up with a consistent alibi are games of pure coordination, where everyone's interests are aligned and any joint solution is as good as any other.

Often interests conflict, though. Suppose that James and Charlotte each had a strong preference for one café over the other, while still preferring each other's company to sipping alone. In game theory, their predicament is called the Battle of the Sexes, which actually has nothing to do with the sexes other than invoking some gender stereotypes for convenience.[23] But as we have seen, technical terms are conventions, and they can get grandmothered in even if they had not been chosen for what we might consider good reasons.

The Battle of the Sexes refers to a hypothetical scenario like the following. A couple, let's call them Steve and Rebecca, would rather spend time together than apart, but have different preferences as to where to spend that time, Steve preferring to watch the Boston Bruins face off against the Montreal Canadiens and Rebecca preferring to take in a performance of *La Traviata*.[24] Here are the payoffs:

Steve

	Opera	Hockey
Opera	75 / 100	0 / 0
Hockey	0 / 0	100 / 75

Rebecca (row player)

Once again there are two equilibria: if Rebecca goes to the opera, Steve prefers the opera, and vice versa (top left), and if Rebecca goes to the hockey game, Steve prefers the hockey game, and vice versa (bottom right). A matrix with two equilibria means we are in a coordination game, where the two parties are better off in either of them than in the other two cells, and nothing in the numbers will force the pair into one or the other. Unlike Rendezvous, though, the numbers in the two cells differ; each prefers one equilibrium to the other.

Again, they need common knowledge of their intentions to be sure of ending up at the same venue. Direct speech—a phone call to finalize the engagement—would do the trick, though the rub is which equilibrium to make common knowledge, since each would prefer a different one. They could conform to a convention like chivalry and have a night at the opera, or patriarchy and cheer at the game, or fairness and take turns or flip a coin. They could look for a focal point, like which venue was closer or which tickets were cheaper, even if the difference wasn't great enough to overturn their preferences. Alternatively, one of them could force the issue by announcing their intention just before their cell phone went dead, or credibly signaling that they were intransigent about their preference out of pride or superstition or sheer mulishness—that "it's my way or the highway." Since a second-choice date is better than none, the pighead has the compromiser over a barrel. Schelling called these voluntary sacrifices of control "paradoxical tactics," and they are an endless source of fascination to those who want to make sense of human senselessness.[25]

The Battle of the Sexes plays out in real life when people engage in bargaining. When a buyer and seller haggle over a price, there is a range of values that make it worthwhile for the two of them to consummate the deal rather than walk away. But the seller prefers a high price in the range and the buyer a low one. They might find their way into one of these equilibria with the help of a focal point, like splitting the difference or settling on a round number, or by one of them paradoxically forfeiting control, such as a car salesman who conveniently needs the approval of a stubborn manager or a car buyer who conveniently needs the approval of a stubborn loan officer. The

Battle also plays out in the adoption of technical, legal, and financial standards. Everyone would prefer there to be a single kind of connector for cell phones and earbuds to replace the spaghetti of cables that now stuff our drawers, but Apple would profit if it was Lightning while other companies would lobby for USB-C.

⚬⊱⚬

Though game theory was invented in 1944 by John von Neumann and Oskar Morgenstern, the insight that the costs and benefits of a choice may depend on the choices of others was anticipated, like so many other great ideas, during the Enlightenment. In 1755 Jean-Jacques Rousseau originated another coordination scenario, logically distinct from the ones we have considered so far:

> When it came to taking down a stag, everyone knew he had to do his part faithfully, but if a hare happened to cross the path of one of them, no doubt he would have chased it without scruple, and once he caught his prey, not cared that he had let his companions lose theirs.[26]

The game that was loosely inspired by this sentence is called the Stag Hunt.[27] In Rousseau's version, every hunter is tempted by selfishness and impatience to pursue a small but sure reward, the hare, over a larger but less certain reward, the stag, which he could have taken down if he had hunted with the others. The uncertainty comes not from the possibility that the stag might escape from the team of hunters (let's assume that, working together, they can always ambush it) but from the possibility that any of the *other* hunters might go after a hare, too, if only from *their* fear that some *other* hunter might do so. When there are only two hunters and they agree to divide a carcass in half, they face the following payoffs, reckoned in pounds of meat:

François-Marie

	Cooperate (hunt stag)	Defect (hunt hare)
Cooperate (hunt stag)	30 / 30	3 / 0
Defect (hunt hare)	0 / 3	3 / 3

Jean-Jacques

The theme of forgoing a large reward by defecting on a partnership makes it sound a bit like a Prisoners' Dilemma, but it isn't, because in the Dilemma, the best thing you can do is defect when the other guy cooperates (going free by snitching when he stays mum), but in the Hunt, the best thing you can do is cooperate when the other guy cooperates (joining forces to fell a meaty stag instead of a puny hare). More important, a Prisoners' Dilemma has one Nash equilibrium (mutual defection), whereas a Stag Hunt has two: if François-Marie hunts hare, Jean-Jacques is best off hunting hare, and vice versa, but if François-Marie hunts stag, Jean-Jacques is best off hunting stag, and vice versa. The twofold equilibria tell us we are in a coordination game.

The coordination dilemma is camouflaged by the language of cooperation and defection and by Rousseau's judgmental framing of the parable in terms of scruples and thoughtlessness. But the tension in a Stag Hunt lies not as much in betrayal as in uncertainty. A less moralistic cover story has the two hunters deciding every morning before meeting up whether to bring the heavy weaponry needed to fell a stag in cahoots or the light weaponry sufficient to bag a hare each on his own. Jean-Jacques would be happy to bring his shotgun if he could be sure that François-Marie would too, and vice versa, but each worries about being weighed down by the cumbersome weapon if the other came with just a slingshot, which he might have chosen as the failsafe option if he worried that the first might have done so, and so on down the mental hall of mirrors. Common knowledge would get them out of their predicament, but cell phones would not be invented for another two hundred years. (Cheap talk on the call would be enough as long as neither had anything to gain from the other hunting stag while he himself hunted hare.[28]) Without common knowledge, the hare-hunting equilibrium is tempting to each, despite its paltry payoff, because going after hare is the sure thing, while gearing up for stag incurs the risk that the other hunter will not so prepare, if only because he is risk-averse, too. What they need is common assurance. For this reason the Stag Hunt is often called the Assurance Game, or sometimes the Trust Dilemma.

The dilemma of a Stag Hunt is far from hypothetical. The anthropologists Michael Alvard and David Nolin studied an Indonesian people called the Lamalerans, who hunt whales in teams of eight to fourteen men which divide up the tasks of rowing, bailing, helming, and harpooning.[29] Only if they work together can they land a whale. But in a twist that could have been scripted by Rousseau, they also have the option of foraging alone or in smaller groups for fish. The Lamalerans' version of the Stag Hunt is particularly acute because when such a big team is required, all it takes is one member failing to show up for the hunt to fail.

The Lamalerans solve their coordination dilemma with a convention stipulating which men are expected to hunt in which boat.

Members of a patrilineal descent group (paternal relatives, descended from the same grandfather or great-grandfather) hunt together. This crisp convention can easily become common knowledge because everyone can tell who's in and who's out, and they can expect that everyone else can tell, too.[30] It contrasts with mere kinship, which peters out as relatives become more distant, leaving it a matter of opinion who counts as a relative. (My profile on a personal genomics website lists more than five thousand "relatives" varying in the amount of DNA we share from 0.07 to 16.79 percent, including dubious kinfolk such as the columnist David Brooks, the lawyer Alan Dershowitz, and the actress Mayim Bialik. But it lists exactly 116 men who share my Y chromosome, inherited from a common great-great-etc.-grandfather.[31]) A patrilineal descent group also contrasts with a scheme that might appear more logical, namely assembling teams with complementary skills, but which is also more subjective and therefore vulnerable to discoordination.

If the nervousness of the two hunters in the original scenario feels like déjà vu, it's because we've seen this game in various isomorphs in earlier chapters.[32] The Coordinated Attack problem of chapter 2 is a Stag Hunt, where attacking together is hunting stag, staying put is hunting hare, and attacking alone is showing up with a shotgun and coming home empty-handed.

So are the bank runs and asset bubbles of chapter 1: investors stay in and enjoy stag-sized returns if they have reason to believe that all the other investors are staying in, but run for the exits in the hope of getting out early with a hare rather than late with nothing if they fear that other investors are worrying about the same thing.

Ditto with protests: if enough other protesters show up, they all enjoy the stag of regime change, but at the risk of being imprisoned or gunned down if they are outnumbered, tempting them to stay home with their hares grumbling about the regime. The challenge for leaders of movements for change is not just to generate common knowledge of the shared grievance (say, by handing out leaflets or opening umbrellas) but to entice the onlookers to join the hunt by generating common expectations of success that can become self-fulfilling: *We shall never surrender*; *We shall overcome*; *We shall not be moved*; *I have a dream.*

And yet another familiar Stag Hunt comes from the Prisoners' Dilemma itself when it is repeated, giving each prisoner an opportunity to reward or punish the other for what he did on the last round. In that case a pair of distrustful prisoners might still find themselves boxed into an equilibrium in which they defect on each other over and over. But if they start out cooperating and then play Tit for Tat, defecting only to punish the other guy for defecting, they can remain ensconced in a happy cooperative equilibrium instead. In *The Stag Hunt and the Evolution of Social Structure*, Skyrms argues that the evolution of societies from an anarchic state of nature to a mutually beneficial social contract can be likened to a dynamic in which citizens learn, connive, congregate, or blunder their way into hunting stag together instead of hare alone.

The last of the evocative coordination games also takes its name from the animal kingdom, but this one from the avian rather than the mammalian class. Or, more accurately, its two names, because two stereotypes of conflict with the same array of dangers and rewards are named after birds.

The more familiar one is called Chicken, after the alleged pusillanimity of the fowl. Two teenagers drive toward each other at high speed on a highway, and the first to swerve loses face as the "chicken." The payoffs, with players named after the characters in *Rebel Without a Cause* who carried out a similar game,[33] are shown in the grid below.

Buzz

		Swerve	Proceed
Jim	Swerve	Anticlimax 0 / Anticlimax 0	Win 10 / "Chicken" −10
	Proceed	"Chicken" −10 / Win 10	Crash −100 / Crash −100

In a gentler and more realistic scenario, two drivers converge on an unmarked intersection, or two walkers approach in a narrow hallway, and one incurs the inconvenience of waiting to let the other one pass. There are two equilibria, though they are not the cells along the main diagonal in which players try to match each other's choices. On the contrary, if the other guy swerves, you want to proceed, and if the other guy proceeds, you want to swerve, so the cells that neither driver wants to switch out of are the cells in which they make opposite choices. The tragedy is that each driver prefers the equilibrium in which he persists and the other is the chicken, but if they both pursue that preference, they end up in the cell they have a common interest in avoiding, a disastrous crash.

The game of Chicken became famous in the 1950s, not just from the James Dean movie but because Bertrand Russell had likened it to the confrontation between the United States and the Soviet Union. As the humorist Dave Barry later put it, the cold war consisted of "258 crucial world hotspots, where at this moment the United States and the Soviet Union, each with one hand on the steering wheel and the other on the horn, are simultaneously edging into the same parking space."

Joshua Goldstein, the international relations scholar, has argued that the metaphor is apt.[34] Many trade wars, debt crises, saber-rattlings, and shooting wars fall into the pattern of a Chicken game rather than a Prisoners' Dilemma, which superficially resembles it because two actors pursuing their self-interest end up worse off than if they had cooperated. But in a Prisoners' Dilemma the worst possible outcome is to cooperate while the other party defects, whereas in Chicken the worst outcome is for both parties to defect (that is, proceed to a crash). Plausible real-life examples include the confrontations between Hitler and Chamberlain in 1938, the Soviet Union and its breakaway republics in 1990, the United States and Iraq in 1991 and 2003, and the United States and the Soviet Union during the Berlin blockade of 1948 and, most famously, the Cuban Missile Crisis of 1962. At the time of this writing, the United States and NATO are trying to prevent the war in Ukraine from turning into a game of Chicken between them and Russia.

The second conflict prototype, an isomorph of Chicken, literally comes from biology. It was named by the inventor of evolutionary game theory, John Maynard Smith, after two species of birds whose names are metonyms for aggression and conciliation, the hawk and the dove.[35] The terms shouldn't be taken literally—doves are in fact rather aggressive birds, and the antagonists in a Hawk–Dove game generally belong to the same species.

Suppose two magpies face off over a territory that both want to occupy. Each can either squawk and spread its wings (Dove) or claw and peck the other (Hawk). If the two just dovishly display, they split the territory.[36] If one displays and the other attacks, the dove concedes to the hawk. If they both attack, feathers fly and the two are mortally wounded.

Jeckle

		Dove	Hawk
		Split 50	Win 100
Heckle	Dove	Split 50	Concede 0
		Concede 0	Fight −100
	Hawk	Win 100	Fight −100

As usual, the numbers in the boxes are meant to show the relative magnitudes of the outcomes, not their absolute values, and it's easy to see that the ordering of the four boxes is the same as in Chicken. Of course, in reality the values do matter: when people or magpies face off, they weigh the benefit of the contested resource against the potential cost of conflict and the likelihood of winning to decide whether the resource is, as we say, worth fighting over.

Natural selection favors winning, but it favors even more strongly not dying in a fight. That's why real animals of the same species seldom fight to the death (though they do sometimes). Evolutionary biologists have been curious about how they manage to avoid the mutual fighting cell with its Shakespearean tragedy of a stage strewn with bodies. One option is to evolve a conditional strategy that sorts the animals into one of the two equilibria: first strut your stuff to see who's bigger and stronger, then play Hawk if it's you or Dove if it's the other magpie. Mortal combat takes place when each of the animals thinks it's stronger, one of them mistakenly, a tragedy analogous to the many catastrophic wars in human history that were triggered by mutual overconfidence.[37]

Alternatively, antagonists may settle into an equilibrium with the help of our familiar tie-breaker, common salience or a focal point. The most common focal point is sheer precedence: the animal that shows up first in a territory acts like he owns it and stands his ground while the interloper concedes. Maynard Smith whimsically called this strategy Bourgeois, but many thinkers, starting with David Hume, have argued that it literally is the rationale behind the human convention of property.[38] Legal property rights hinge not on a judgment of who "deserves" the resource but on common knowledge of who is recognized as having the right to keep and use it. As with the Bourgeois strategy, possession is nine-tenths of the law: in cases of uncertainty, the courts generally recognize the party holding or squatting on the resource as its owner. Regardless of whether they are just or unjust in some cosmic sense, commonly known property rights prevent endless robberies and reprisals.

With the fate of the world literally hanging on the answer, scholars and leaders alike take an interest in how players in a game of Chicken can avoid the crash cell and get into one of the two equilibria (or best of all, the compromise cell).[39]

Furnishing the teenagers with cell phones so they can exchange cheap talk won't help, because if one says "I'm not swerving, suckahhh!" the other could call his bluff, knowing he has no interest in carrying out the threat. One tempting but perilous alternative is the paradoxical tactic of forfeiting rationality or control. One of the drivers could conspicuously lock his steering wheel and put a cinder block on the accelerator, forcing the other to swerve or kill them both. In international relations it's called the Madman strategy, and has been attributed at various times to Richard Nixon,

Saddam Hussein, the Kims of North Korea, and Donald Trump. One peril in the strategy is obvious: both drivers might lock their steering wheels at the same time. Another is that the sacrifice of control may be private rather than common knowledge—if, say, the second driver did not notice or believe that the first had locked his wheel.

In the darkest joke in the history of cinema, the movie *Dr. Strangelove* showed how a lack of common knowledge could destroy the world.[40] The Soviets have deployed the ultimate paradoxical tactic, the Doomsday Machine, a network of nuclear bombs capable of destroying all life on Earth and triggered to go off automatically if the country is attacked. A rogue American officer, unaware of the deterrent, launches an irrevocable attack, and as it is under way the brilliant game theorist Dr. Strangelove confers with the American president and the Soviet ambassador:

> STRANGELOVE: There is only one thing I don't understand, Mister Ambassador. The whole point of the Doomsday Machine is lost if you keep it a secret. Why didn't you tell the world?
> AMBASSADOR: It was to be announced at the Party Congress on Monday. As you know, the Premier loves surprises.[41]

There are safer ways to navigate a game of Chicken. If the players live to play another day, and the day after that, and so on, they can play Tit for Tat or some other retaliatory strategy that can make mutual conciliation an equilibrium.[42] Or they could bargain, that is, offer to change the payoffs (such as by agreeing to divide a resource rather than fighting for all of it) and turn the game into a Battle of the Sexes. Yet another alternative was favored by Bertrand Russell, Albert Einstein, and other intellectuals in the 1950s. They argued that nothing short of a world government with the power to rewrite the payoffs by punishing aggressors, with nuclear weapons if necessary, could save the species from annihilation.

But in practice it seems to have been convention and common salience that solved the unsolvable. Political scientists have examined which historical developments deserve credit for the Long Peace, the decline in interstate wars after World War II.[43] A major contender is a historically novel convention, the territorial integrity norm.[44] War is no longer treated by the international community as a legitimate means of rectifying borders: United Nations members have pledged not to wage war except in self-defense or with the approval of the Security Council. International borders, however arbitrary or unjust, are grandfathered in, or, when new nations emerge, are carried over from provincial or colonial boundaries.

Could these toothless norms really have deterred the hawks and kamikaze drivers that populate the tough neighborhood known as the global system of nation-states? Not always, of course, as we saw in Russia's 2022 invasion of Ukraine. But the logic of common salience in coordination games makes it plausible that focal points could make a difference. Good fences make good neighbors. In a Hawk–Dove game in which the weaker party can threaten real damage (since they have more to lose), both parties may seek safety in a focal point like "stick with the border already on the map" rather than risk escalation to a mutually ruinous war. Indeed, in a sharp break from centuries of history, no UN member state in the postwar period has gone out of existence through conquest, and little territory has permanently changed hands (other than some small islands and sparsely populated hinterlands). When one nation has tried to absorb a conquered territory (such as Israel with the Golan Heights), the international community has refused to recognize the annexation. Diplomatic recognition itself is a convention ratified by common knowledge: what it means for a country or border to be "recognized" is that every country knows that every other country recognizes it, and knows that, and so on.

Together with the territorial integrity norm, another focal point that countries may gravitate to is the stipulation of a mediator or arbitrator.[45] The United Nations, the United States, and the Vatican have occasionally played this role (notwithstanding Stalin's sarcastic question "How many divisions does the Pope have?"). In the 1995 Dayton Accords, the American negotiator Richard Holbrooke enticed the Serbs and Bosnians to end their war with the help of yet another focal point: a 51–49 percent territorial split that gave the Bosniak-Croat portion of the Bosnia-Herzegovina federation a majority of the nation's area.

The soft power of powerless agents is common in human history. The International Court of Justice has a high success rate in adjudicating territorial disputes, even though, like the Pope, it has no armed divisions.[46] So do religious councils like rabbinical and shariah courts, together with the historical legal systems in many parts of the world that took root before their rulings could be enforced by police and prisons. Communities of ranchers, herders, and fishers in lawless frontiers commonly developed unwritten rules for settling their disputes.[47] The common knowledge may be captured in a pithy saying, like the whalers' law in *Moby-Dick*: "A Fast-Fish belongs to the party fast to it; a Loose-Fish is fair game for anybody who can soonest catch it." In all these cases, disputants may adhere to a ruling because it is a focal point which generates self-fulfilling expectations in their Hawk–Dove game. The winner stands his ground because he expects the loser to cede it and vice versa, both of them preferring that outcome to a ruinous feud.

McAdams argues that the magic of focal points can explain a long-known feature of legal systems: they are not just coercive but expressive. Democratic governments couldn't possibly enforce their laws with a vast network of officers, snitches, and telescreens that disincentivize lawbreakers by catching and punishing them every time. Instead, as with the law that mandates driving on the right, merely stating an expectation can create it and render it self-enforcing. Antagonists in various Hawk–Dove games use the law as a focal point, which stipulates who should concede to whom if they both want to avoid a conflict. A recent example is the law against smoking in public spaces. Probably no one was ever arrested and convicted for smoking in a lecture hall or airport terminal. But once NO SMOKING signs were posted, nonsmokers, who previously would not have wanted to create a scene, were emboldened to look daggers at the violators or ask them to stop, and they didn't push back.

None of this means we should defund the police.[48] Parties that always find themselves in the role of Dove, or who are strong enough to play Hawk without suffering much damage in a conflict, may blow off the convention and take the law into their own hands. And when unwritten codes do work, they often are enforced with a little vandalism and intimidation, with the constant danger of escalating into a bloody vendetta. So a fear of predictable penalties that neutralize the expected gains from aggression is important too. The expressive function of law doesn't refute a conception of people as rational actors responding to incentives. But it does broaden that conception to include the counterintuitive strategies that rational actors may deploy when interacting with other rational actors in coordination dilemmas.

The games explored in this chapter can't be taken too literally. I've left out a lot of game theory, including probabilistic strategies, mixtures of players with different strategies, games that unfold into still other games, and much else. And even in the simplest cases, it's never obvious how to reduce a complex outcome, with its assortment of material and psychological rewards, to a single number. As they say, it's only a game.

But I hope to have convinced you that coordination games, with their historical, cultural, and psychological solutions to otherwise unsolvable problems, can illuminate many mysteries of the human condition. Common knowledge can make frivolity important, aesthetics practical, powerlessness empowering, profligacy efficient, and arbitrariness systematic.

4

Reading the Mind
of a Mind Reader

*Bystanders, bank runs, beauty contests,
and other ways we get inside each other's heads*

Whenever I try to explain the concept of common knowledge to someone—"You see, it's when I know something, and you know it, and I know that you know it, and you know that I know it, and I know that you know that I know it . . . "—my listener's lips curl into a little smile. It's an acknowledgment that human curiosity about what other humans are thinking about them is inexhaustible, together with a sense that the curiosity ultimately is futile because the mind starts to stagger as we plumb the depths of thoughts about thoughts about thoughts.

The tension between our interest in other people's mental states and our difficulty in keeping track of them is sometimes put to whimsical use. This old poem, which ends with three layers of thoughts within thoughts, is fairly easy to follow. (We can count the layers of mentalizing by adding up the mental-state verbs in the most complex clause, in this case *she knew*, *I knew*, and *she meant*.)

> 'Twas a long time ago, many years intervenes,
> Since I courted a lass who was yet in her teens.
> Go to Father, she said, when I asked her to wed,
> when she knew that I knew her father was dead,
> but she knew that I knew what a life he had led.
> So she knew that I knew what she meant when she said, Go to Father.[1]

It's a greater challenge with four layers, as in this 2010 subway ad for the now-defunct BlackBerry smartphone:

With a bit of thought, a straphanger can see that the ad was touting a (rather dystopian) feature of the device called "conversation confirmation," in which the receiver of a message cannot deny to a sender that he or she had read it.

The difficulty of a four-layer thought was played for laughs in a well-known episode of *Friends*, the situation comedy about six platonic friends and their romantic entanglements. Monica and Chandler have begun a clandestine sexual liaison, but Joey has stumbled upon evidence for it, and Phoebe and Rachel have spotted them *in flagrante* but decided to keep their knowledge a secret so they can tease the couple with practical jokes. The couple catches on and lets Joey know about it so they can turn the tables and play along. When Phoebe and Rachel discover that the slow-witted Joey is aware of the affair, they confront him:

> RACHEL: Joey, do they know that we know?
> JOEY: They know you know.
> RACHEL: Ugh, I knew it! Oh I cannot believe those two!
> PHOEBE: They thought they can mess with us! They don't know that we know they know we know! Joey, you can't say anything!
> JOEY: I couldn't even if I wanted to.[2]

With six layers of mental states, the absurdity of keeping track of them inspired a *New Yorker* cartoon about marital relations by Bruce Eric Kaplan:

"Of course I care about how you imagined I thought you perceived I wanted you to feel."

And with still more layers, the futility of comprehending the thought can serve as a wry subtext that we may be best off not even trying to understand each other that deeply. The poem "Knots" by the psychiatrist R. D. Laing contains the lines:

So Jill does not know
   she does not know
   that Jack does not know
   that Jill thinks
   that Jack does know
and Jack does not know he does not know
   that Jill does not know she does not know
   that Jack does not know
   that Jill thinks Jack knows
what Jack thinks he does not know

The next verse concludes, "They have no problem."

This chapter is about the cognitive processes that allow us to think about what other people think about what other people think. If common knowledge is as big a deal in human affairs as I have been claiming—nothing short of a prerequisite to social coordination—and if common knowledge consists of everyone knowing that everyone knows that everyone knows something, ad infinitum, then humans must be adept at this recursive mentalizing. Yet as the whimsical examples show, any instance of he-knows-that-she-knows which embraces more than a few levels of embedding is fiendishly difficult to think. How can people be so good at coordinating their choices if the necessary cogitation requires superhuman mental stamina?

Logicians have tried to pin down exactly how common knowledge should be represented, that is, how it can be captured in a precise statement, and whether the various possibilities are logically equivalent or pick out different versions of the concept. And being human, they can't help but wonder which of these formulations might be the thoughts that we mortal humans actually think when we have common knowledge. This last question is the one that animates cognitive scientists, and it's the topic of this chapter. Let's begin by looking at the three main theories.[3] (As usual, I will gloss over the difference between common knowledge and common belief.)

The most straightforward representation of common knowledge is a list of *iterated* or *recursive* propositions ("recursive" means "containing an example of itself"):

> Amy knows that *x*.
> Brad knows that *x*.
> Amy knows that Brad knows that *x*.
> Brad knows that Amy knows that *x*.
> Amy knows that Brad knows that Amy knows that *x*.
> Brad knows that Amy knows that Brad knows that *x*.
> Amy knows that Brad knows that Amy knows that Brad knows that *x*.
>
> . . .

There are two obvious objections to such a list as a mental representation of common knowledge. One is that an infinite number of propositions cannot fit into a finite skull. The other is that each proposition is longer and more convoluted than the one before, and after the first few on the list no flesh-and-blood human can even understand them.

The first objection might be met by noting that the three dots at the end of the list, or their linguistic equivalents *and so on*, *et cetera*, or *ad infinitum*, can capture the idea of the infinite series. It's similar to the way we express the idea of an even number as "0, 2, 4, 6, 8, . . . "[4]

The second objection might be met by using symbols to stand for entire propositions, so that the propositions don't have to increase in length, like this:

(1) Amy knows that *x*.
(2) Brad knows that *x*.
(3) Amy knows that (2).
(4) Brad knows that (1).
(5) Amy knows that (4).
(6) Brad knows that (3).

. . .

Now that we have symbols that stand for entire propositions at our disposal, we can dispense with an infinite list altogether, as long as we allow a proposition to contain a symbol referring to itself. This gives us a second way to capture common knowledge, called the *reflexive* or *fixed-point* representation. It might look like this:

(*n*) Amy and Brad know *x*, and Amy and Brad know *n*.

The advantage of this self-referential proposition is that it does away with the annoying infinitude of a list. The disadvantages are that it is still cognitively unintuitive, and perhaps paradoxical. It's not that people can't understand self-referential sentences at all. *This sentence has five words* is pretty clear, and people smile when they learn about Hofstadter's Law: "It always takes longer than you think, even when you take Hofstadter's Law into account." But proposition (*n*) is not particularly intuitive, and while some philosophers (such as Gilbert Harman and Jon Barwise) have proposed it as a plausible finite representation of common knowledge, others (such as Robert Aumann of can't-agree-to-disagree fame) believe it is circular, and not a definition at all.[5]

The third possible rendering of common knowledge hinges on *self-evidence* or *conspicuity* (sometimes, *shared basis*).[6] A self-evident event is one that can't occur without people knowing it occurred. Having a conversation, for example, is self-evident to the conversationalists, and signing a contract is self-evident to the signers. Similarly, when we call an event "public" or "conspicuous" or "salient" or "out there," or we say "You can't miss it!" we're implying that the event is self-evident: when it happens, people know it by definition. Then common knowledge of *x* can be represented in the following way:

Amy and Brad experienced a self-evident event that implies *x*.

When the host of a dinner party announces, "Amy has spinach in her teeth," it's self-evident to all those present that the host has said it, and it implies that Amy really does have spinach in her teeth. That's enough for the spinach in Amy's teeth to be common knowledge. The fact that the event witnessed by the pair is self-evident would allow Amy to infer that if she knows it, Brad knows she knows it, and vice versa, for as many levels as she cared to reel out—though she needn't reel out any if she was not in the mood; the mere knowledge that she and Brad experienced a self-evident event is enough.

Indeed, all three formats obviate the need for the knowers to get lost in an endless spiral of "I know that she knows that I know . . ."

thoughts until the end of time. With the recursive representation, they could stop at some point and think "and so on." With the reflexive one, they could note that the self-reference in the proposition allows it to be spun out into as many propositions, as deeply self-embedded, as they would ever want. With the self-evident proposition, the ability to spawn these propositions is self-evident. With any of these possibilities, we can say that the knower has *reason to believe* the infinite set of multiply embedded propositions that make up "common knowledge," namely that they would have rational grounds to assent to each one if they ever had to, even if they don't literally *believe* them in the sense that those thoughts are running through their minds.[7] By analogy, as soon as I learned about even numbers as a child, I had a reason to believe "847,576,954 is an even number," even though that thought had not crossed my mind until the moment I typed that sentence.

The question for us now is: Do people actually hold any of these representations in their heads, and if so, how adeptly, and how easily can they switch from one to the other? Let's look at the representations in turn.

Though people can't hold an endless series of "He knows she knows he knows . . . " thoughts in their minds, we have seen that they can hold a few. The talent for recursive mentalizing emerges in the early school years. This was shown by a pair of psychologists, Josef Perner and Heinz Wimmer, who had previously become famous for demonstrating the age at which children showed signs of simple mentalizing, that is, just thinking about other people's thoughts. (As I mentioned, mentalizing is also called theory of mind, where the "theory" refers not to the scientist's theory but to the child's intuitive or folk theory of what goes on in other people's heads.)

To show that a child has the power to mentalize, one can't simply ask her whether someone else knows some fact, because if the fact is common knowledge, there's no difference between what the other person knows and what the child herself knows—they're thinking about the same world. Wimmer and Perner were inspired by an observation by the philosopher Dan Dennett that a stringent test of the ability to mentalize would be to probe whether children understand that someone can hold a belief that they themselves know to be *false*:

> Very young children watching a Punch and Judy show squeal in anticipatory delight as Punch prepares to throw the box over the cliff. Why? Because they know Punch thinks Judy is still in the box. They know better; they saw Judy escape while Punch's back was turned. We take the children's excitement as overwhelmingly good evidence that they understand the situation—they understand that Punch is acting on a mistaken belief (although they are not sophisticated enough to put it that way).[8]

Dennett suggested an experiment that would use this logic to test whether a child of a given age (or, for that matter, a chimpanzee) has a theory of mind: stage an event in which an object was moved when a character's back was turned, and see whether the child expects the character to look in the original place (where the character thinks it is) or the new place (where the child knows it is). Wimmer and Perner did the studies.[9] The child sees a little play acted out with toys in which (say) Mary wants to buy ice cream from a truck in the park but has to go home to get the money, and while she's gone the truck moves to a church. The child has seen the truck move to the church, but Mary hasn't, so Mary still thinks the truck is in the park. Now the experimenter asks the child, "Where will Mary go to buy ice cream?" Wimmer and Perner's famous result is that three-year-olds say, "To the church," presumably because they are foggy about the fact that other people have their own minds with their own, possibly false, beliefs. But four-year-olds can distinguish their thoughts from other people's and say, "To the park."

The simplest interpretation is that children grow a theory of mind between three and four. But that turns out to be too simple. On one side of the transition, young children are not always that oblivious. The psychologists Kristine Onishi and Renée Baillargeon have shown that even infants appear to be surprised when they see a person look for an object in the spot it was moved to while the person was out of the room.[10] On the other side, adults are not always that sophisticated. They often blithely assume that what they know is known to everyone else, a habit called the curse of knowledge.[11] (In *The Sense of Style*, I suggested that the curse of knowledge is the main cause of bad prose. Writers use jargon, abbreviations, abstractions, and glosses that are obvious to them but not obvious to anyone else.) This suggests that the problem for the three-year-olds in the classic false-belief study is not an utter inability to conceive of other people's mental states but a difficulty in consciously reasoning about them. Mentalizing is possible but strenuous when their own knowledge differs from someone else's and they have to keep the two worlds straight. In any case, the findings in the false-belief task are highly replicable, and they set the stage for an investigation of the development of *recursive* mentalizing.

In the new study, Perner and Wimmer had children watch a different little play, this one with an additional character.[12] A second child, John, is in the park with Mary, and while she is at home fetching the money, the ice cream vendor tells John he's going to drive to the church. Fortunately for Mary, the driver passes her house while she's there and independently tells *her* that he's heading for the church. Since John and Mary have each been informed out of sight and earshot of the other, their knowledge is private, not common: they both know, but neither knows that the other knows. The key question is: Does the child know that John doesn't know that Mary knows—a second-order belief that would require recursive mentalizing?

In the narrative, John now wants to find Mary, and is told only that she went to buy ice cream. The child is asked: "Where does John think she has gone?" Seven-year-olds, despite having understood what other people believe since they were four, can't keep track of what other people believe about what still *other* people believe. They respond that John will look for her at the church—where John knows the truck is, and where in fact Mary knows the truck is, but John had no way to know that. Eight-year-olds get it right more often than they get it wrong, and ten-year-olds always get it right.

Is there anything special about the age of seven or eight that would explain why children start to recursively mentalize around then? Perhaps. It coincides more or less with the onset of what the developmental psychologist Jean Piaget called the Concrete Operations stage of cognitive development, when children's thought processes become organized into systems.[13] It has also been called the Age of Reason, the milestone at which children in traditional cultures were considered ready to start school or an apprenticeship and to be treated as moral agents (as in the Catholic First Communion).[14]

The story about the ice cream truck requires two levels of embedded knowledge (John thinks that Mary thinks). How high can people go? A study by the psychologists Peter Kinderman, Robin Dunbar, and Richard Bentall presented college students with stories whose characters had to deal with various surprises, bluffs, and subterfuges that made their beliefs differ from one another's and from reality.[15]

Then they asked them questions that varied in the number of levels of embedded knowledge (which, recall, corresponds to the number of mental-state verbs in each sentence):

First-order: John <u>wanted</u> to go to the pub after work.

Second-order: John <u>thought</u> Sheila would <u>like</u> to go out to the pub with him.

Third-order: John <u>thought</u> that Penny <u>knew</u> what Sheila <u>wanted</u> to do.

Fourth-order: Penny <u>believed</u> that John <u>thought</u> she would not <u>know</u> what Sheila would <u>want</u> to do.

Fifth-order: John <u>thought</u> that Penny <u>thought</u> that John <u>wanted</u> Penny to <u>find out</u> what Sheila <u>wanted</u> to do.

The participants had no trouble with thoughts requiring up to four levels of mentalizing, but their performance fell off a cliff with the fifth-order questions, that is, thoughts about thoughts about thoughts about thoughts about thoughts.

The simplest conclusion is that the adult mind has four slots for keeping track of thoughts about thoughts. In the snippets at the beginning of the chapter, that was the dividing line between sentences that are understandable with a bit of effort (like the BlackBerry ad and the *Friends* dialogue) and those that are altogether baffling (like the Kaplan cartoon and Laing poem). Consider how much easier the Kaplan cartoon would have been with four levels rather than six: "Of course I care about how you perceived I wanted you to feel." A real-life example is a notorious four-level disclaimer that has been attributed to various public figures over the years: "I know you think you understand what you thought I said, but I'm not sure you realize that what you heard is not what I meant."[16] Evasive, but intelligible.

But a hard stop at four is too simple a conclusion; the exact number depends on the person and the content. Recursive mentalizing improves from early to late adolescence and then into adulthood. And it's better in people with greater working memory capacity, with better language skills, and with a lower position on the autism spectrum (that is, with greater social perspicuity).[17]

The ease of recursive mentalizing also depends on what's being mentalized. Of course, it's harder to keep track of thoughts within thoughts as the number increases. But the plunge into unintelligibility with deeply embedded sentences is not just a matter of the number of thoughts exceeding the number of slots in memory. Remember the puzzle of Cheryl's birthday from chapter 1, which requires just two levels of mentalizing but can't be solved without pencil and paper. Or the Spinach-in-Teeth problem from chapter 2 ("the hardest logic puzzle in the world"), which boggles the mind with just two or three levels. Or consider Amy, who tells Brad that their car is parked across from the school, but actually it's been towed to a police lot, and the person at the lot calls Brad and Amy separately without telling the other. Where does Amy think that Brad thinks that Amy thinks that Brad thinks the car is? Not such a complicated scenario, but answering the question is strenuous.

The peculiar difficulty of thinking thoughts about thoughts lies deep in the computational architecture of human cognition. The handicap is not that the mind can't represent complex chains of ideas connected to other ideas. Even children can visualize the images in these familiar verses:

This is the cow with the crumpled horn that tossed the dog that worried the cat that killed the rat that ate the malt that lay in the house that Jack built.

Then came the Holy One, blessed be He, and destroyed the angel of death that slew the butcher that killed the ox that drank the water that quenched the fire that burned the stick that beat the dog that bit the cat my father bought for two zuzim.[18]

In these recursive sentences, each embedded clause serves to narrow down the identity of the noun it modifies. But the concepts behind the nouns are not *defined* by the modifying clause (it's not in the very nature of the rat that it ate some malt), so there's no need to hold the entire string of verbs in mind simultaneously to understand it. Each entity can be mentally identified and set aside in long-term memory, allowing attention to be turned to the next. With recursive mentalizing, in contrast, you can't understand exactly what it is that Amy is thinking without grasping the entire Russian doll of nested phrases that comes afterward.

And this requires keeping straight multiple instances of the same concept, in this case the concept "believes." That requirement is particularly taxing for human cognition. In theory it needn't be. A digital computer easily distinguishes multiple instances of a concept; they are simply stored in separate slots in memory, each with a unique hardware address. That makes it easy to list a set of distinct propositions and their logical connections. Amy's fourth-order thought, for example, could be represented as something like this, where each line shows a memory address and its contents:

Address   Contents
```
05cffc48  believes(Amy,[77f9d022])
77f9d022  believes(Brad,[008b6f00])
```

```
008b6f00  believes(Amy,[4e7dc19a])
4e7dc19a  believes(Brad,[05dd764e])
05dd764e  location(car,school)
```

The first memory cell, 05cffc48, contains the proposition "Amy believes the contents of memory cell 77f9d022." The entire knowledge base keeps everything straight because we have a clean separation between the identity of a proposition (each line in the knowledge base, identified by its address) and the contents of that proposition (Amy, Brad, the predicate "believes"). Digital computers are designed to make this easy. They have registers and memory slots that may be filled with symbols, some of which point to other memory slots, and a processor that can work through the list keeping track of which symbol points to which slot by consulting a memory structure called a stack. But the human brain doesn't seem to work this way: it does not have preexisting memory locations that may be dynamically filled with arbitrary contents. Instead the contents *themselves* define the locations, a computational architecture called content-addressable memory.[19]

In the simplest model of content-addressable memory, a concept, in this case "believes," is represented just once in the entire brain, in a single neural circuit.[20] When the person is thinking about that concept, those neurons are activated; otherwise they are quiescent. The lack of an abstract address, or label, or variable that stands for a thought may explain a cognitive phenomenon first noted by Fyodor Dostoevsky and confirmed experimentally more than a century later by the psychologist Daniel Wegner: "Try to pose for yourself this task: not to think of a polar bear, and you will see that the cursed thing will come to mind every minute."[21] If the concept of a polar bear occupied slot 03cffc481 in memory, we could simply program our train of thought not to look up the contents of slot 03cffc481. But that appears to be impossible; to consider a thought means to think it.

This means that our system for handling mental representations is afflicted with a bug: it can't easily represent multiple instances of the same concept, each with a different set of participants (in this case, the relevant thinker and thought). The different instances are superimposed onto a single symbol, collapsing the representation upon itself:

```
believes (Amy & Brad, [LOCATION (car, school])
```

Now, all this is an exaggeration; we'd be cognitively crippled if our brains did not have *any* means to distinguish several exemplars of a single concept at a given time. The point is just that entertaining an idea is easy, whereas packaging that idea so that it may be inserted as a component inside another idea (especially another idea of the same kind) requires an effortful cognitive process. It's an effect that has been widely appreciated by cognitive scientists ever since the linguist Noam Chomsky and the psychologist George Miller noted the marked difficulty people have in understanding "self-embedded" sentences,[22] ones in which phrases are successively nested inside phrases with the same grammatical structure:

> The rat the cat the dog chased ate died.
> The rapidity that the motion that the wing that the humming-
> bird has has has is remarkable.
> That that that he died is tragic is obvious is dubious.

Though technically grammatical, the sentences collapse into unintelligibility as people try to identify the referents of the layers of clauses inside clauses.

If recursive mentalizing is so computationally demanding, how do we do it at all? A basic law of cognitive psychology is that the human mind can overcome its processing limitations by fusing a collection of simple ideas that frequently occur together into a well-learned cognitive assembly called a chunk.[23] Chunks can be assembled into still larger chunks, and so on. (It's related to the techniques in computer science known as macros, caching, subroutines, and memoization.) People are best at remembering phone numbers if they don't try to rote-memorize a string of fifteen digits but rather chunk them into the country code, the area code, the local number (further divided into the three-digit exchange and four-digit line number), and the extension. In learning to play a piece of music, a student does not tackle the entire piece from its first note to its last in one go but may practice individual chords and intervals until they become automatic, then recurring phrases and motifs, then entire lines, then verses, bridges, choruses, movements, and so on.

In a similar way, as we navigate the social world we chunk combinations of thoughts about thoughts into single mental units, sparing us from having to assemble them in real time on every occasion. Many of these chunks have acquired their own English verbs:

> *bluff*: Amy wants Brad to believe that Amy believes something which Amy doesn't believe.
>
> *conceal from*: Amy wants Brad not to know something Amy knows.
>
> *deceive*: Amy wants Brad to believe something Amy doesn't believe.
>
> *doubt*: Amy thinks Brad believes something that Amy doesn't believe.
>
> *humor*: Amy wants Brad to think Amy believes something that Brad believes although Amy doesn't believe it.
>
> *persuade*: Amy wants Brad to believe something that Amy believes.
>
> *suspect*: Amy thinks Brad wants Amy to believe something that Brad doesn't believe.

These may in turn be combined into ideas about recurring human plotlines, called scripts or schemas. In an "affair," for example, two people conceal a sexual liaison from their partners; in a "scandal," people come to know about something that a well-known figure tried to conceal; in an "argument," each of two people wants to persuade the other; and so on.

The availability of mental scripts with prepackaged beliefs-about-beliefs may explain why some of the chains of recursive mentalizing we've seen, like the plots of "The Purloined Letter" and the episode of *Friends,* are reasonably easy to follow: they involve familiar human scripts like criminal deception, clandestine sex, and practical jokes. Moreover, when a narrative unfolds event by event, readers who have learned about one character's belief about another's belief can store this chunk in long-term memory as they follow the developing plot, and the chunk is there to be embedded still deeper as subsequent events unfold. Knowing that Monica and Chandler's secret liaison has been discovered by the three friends, the audience can easily handle an additional layer when the couple surreptitiously learns about that discovery.

The baffling brainteasers, in contrast, introduce arbitrary contrived scenarios and generic knowers like the alphabetic Amy and Brad or Xavier and Yolande. Then the entire onion of thoughts within thoughts is dumped on the reader at once. It's an example of the contrast I drew in my book *Rationality* between "ecological rationality," the horse sense about common human predicaments which comes naturally to us, and "formal rationality," the application of abstract logical and statistical formulas to arbitrary subject matter.[24]

So automatic is the process of grasping familiar combinations of thoughts that it's easy to forget that even the simplest act of communication requires recursive mentalizing. I've been writing as if seeing (or hearing) a proposition is believing it, but of course we don't allow people to surgically implant ideas in our brains. We always evaluate their speech in the context of their intentions (more on this in chapter 7).[25] Philosophers of language note that "Amy says x to Brad" roughly means "Amy wants Brad to believe x by getting him to recognize that she wants him to believe it." This implies that you can give yourself credit for at least an additional four layers of mentalizing on top of however many you exercised in understanding the examples in this book. Those layers are baked so deeply into the process of understanding that they rarely register in our consciousness unless we find ourselves confused or suspicious about what a speaker is up to.

⚬⚬

We have seen that older children and adults can recursively mentalize up to a point, get bogged down when the layering of thoughts within thoughts gets too deep or self-similar, but can stretch those limits when a combination of thoughts is part of a stereotyped script. None of this gets us to common knowledge, where the number of layers is infinite—or at least, thinkers come to realize it is, since they obviously can't think an infinitely layered thought.

According to an apocryphal story that academics love to tell (commonly attributed to William James or Bertrand Russell), after a public lecture on cosmology, a professor is accosted by an old lady who offers an alternative theory of the solar system: the Earth, she tells him, rests on the back of a giant turtle. Humoring the woman, the lecturer asks her what supports the turtle. She confidently replies that it rests on the back of a second turtle. When he skeptically asks what the second turtle rests on, she crows, "It's no use, professor; it's turtles all the way down."[26] For recursive mentalizing to result in common knowledge, the mentalizer has to make the leap to "et cetera," "and so on," "ad infinitum," or "turtles all the way down." Note that the leap is not necessarily warranted, nor is it innocuous. As we saw in chapter 2 with James and Charlotte trying to rendezvous, and two armies or fighter pilots trying to coordinate an attack, no finite number of knowledge levels guarantees common knowledge in all its infinite glory. But while fallible, in some circumstances the conclusion that it's turtles all the way down may be reasonable.

Before we consider how readily people make such leaps, let's consider the other two theories of how people might mentally represent common knowledge.

⚘

The second possible representation for common knowledge is a reflexive or self-referential statement like "(*n*): Amy and Brad know *x*, and Amy and Brad know *n*." This seems particularly unintuitive. Our look at recursive mentalizing suggested that people don't easily assign a mental symbol to a proposition in order to keep track of multiple instances of it. A reflexive proposition imposes the additional demand that the symbol simultaneously label a proposition and appear inside that very proposition. Certainly it bears no resemblance to any aperçu or epiphany that ever makes an appearance before the footlights of consciousness.[27] Perhaps the mind entertains a reflexive proposition unconsciously, but I can't think of any evidence that it does.

And this brings us to the third possibility for representing common knowledge, self-evidence.[28] This is the idea that something is common knowledge if the event which reveals it is, by definition, known to one and all. That is, it's in the very nature of the event that the event is known to have happened. When people perceive the event, what they're perceiving includes the fact that other people are perceiving it—which entails that those people, too, are perceiving that the event is being perceived, and so on. The knowledge derivable from the event is common knowledge.

What counts as "self-evident" is not always self-evident, so let's consider some examples. One is an event that is *public*, not just in the sense that everyone sees it, but that everyone can see everyone else seeing it. The first three drawings in chapter 1 (pages 2–3) show the difference with two observers: the first two depict private and reciprocal knowledge; the third, with its triangle of gazes, depicts a public event, which generates common knowledge. Psychologists call this situation "joint attention," and have proposed that it allows children, starting around the age of one, to learn the linguistic and social skills of their culture.[29]

When there are more than two onlookers, the contrast may be depicted by the pair of diagrams below. The hub-and-spoke scenario on the left (which might occur if, say, apartment dwellers all espied someone in a courtyard at night by peeking through a gap in their curtains) depicts private knowledge. The polygon mesh on the right, which indicates a truly public happening, implies common knowledge.

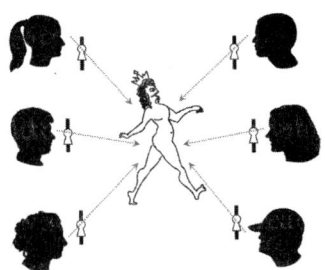 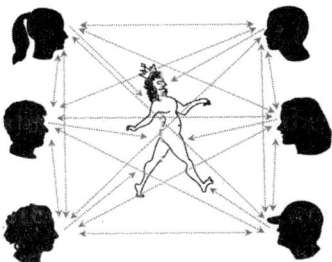

Another kind of self-evident event is an act of verbal communication. As long as the speaker is talking *to* the listener and not *at* her (as he might if she didn't understand English), an act of communication implies there is a comprehender at the other end, and his intention to convey some idea is common knowledge between them.[30]

A different kind of self-evident phenomenon is the focal point: a conspicuous landmark that pops out to an observer, from which he can reasonably surmise that it pops out to everyone else. A focal point, while it falls short of common knowledge, creates common salience, and as we saw in chapter 3, it can suggest itself as an effective solution to a coordination dilemma, as with the separated couple who meet at Grand Central Terminal at noon.[31]

The cognitive demands of self-evidence are minimal, and the psycholinguist Herbert Clark and others have argued that it's the most plausible psychological implementation of common knowledge.[32] It's the "sense organ for common knowledge" that I hinted at in chapter 1, and it's closest to the conceptual metaphor of common knowledge as a conspicuous object or sound, like *It's out there*. Though a self-evident event entails common knowledge, the person need not think through that chain of implications. The infinite layer cake of propositions entailed by a public event is something which observers have a *reason to believe* (in theory) even if they never go to the bother of believing it.[33]

We can see this in a case where a focal point solves a coordination problem among creatures that don't believe anything at all, indeed, that don't even have a brain to believe things with: the lowly coral. Coral organisms, anchored as they are to the ocean floor, face the problem of getting their eggs and sperm to other coral. They resort to "broadcast spawning," spewing massive numbers of eggs and sperm into the water as if hoping for the best. Since gametes are expensive to produce, they cannot spew them 24/7/365. This puts them into the ultimate game of Rendezvous, where every coral on the reef would do best to broadcast its gametes on the same night, any night, as all the other coral do, so the gametes have a fighting chance of finding their counterparts floating somewhere in the briny. In what marine biologists call the Great Barrier Reef's Annual Sex Festival, corals from all over the reef spew their sperm and eggs into the water at the same time a fixed number of days after the season's full moon (with different lags for different species). There's nothing special about that night other than that all the coral can settle on it, which they do with the help of photoreceptors called cryptochromes that detect moonlight. The full moon is their focal point.[34]

The moral is that conspicuous (hence self-evident) events can generate the commonly perceived information necessary for solving coordination dilemmas without the need for involuted layers of embedded propositions or a confusingly self-referential formula. At the same time, we have seen that human beings are capable of recursive mentalizing, at least up to a point. How do these two talents—noticing a self-evident event, and thinking about thoughts—lead to the epiphanies of common knowledge that make coordination possible?

⋯❧⋯

To probe people's ability to get to common knowledge, I have worked with a team of social scientists starting when they were graduate and postdoctoral students: Julian De Freitas, Peter DeScioli, Omar Sultan Haque, Yuhui Huang, James Lee, Miriam Lindner, Lawrence Ian Reed, Kyle Thomas, and Dylan Tweed.

In our first study, Thomas, DeScioli, Haque, and I had people engage in an online fantasy version of a Stag Hunt.[35] Recall from the preceding chapter that this game pits a small sure reward from working individually against a larger but riskier reward from working together, the risk coming from a lack of common knowledge that both partners intend to coordinate. We recruited several thousand internet users to imagine that they were a butcher or a baker. Every day they could earn a sure profit by individually preparing chicken wings or dinner rolls, respectively, but on some days, depending on the market price, they could earn a larger profit by making the sausages and buns for hot dogs, neither of which was saleable without the other. That is, if the price of hot dogs was high, the butcher could earn a larger profit making sausages, but only if he could count on the baker also knowing that the price was high (and knowing that he knew, and so on) so that he would confidently make the buns. We were interested in what kind of information would reassure them about the other's knowledge (and knowledge about their knowledge, and so on) so they would take the chance at a larger profit. A quarter of them, picked at random, got one of the following notices (imagine you are playing the baker):

Private knowledge: A messenger boy tells you the market price for hot dogs today is high. But he has not seen the butcher, so he can't tell you anything about what the butcher knows.

Second-order (detected) knowledge: A messenger boy tells you the price today is high, and mentions that he also told the butcher the price—but forgot to mention to him that he was coming to see you, so the butcher doesn't know that you know the price.

Third-order (reciprocal) knowledge: A messenger boy tells you the price is high, and is heading over to the butcher to tell him that too. He'll also tell the butcher that he just told you the price, but he won't tell him that he told you he was heading over there. So while the butcher is aware that you know today's price, he is not aware that you know he knows that.

> **Public (common) knowledge:** A loudspeaker announces that
> the price is high.

In an homage to Rousseau, we also ran a version in which the players imagined themselves as hunters who could stalk rabbits individually or who could hunt deer together, one as an archer and the other a tracker. As before, an occasionally absent-minded messenger conveyed information about the payoffs, in this case whether deer had been sighted in the area that day, or it was made public by smoke from a signal fire.

The question was which states of knowledge gave the participants the confidence to agree to coordinate with their counterpart for a bigger profit. If they were fully rational and knew that the other participant was fully rational, they would work together only when the high price was common knowledge; anything short of that would put them at risk of going home empty-handed. Assuming that they interpreted a public signal as a common-knowledge generator, they would opt to work together only when they perceived the loudspeaker or smoke signal, but not when they had any of the lower orders of knowledge conveyed by the messenger.

It was not a foregone conclusion that participants would coordinate only with public knowledge. If people are damned by a curse of knowledge, they would project their private knowledge onto their counterpart and foolishly try to coordinate even when the messenger told no one but them the price. And if they prematurely generalized that it's turtles all the way down, they would leap from second- or third-order knowledge to common knowledge and recklessly try to coordinate in these conditions.

How did they do? As in many other experiments on rationality, people acted more or less rationally, though with some blind spots. With private knowledge, fewer than 20 percent of them attempted to coordinate; with public knowledge, more than 80 percent did. And indeed, in these bookend conditions, the participants earned around 85 percent of the theoretical maximum—not bad for distractible internet users playing make-believe for a few bucks.[36]

But to our surprise, a bit more than half of the participants in the intermediate knowledge conditions also gambled on working together, and they paid a price, earning nothing whenever their counterpart played it safe by working alone. Some of them may have committed a turtles-all-the-way-down fallacy, which we can also think of as a curse of second- or third-order knowledge: "If I know that he knows the price, then he must know that I know that he knows, and so on."[37] But we have reason to believe that most did not. When psychologists run experiments online, they always give participants a little quiz about the details of the procedure to ensure that they've been paying attention (and to weed out bots). In our Who-knows-what quiz (for example, "Does the Butcher know that you know that he knows the price of hot dogs today?"), few of the participants were confused when they had private or public information, and almost none made the turtlish leap from second- or third-order knowledge up to common knowledge. But as you might appreciate from your own efforts to keep track of the conditions, it's mentally demanding to keep three layers of recursive knowledge straight, and the understanding of the participants who were given third-order knowledge often collapsed downward into second-order knowledge. We concluded that private knowledge and common knowledge are distinctive mental states, which reliably light up in the mind free from the cognitive burden of recursive mentalizing.[38]

Though people seem to avoid the fallacy of leaping from finite levels of recursive knowledge up to common knowledge, do they correctly reason in the other direction, deducing that if something is common knowledge—as ascertained by its being public or self-evident—then each of the knowers knows that the other knows it, and knows that, and so on?

It's hard to test because people get overwhelmed by too many layers of recursive mentalizing, but De Freitas and I gave it a shot.[39] We presented participants with a description of a conspicuous public event, like a car crash in plain sight of two witnesses, Sally and Edward, and compared their understanding of who knew what with a scenario in which the two had witnessed the event separately and a scenario in which one of them had learned about it from a second-hand report. We then asked them whether Edward was thinking each of the following:

1. A car crash just happened.

2. Sally knows I'm aware of the car crash.

3. Sally knows I'm aware of the car crash. And she understands that I realize that she knows it.

4. Sally knows I'm aware of the car crash. And she understands that I realize that she knows it, and also that I know that she knows this.

As the knowledge states get embedded increasingly deeply, of course, they get harder to keep track of. Not surprisingly, in the scenarios where Edward learned about the event through hearsay, the participants' confidence in what he knew plummeted as the levels deepened. But when the event in the story was public, the participants were almost as confident about Edward's fifth-order knowledge (#4) as they were about his knowledge of the event itself (#1).[40]

Now, we tried to make it easy for them to keep track of these layers, by leading up to the fifth-order statement one step at a time and by keeping the syntax relatively simple. But we didn't really credit them with mentally tracking the layers upon layers. More likely, they sensed that if something is public, it just follows that each perceiver knows that the other knows that she knows what the other one knows, and so on. To see if our participants really did have the sense that a public event entails any number of embedded knowledge states, we presented them with a silly sentence with eighteen layers of thoughts within thoughts, and asked them to consider whether Edward thinks it:

> Sally knows that I'm aware that she realizes that I understand that she recognizes that I know that she's aware that I realize that she understands that I recognize that she knows that I'm aware that she realizes that I understand that she recognizes that I know that she understands that I'm aware of the car crash.

Of course we didn't expect them to follow this ridiculous sentence; we just wanted to assay their intuition as to whether the public nature of the event gives them a reason to believe it. And so we asked whether they agreed with Art, a commentator who infers that this sentence must be true even if he finds it difficult to follow; with Bart, who is sure it must *not* be true; or with Hart, who has no opinion one way or the other. For events that were public, a majority of the participants agreed with Art: a public event gives an observer a reason to believe any number of embedded thoughts.

These experiments were designed to see how recursive mentalizing and public events might give rise to common belief about an objective fact. When the fact is a price, as in the butcher–baker studies, the question has obvious relevance to economics. But economists are also intrigued by the mental processes that go into a common *expectation*, namely a belief about other people's beliefs about other people's beliefs, untethered to any objective fact in the world.

The interest began with a famous analogy drawn by John Maynard Keynes in 1936 between the stock market and a certain kind of beauty contest that may have appeared in British newspapers of the day.[41] The contest was not like Miss Rheingold, the annual campaign sponsored by an American brewery from 1941 to 1964 in which people voted on which of six young women displayed in their ads was the prettiest. Instead, Keynes explained,

> Professional investment may be likened to those newspaper competitions in which the competitors have to pick out the six prettiest faces from a hundred photographs, the prize being awarded to the competitor whose choice most nearly corresponds to the average preferences of the competitors as a whole; so that each competitor has to pick, not those faces which he himself finds prettiest, but those which he thinks likeliest to catch the fancy of the other competitors, all of whom are looking at the problem from the same point of view. It is not a case of choosing those which, to the best of one's judgment, are really the prettiest, nor even those which average opinion genuinely thinks prettiest. We have reached the third degree where we devote our intelligence to anticipating what average opinion expects the average opinion to be. And there are some, I believe, who practise the fourth, fifth and higher degrees.

Do people really mentalize to four, five, and higher degrees of expectations about expectations? Do they even get to two or three? You can try it yourself. First, name a flower, any flower. Now a year, any year. A day of the year. A car maker. A number. A color. A city. Now suppose you are paired with a person more or less like you, and you get a reward for each answer *if* it is the same as the other person's, who will also be rewarded if his or her answer matches yours. Do you make the same choices?

The economists Judith Mehta, Chris Starmer, and Robert Sugden tried this experiment on British university students,[42] inspired by an informal study that Thomas Schelling had reported in 1960. (I mentioned it in chapter 3, noting that when Schelling's respondents had to match their counterpart's guess of heads or tails, most picked heads.) It's a kind of Rendezvous game, and solving it requires common knowledge, which is unavailable to the respondents. If their only workaround was salience, without any recursive mentalizing, their answers would be the same in the two conditions: whatever popped into a respondent's head would be his or her best guess as to what would pop into the other's.

But in these experiments (as in Schelling's decades earlier), people adjusted their guesses in anticipation of others doing the same, and they made far more matches than if they had simply proffered their private guesses and hoped for the best. When people had to name a flower, they offered "rose," the prototypical blossom, about a third of the time; the majority of choices were spread across a range of personal favorites such as "daisy," "tulip," and "daffodil." But when the task was to anticipate another's choice, people narrowed down their fancies and offered "rose" two-thirds of the time. When choosing a day and a year, most went with their birthdays. But they knew that those wouldn't work with other choosers, so they tried to coordinate by choosing Christmas Day and the current year. The color they most often suggested on their own was "blue," presumably because it's the most common favorite color; the one they selected in anticipation of others' selections was "red," presumably because it's the most common color word in the language.[43] The choices "Ford" for a car, "John" for a boy's name, and "London" for a city barely edged out other responses in the simple offerings but trounced them in the attempted matches. Even people's choice of a number reflected mentalizing. "1" is rarely anyone's favorite number, nor is it a stereotype of a positive integer. But it is a special number—it's first, and smallest—and so respondents piled on it as their most popular attempted match.

The results suggest that when people need elusive common knowledge in a coordination problem, they are smarter than coral, which just respond to a conspicuous cue and are rewarded fortuitously when their counterparts do the same. And people are not crippled by a curse of knowledge, projecting their private preferences onto everyone else. Instead, they try to get into each other's heads deeply enough to weed out what they anticipate might be idiosyncratic picks, and when there is a prototypical choice, they come down strongly on it. When there isn't, as with a number, they search for a distinction that picks out a unique examplar which might commend itself to others. This shows, by the way, that a focal point for coordination isn't the same as the item that is most salient to an individual. People differentiate salience from *common* salience, and that requires mentalizing.

How much mentalizing? In these studies it was just one or two layers down, but another economist, Rosemary Nagel, tried to see how deep people can go.[44] She tried the following variation: pick a number from 0 to 100, but this time the prize goes to whoever's guess is closest to two-thirds of the average of all the guesses. Try it yourself now, while assuming that all the other guessers are trying it too.

The answer you should arrive at is 0. You could get there in either of two ways. The first is to sucessively rule out the impossible solutions. What's the highest number that two-thirds of the average could be? If everyone else picked the highest possible number, 100, it would be 66.67, so the answer could not possibly be higher than that. Everyone else can figure that out too, so the highest any rational guesser will guess is 66.67—but even if everyone guessed that maximum, the largest possible solution would be two-thirds of *that*, or 44.44. But if *that* is the highest rational guess, then the winner can be no higher than two-thirds of that, and so on, corkscrewing closer and closer to 0, the only viable solution.

The other way to mentalize your way to a solution also requires the epiphany that it's turtles all the way down. Start by supposing that everyone else makes their first choice at random. That would make their choices average out to 50. But being rational mentalizers, they have figured this out, so they calculate two-thirds of that, or .33. Now they realize that the other rational choosers will have done that too, so they calculate two-thirds of the second guesses, or 22.22. This race to the bottom can only end at 0—not that the guessers will creep toward 0 forever, like Zeno's paradoxical arrow, but they should see that that's where all the mentalizing must end up.

What did people actually do when faced with this challenge? No one chose 0, and though lower is better, very few even chose less than 10. The mean answer was 36.73, and many of the choices piled up around 33 and 22. This suggests that people first guessed the average of everyone else's first guesses, which they assumed were random, averaging out to 50, then multiplied by two-thirds. Some went a layer deeper and took two-thirds of *that*, but their recursive mentalizing stopped there, as if they thought they needed to be just a wee bit deeper a thinker than everyone else. Even when they were shown the results of a round of guessing, and most could see that their guesses were too high, they bumped their guesses downward just a bit on the following round. What they did not do was recursively multiply all the way down toward 0.

Nagel and her collaborators got similar results when they ran the game as an actual contest in newspapers in Britain, Spain, and Germany.[45] In these real-world contests, about 15 percent of the respondents chose 0. Ironically, while 0 is the rational choice for a recursive mentalizer when all the other choosers are rational recursive mentalizers (and their rationality is common knowledge), it's not necessarily the best choice when everyone else is a human, with all their cognitive limitations. When everyone else peters out somewhere along the spiral of anticipation, the best guess is to go no lower than two-thirds of that floor. As a result, the recursively rational zero-guessers were outcompeted by the mere lowballers. And since there's no way of predicting from one's armchair how deep everyone else will go, the most successful contestants were those who took it upon themselves to run little experiments among their friends and go with two-thirds of the average they got in their own data.

It's no anomaly that the first scholar to ponder the psychology of recursive mentalizing was not a psychologist but an economist, because a surprising number of economic phenomena are driven by Keynesian beauty contests, as these cycles of psyching out are now called. Indeed they are a major reason (perhaps *the* major reason) why markets don't always follow predictable curves governed by the fundamentals of production, consumption, and investment but are instead vulnerable to bubbles, crashes, runs, attacks, manias, shortages, animal spirits, and irrational exuberance.

These lurches are driven by the self-fulfilling psychology of common knowledge: "We devote our intelligence to anticipating what average opinion expects the average opinion to be." And while some actors exercise this power recursively ("to the fourth, fifth and higher degrees"), most home in on conspicuous public events or focal points that allow them to anticipate others' choices without these mental gymnastics.

Keynes singled out investing as a beauty contest, but he was not referring to the choice of buying shares or bonds in anticipation of a return on a productive investment, like the future earnings of a company that plants a forest or builds a factory. He had in mind speculative investing, in which investors predict that other investors will want to buy in later, driving up the price. As we saw with Aumann's agree-to-disagree theorem, this cannot be rational for everyone, because when investors share an understanding of the world and prices are common knowledge, they should all agree on the appropriate price, and no one should want to buy or sell (other than for boring reasons like wanting to earn interest and dividends or needing the money now). But as we saw in chapter 1, speculation that is set off by noticing that other investors are starting to bid up the price of an asset, or by witnessing an event that other investors are witnessing which suggests that still other investors may bid it up (like a Super Bowl ad for cryptocurrency), can be rational for a while. It can inflate a bubble until the market runs out of greater fools and the bubble pops.

The behavioral economist (and Nobel laureate) Richard Thaler has a favorite example of how bubbles can be set off by any event that brings an asset into the consciousness of enough investors.[46] Now, it's always hard to know whether a run-up in prices is a self-inflating bubble or a rational response to an actual change in the value of the asset. One kind of security that does allow these to be distinguished is the closed-end mutual fund, a fixed bundle of stocks which trades on the market, sometimes for more or less than the sum of the prices of the stocks themselves. An example is the Herzfeld Caribbean Basin Fund, stock ticker symbol CUBA, which held shares in companies in several countries around the Caribbean, though not Cuba itself, since that had been illegal for American companies since 1960. (The symbol had been picked because Cuba was the largest island in the Caribbean.) Thaler noticed that the fund had long traded at around 10 percent below the value of its shares, until December 18, 2014, when the price shot up to 70 percent *above* that value: "Whereas it had previously been possible to buy $100 worth of Caribbean assets for just $90, the next day those assets cost $170!" What had changed? President Barack Obama had announced that he intended to relax diplomatic relations with Cuba (the country). The price jump reflected nothing but the expectations of investors, whose heads had been turned by the fund's nickname.

The rise of social media has given rise to a new kind of bubble, the meme stock. These are shares of a company with dubious fundamentals which go through the roof when the stock is talked up by a viral influencer on a social media platform. That happened in 2021 with GameStop, a brick-and-mortar videogame retailer touted by the YouTube persona "Roaring Kitty" (in real life, Keith Gill). By May 2024 the shares had returned to earth, but then Roaring Kitty tweeted a cartoon of a man suddenly leaning forward in his chair. That focal point was all it took: two days and twenty-four million views later, the price of the stock had tripled.[47]

The mirror image of bubbles are crashes, squeezes, panics, and runs for the exits. The clearest example is a bank run.[48] People deposit money in their local credit union or bank branch or savings and loan, rather than stuffing it in a mattress, and expect to be able to withdraw it whenever they need it. The bank, for its part, doesn't just pile up the deposits in a mountain of cash like Scrooge McDuck; it lends the money out with interest to homebuyers or businesses for various stretches of time, locking it up until the loans are paid off. As long as the payback dates are staggered over time and not all the depositors want their money back at once, the deposits and loans more or less balance out, and the bank can keep jogging on this treadmill indefinitely. But if everyone decided to withdraw their savings at the same time, the bank would run out of cash after it paid the first few, and the rest would be left empty-handed. The instant this nightmare possibility occurs to depositors, they realize it must have occurred to all the other depositors. They don't want to be the latecomers holding the bag, so they scramble to withdraw their savings while there are savings to withdraw. It's called a run on the bank, and it can be contagious, as depositors in other banks worry that the same thing can happen to them, which ensures that it does happen. Before long there are breadlines and shantytowns and songs called "Brother, Can You Spare a Dime?"

As we saw in chapter 3, a bank run is a Stag Hunt: a game with two equilibria, one much better than the other (two hunters cooperating to hunt stag together rather than defecting to hunt rabbits alone), but in the absence of common knowledge like a smoke signal, each hunter worries about the worst-case scenario of being the lone stag hunter, and the two are likely to end up in the inferior equilibrium of each going after rabbits. The depositors in a bank that's vulnerable to a run also seek one of two equilibria.[49] It's best for everyone if they all leave their deposits in the bank and keep their savings and interest, and second-best to withdraw early in the run and at least keep their savings. Their worst case is to try to withdraw late in the run while others have withdrawn early and thus to go home empty-handed. Recall that a Stag Hunt is also called an Assurance game. Here the depositors are perfectly happy to keep their money in the bank if they are assured that everyone else will keep it there, but may withdraw out of fear that others will withdraw, if only because *they* fear that others will withdraw. In the words of Douglas Hofstadter, they are overcome by reverberant doubt.[50]

To prevent bank runs, people must have confidence, and have confidence that everyone else has confidence, that the bank can cover its withdrawals. One way that banks traditionally tried to accomplish this was with conspicuous opulence. Even in small towns, banks had impressive classical architecture with marble pillars, spacious lobbies, and gilded signs and fixtures. The union song

"The Banks Are Made of Marble," performed by Pete Seeger and his folk music group The Weavers, protested this apparent insult to hardworking farmers and miners. But the marble may have worked to their advantage, creating common knowledge that the banks had money to spare and so their savings were safe from self-fulfilling bank runs.[51]

Not safe enough, obviously. After the bank runs that deepened the Great Depression, Franklin Roosevelt's declaration "The only thing we have to fear is fear itself" was not a feel-good bromide but literally true: the fear of fear itself was the immediate cause of the bank runs (and of the stock market crash before them).[52] A quick fix was the "bank holiday," which prevented depositors from withdrawing their money for a fixed period, to everyone's advantage. A longer-term fix was federal deposit insurance, which guarantees that depositors get their money back should the bank fail (underwritten by the government's limitless power to raise money by taxes), thereby making it less likely that the bank will fail. In place of the marble pillars, American banks now generate common knowledge of the safety of customers' deposits with prominent brass plaques or window decals emblazoned with the seal of the Federal Deposit Insurance Corporation.

FDIC insurance is small potatoes (currently $250,000 per account), and larger banks and investment firms with seriously rich depositors are still vulnerable to runs even when they are financially sound. The self-fulfilling fears may be set off by gossip, rumors, tweets, vaguely related news items, or other unpredictable yet publicly visible events, which economists call sunspots. When the Silicon Valley Bank, which served many tech and healthcare startups, collapsed in 2023, some analysts raised doubts about the bank's lending practices. But the financial journalist Matt Klein noted that "this was more a case of a 'bank-run by idiots' rather than a 'bank run by idiots'" (a nice addition to my collection of syntactic ambiguities).[53] When banks or investment firms are "too big to fail" (because they would take the economy down with them), the closest equivalent to deposit insurance is a bailout or loan guarantee by the government, acting as a "lender of last resort." (Of course, this introduces a new problem, the "moral hazard" or perverse incentive to take crazy risks, knowing the government is there to bail you out.)

Sometimes an entire country may face the equivalent of a bank run, when investors fear it may not have enough reserves to convert its own currency to a foreign currency at the current fixed rate.[54] They may dump their holdings before the country devalues the currency, or even hurry the devaluation along with a speculative attack, taking out huge loans in the currency and planning to pay them back at the cheaper exchange rate. All the other holders of the currency, fearing a devaluation, scramble to dump theirs too, each fearing that the others will do so first. Rich countries or international banks may have to step in as the lender of last resort to damp down the reverberant doubt and prevent it from spreading to other countries.

Several other macroeconomic phenomena are driven by common expectations arising from a back-and-forth between recursive mentalizing and conspicuous focal points. Inflationary spirals are set off when merchants increase retail prices in anticipation of the increased wholesale prices they think suppliers may charge and the increased wages they think workers may demand, and vice versa. Recessions may feed upon themselves when consumers put off buying out of fear of losing their jobs and employers put off hiring out of fear of a drop in sales.

Since the economic actors couldn't possibly probe deeply enough into one another's psyches to divine their fears about fears about fears, they may develop hypersensitive antennae for any public event that could serve as a focal point which sets off or damps down a vortex of common expectations. This in turn puts prominent economic officials in the role of oracles, mystics, and occasionally comedians, who must wordsmith their pronouncements into precise vagueness. Alan Greenspan, chairman of the Federal Reserve from 1987 to 2006, once said, "Since I've become a central banker, I've learned to mumble with great incoherence. . . . If I seem unduly clear to you, you must have misunderstood what I said."[55] The economist Alfred Kahn, Jimmy Carter's inflation czar, had been told by his boss to avoid the self-fulfilling word *depression*, so he warned, "We're in danger of having the worst banana in 45 years."[56] (When banana producers protested, he switched to *kumquat*.)

Yet the strangest self-fulfilling economic phenomenon in recent memory may have taken place in 2020, when on top of all the other indignities of the Covid-19 pandemic, consumers faced a sudden shortage of toilet paper.[57] The shortage could not be explained by economic fundamentals. Though the supply chain had been temporarily disrupted when people started sheltering at home and used more consumer-grade toilet paper rather than the jumbo rolls stocked in schools and offices, the manufacturers quickly stepped up production. Nor could a response to the coronavirus itself explain the shortage, since it afflicts an orifice at the other end of the body. The economist Justin Wolfers suggested that the major reason was panic buying: consumers hoarded toilet paper out of fear that other consumers were hoarding it out of fear that still others were hoarding it, which might leave the store shelves bare, and soon enough did.[58] Somehow it had become conventional wisdom that toilet paper is a commodity that is particularly vulnerable to shortages; people often hoard it when a hurricane or snowstorm is predicted, too.

According to one explanation, the conventional belief can be traced to a common-knowledge generator almost as salient in its day as the Super Bowl. From 1962 to 1992, Johnny Carson was "the King of Late Night," hosting *The Tonight Show* in an era when Americans could choose from just three commercial television networks, and many tuned in at 11:30 p.m. every night to watch him. Catchphrases from the show like "Heeeere's Johnny!" entered the national lexicon, and his jokes and interviews were often discussed around the water cooler the following day. One night in December 1973, when the nation had endured shortages of gasoline, beef, sugar, and other staples, Carson quipped in his monologue, "You know, we've got all sorts of shortages these days. But have you heard the latest? I'm not kidding. I saw it in the papers. There's an acute shortage of toilet paper!" It wasn't true at the time, but it quickly became true when viewers, knowing how many other Americans were viewers, snapped up the supply. Ever since then, toilet paper has been thought of as something to hoard in an emergency.[59] Though the nation has no Strategic Reserve of Toilet Paper or other provider of last resort, shopkeepers ended the 2020 shortage by imposing their own version of a bank holiday. Signs restricted customers to three packages, which didn't so much alleviate the shortage by throttling demand as signal to customers that their fellow customers could not strip the shelves bare.

Though the concept of a Keynesian beauty contest emerged from economics, the contests, with all their strange, self-fulfilling dynamics, may be found in many other realms. In one case it was made into an actual contest. One of the longest-running and most popular quiz shows in the history of television is *Family Feud*. Two competing families are given questions and earn points by guessing the answers that were most popular in a survey of a hundred people like them. Since the game show lacks a control condition in which the families simply offer their own best answers, we can't tell whether their answers come out of recursive mentalizing or are simply the first things that come into their minds, which may be the first things that come into everyone else's minds, especially since the family members confer, giving them a sample of five. But the experiments by Schelling and his successors suggest that people in this situation do engage in some recursive mentalizing. That means that some of the odder answers—such as that Benjamin Franklin was an American president, spiders are a kind of insect, and penguins are animals found at the North Pole—reflect a mixture of typical Americans' beliefs and typical Americans' beliefs about other typical Americans' beliefs. One of the show's biggest fans is the humorist Fran Lebowitz:

> It was like going to a mall without having to leave the house. One of my favorite questions they ever had was, "Name five famous American intellectuals" and the first answer from the winning team was "John Kennedy," a well-known intellectual, and it was on the board! In answer to the question, "Name a famous Rudolph," a guy jumped up and yelled, "Rudolph Hitler!"[60]

A more consequential instance is the strange American process for choosing the presidential nominees of the two major parties, the primary system. Though journalists call it a "horse race," it's really a Keynesian beauty contest.[61] Voters don't just express their preference among candidates but try to anticipate which of them are most preferred by other voters—which are most "electable"— so they won't "waste their vote" on merely helping to decide who finishes in eighth versus ninth place. The dozen or more candidates are winnowed down in a series of heavily hyped statewide elections. These begin in the January of an election year with the caucuses in Iowa and the primary in New Hampshire, despite the fact that those white, rural, and sparsely populated states are hardly a representative sample of the nation. The capricious results from these early small samples can nonetheless grant or deny a candidate the precious elixir called "momentum" and end the campaign of a front-runner while launching a dark horse into the lead. And as with all coordination games, a conspicuous focal point, no matter how inconsequential, can be the magnet that gets everyone on the same page. Trivial gaffes, indiscretions, or exhausted lapses (like Ed Muskie's apparent tears in New Hampshire in 1972, or Howard Dean's third-place victory scream in Iowa in 2004) can go viral and make voters suspect that all the other voters are about to jump ship. In the other direction, a lucky break, such as Representative Jim Clyburn's endorsement of Joe Biden just before the South Carolina primary in 2020, can embolden them to join what feels like the swelling ranks behind a new front-runner.

In electoral politics, common knowledge giveth and common knowledge taketh away. By early June 2024, the eighty-one-year-old Biden was widely suspected of suffering cognitive decline on the eve of an election that could have kept him in office till he was eighty-six. Many of his advisors privately knew of the decline, and a majority of voters told pollsters they were worried about it, but Biden, his allies, and the Democratic Party supported his reelection bid as if all was normal. Later that month Biden turned in a stumbling performance in a widely watched debate with Donald Trump. Though the percentage doubting his competence crept up by only a few percentage points, the private knowledge was now common knowledge, and after four weeks of snowballing pressure, Biden bowed out of the race.[62]

Let me end the chapter with another study of recursive mentalizing I ran with Thomas, De Freitas, and DeScioli, this one inspired by one of the iconic events of the 1960s.[63] On March 27, 1964, a *New York Times* headline proclaimed "37 WHO SAW MURDER DIDN'T CALL THE POLICE," with the subheading "Apathy at Stabbing of Queens Woman Shocks Inspector."[64] "For more than half an hour," the article began, "38 respectable, law-abiding citizens in Queens watched a killer stalk and stab a woman in three separate attacks in Kew Gardens." The story about the New Yorkers who "didn't want to get involved" as they heard the blood-curdling screams of Kitty Genovese became a parable of the callousness and alienation of modern urban life. It was soon amplified by an article in *Life* magazine titled "The Dying Girl That No One Helped" and a book by the *New York Times* editor A. M. Rosenthal called *Thirty-Eight Witnesses*.

Some journalists never let the facts get in the way of a good morality tale, and the thirty-eighth witness who materialized between the headline and the body of the original story was just one of many humbugs in the report. As the *Times*, to its credit, admitted in a series of follow-ups over the decades, only six people, not thirty-seven or thirty-eight, witnessed parts of the incident, which consisted of two attacks, not three, and some thought the screams were from a quarrel between lovers or drunks. Two people did in fact call the police, and a neighbor ran out and cradled the dying Genovese in her arms until an ambulance arrived.[65]

Still, no one can deny that people often fail to act when they know they should. Many of us have walked by a homeless person, or been awakened by a scream and turned over to fall back asleep, or shirked from refilling a coffee pot in a communal kitchen.

The phenomenon of bystander apathy has been well-documented in a set of classic studies from the golden age of social psychology, when experiments were a kind of performance art designed to raise awareness of the dangers of mindless conformity (this was before committees for the protection of research subjects put the kibosh on the genre). The psychologists John Darley and Bibb Latané suspected that people in the presence of other people might fail to respond to an obvious need not because of apathy but because of a diffusion of responsibility.[66] Everyone assumes that someone else will step in, and that if no one does, the situation mustn't be all that dire. In experiments that have become a staple of the undergraduate psychology curriculum, Darley and Latané brought people into the lab to fill out questionnaires and then staged an emergency, such as a loud crash in an adjoining room followed by agonized moans, or smoke pouring out of a ventilator. If the participant was sitting with a confederate of the experimenter who continued to fill out the questionnaire as if nothing was happening, 80 percent of the time the participant did nothing too. When the participants were alone, only 30 percent failed to respond.

But pondering the game-theoretic payoffs faced by the Good Samaritans and the Don't-Get-Involvers provides a deeper explanation than the nebulous metaphor of diffusion. The sociologist Andreas Diekmann analyzed the bystander effect as a game he called the Volunteer's Dilemma.[67] If someone intervenes, then each bystander enjoys a benefit, namely the reduction of distress at the thought of a person in danger. But the intervener incurs a personal cost in risk, time, and forgone opportunities to do something else. The best outcome for each bystander, then, is for someone *else* to intervene, and the worst is for no one to intervene, with oneself intervening falling in between. Each volunteer would step in if he was certain that no one else intended to, so he tries to discern their intentions while hiding his own. The result is an outguessing standoff, like poker players bluff-ing and calling, generals attacking and defending, or hockey players shooting and goaltending, each hoping to exploit a longstanding habit or momentary tell in the other.[68]

Since predictability is fatal in an outguessing standoff, the best strategy is to roll the mental dice and act randomly, with whatever probability makes your opponent indifferent between *his* two choices (in game theory, choosing one of several moves with certain proba-bilities is called a mixed strategy). The result is a Nash equilibrium, a nervous deadlock in which neither side can do better with any other strategy. In the Volunteer's Dilemma, the strategy is to volun-teer with a probability that depends on the relative costs of no one helping, someone helping, and oneself helping—*and* on the number of potential volunteers. The more volunteers, the lower the odds that you have to spring into action, since it becomes likelier that someone else will spring first. The classic bystander effect—a greater number of bystanders reduces the chance that any one of them will step in—is simply what happens when rational actors in a Volunteer's Dilemma play the most viable strategy.

Notice that the entire scenario presumes common knowledge: the volunteers all know about the need to help, and know the others know. When the knowledge is asymmetrical, everything changes. To see this, imagine renting an apartment from an absentee landlord who needs one of the tenants to change the oil filter on the building's furnace, or else the filter will clog and the whole building will be out of heat and hot water. If you were the only tenant on the premises, you would have little choice. But if other tenants were there and knew of the chore, you might hope that one of them would volunteer, and the more of them there are, the likelier one will step in.

But it's not just the existence of other tenants that should affect your decision but your knowledge about their knowledge, and theirs about yours. Suppose the landlord has not generated common knowledge by posting a sign about the need for the filter change, or sending out a notice to everyone by email, or announcing it at an annual meeting, but instead informs the tenants one by one. As you walk down the hallway you overhear him telling another tenant about the need for someone to change the filter. If you do a quick about-face and tiptoe away before you're noticed, you can leave your neighbor with the burden. You have second-order knowledge (you know that he knows), but he has only private knowledge, so he's on the hook.

Better still, your freedom doesn't depend on how many other tenants know about the need, as long as none of them think you know. With private knowledge, unlike common knowledge, responsibility needn't diffuse as the number of potential volunteers increases.

Now consider a third level. Suppose the landlord tells you about the chore, and tells you that he's telling the other tenants about the chore, while also mentioning to them that he told you. But he doesn't tell the other tenants that he told you he'd be seeing them; as far as they're concerned, you may think you're the only one who knows. You have third-order knowledge (you know that they know that you know about the chore), but they have only second-order knowledge (they know that you know, but they don't know you know they know). So now you're on the hook—you have reason to believe they'll shirk, so you have to act.

Think you can handle a fourth level? The landlord has sent just you and another tenant a notice about the chore, and you see the other tenant opening his mailbox and pulling out the same notice you got. He spots you looking at his envelope, but just before he tries to get your attention, your cell phone rings and you get absorbed in a conversation. Now you have fourth-order knowledge: you know that he knows that you know that he knows about the chore, but he's stuck at three orders: he doesn't know you know he knows you know. You're back off the hook—as far as he's concerned, you have a reason to shirk, so he has to act.

Our team wanted to see whether real people, when placed in a Volunteer's Dilemma, go through the recursive thinking about thinking that would allow them to make the shrewdest decision about whether to volunteer or shirk. We invited internet users to pretend they were merchants in a marketplace and could earn a certain profit every day. But on some days the marketplace owner might need help from one of the merchants, who must sacrifice half his earnings to carry out the chore; if he failed to find a volunteer, he'd fine everyone their entire earnings. As in our earlier experiments with the butcher and the baker, the crucial information (in this case, whether the owner needed help that day) might be public knowledge broadcasted over a loudspeaker, or private knowledge conveyed by a messenger to the merchant alone, or various orders of embedded knowledge about knowledge depending on what the messenger told them he was telling the others. The participants had to decide whether to volunteer and sacrifice half their earnings or shirk and take a chance at earning nothing.

And they behaved, more or less, like recursive mentalizers in a Volunteer's Dilemma should, zigzagging in their volunteerism with the level of embedded knowledge. They volunteered when the messenger gave them private knowledge, shirked when they had second-order knowledge about the other merchants' private knowledge, sprang back into action when they got third-order knowledge, and shirked when they got fourth-order knowledge. When the loudspeaker granted them common knowledge, their rate of volunteering fell in between, as if they mentally rolled the dice.

And in a twist that brings us back to the classic bystander effect, we compared what happened when the participants thought they were one of just two merchants and when they thought they were one of five. With common knowledge, more merchants always led to less helping, just as in the textbook experiments But with private knowledge, and with intermediate levels of embedded knowledge, the size of the volunteer pool made no difference or a very small one. All this is what you'd expect from people trying to read the minds of other mind readers.

So as preposterous as it may seem that I could know that you know that I know that you know something, we appear to be equipped with cognitive processes that strive to do just that. We think about thoughts about thoughts, at least to some number of turtles. Most commonly, we recognize that if something is self-evident, or even salient to us, it's likely to seem so to others. And we jump from one kind of thinking to the other, sometimes when we shouldn't, but often when we should. The fruits of this thinking drive a vast range of human affairs, from game shows and situation comedies to picking presidents, acting in emergencies, and setting off economic bubbles and busts.

5

The Department of Social Relations

*Social relationships as coordination games,
played with symbols, reputation, and face*

The first time I thought about levels of mutual knowledge was in my sixth-grade Sunday school class, when our teacher explained a major idea in Jewish moral philosophy, Maimonides' Ladder of Charity (*tzedakah*).

The Ladder of Charity was the brainchild of one of Judaism's greatest scholars, Rabbi Moshe ben Maimon ("Moses the son of Maimon," Hebrew acronym "Rambam," "Maimonides" in Greek).[1] Maimonides was born in 1135 in Muslim-ruled Iberia and lived in what is now Morocco, Israel, and Egypt, where he died in 1204. He wrote dozens of works on logic, metaphysics, medicine, and astronomy (including a debunking of astrology); distilled Jewish faith into thirteen principles; served as the court physician of the sultan Saladin; wrote *The Guide for the Perplexed*, which tried to reconcile scripture with reason, and Jewish theology with Aristotelian philosophy; and codified Jewish oral law into his *Mishneh Torah* ("second Torah"), the work in which he presented his ladder.[2]

According to Maimonides, the righteousness of a charitable gift cannot be reckoned by the size of the donation alone but depends on the circumstances of giving, particularly the state of knowledge of the donor and the beneficiary. Here's the ladder,[3] in descending order of righteousness, with the levels of knowledge appended:

> 1. A person who strengthens an impoverished member of the community by giving him a starter loan, entering into partnership with him, or finding him work so that he will not have to ask for alms.

> 2. Someone who gives charity to the poor without knowing to whom he gave and without the poor person knowing from whom he received. This type of giving was exemplified by the secret chamber that existed in the Temple. The righteous would make donations there in secret and poor people would derive their livelihood from it in secret. A level close to this is giving to a charity fund.
> **Private donor, private beneficiary**

> 3. The giver knows to whom he is giving, but the poor person does not know from whom he received. An example of this were the great Sages who would go in secret and throw money into the doorways of the poor.
> **Private donor, known beneficiary**

> 4. The poor person knows from whom he took but the donor does not know to whom he gave. An example of this were the great Sages who would bundle coins in a sheet and hang them over their shoulders and the poor would come and take them so that they would not be embarrassed.
> **Known donor, private beneficiary**

5. Giving to the poor person in his hand before he asks.
Common knowledge (donor-initiated)

6. Giving to him after he asks.
Common knowledge (beneficiary-initiated)

7. Giving to him less than what is appropriate, but cheerfully.
Common knowledge (willing)

8. Giving to him grudgingly.
Common knowledge (unwilling)

As an eleven-year-old utilitarian, I could appreciate why Rung 1, which delivered a lifelong stream of benefits, was at the top, and why the rungs with paltry donations (Rungs 7 and 8) were on the bottom. But why, I wondered, should anyone care about the mutual knowledge of the donor and beneficiary, which laid out the ordering of Rungs 2, 3, 4, and 5–8? If you're poor, you can buy the same amount of food whether the coins are taken from a community chest, picked up off a doorstep, pulled out of a rich person's backpack, or placed in your hand. And it being a perquisite of youth to call out the hypocrisy of elders, I demanded to know why, if anonymous giving was so righteous, our very own Temple Beth Sholom was studded with plaques identifying the donor of every pew and fixture.

It being an obligation of elders to prop up their culture's moral norms, my long-suffering teacher conceded that Temple members were only human and should try to do better. Had she been a more erudite *talmid chochem* (wise scholar), she might have explained that another sage of medieval Spain, Rabbi Shlomo ben Avraham (Solomon the son of Abraham, acronym Rashba), had endorsed a *mitzvah l'farsem*, "commandment to publicize," which commends spreading the word about good deeds so that others might be inspired to do the same.[4] But that would only have highlighted the contradiction between the Rashba's call for righteous publicity and the Rambam's call for righteous anonymity. No doubt centuries of rabbis have debated the paradox.

Yet another Jewish sage, Larry David, brought the paradox to life in an episode of his comedy series *Curb Your Enthusiasm*.[5] David, playing himself, donates money for a wing of a nonprofit building, which is named after him. The other wing displays only the inscription "Donated by Anonymous." At the ribbon-cutting ceremony he is chagrined to hear people gushing over his rival Ted Danson, because word had leaked out that Danson was the anonymous donor, earning him the reputational advantages of both the generous gift and the self-effacing anonymity. ("Nobody told me that I could be anonymous and tell people! I would've taken that option, OK?")

The states of knowledge surrounding donations are not just a matter for Talmudic disputation and streaming comedies. In real life, people often criticize donors who seek too much credit for their munificence, as in the outrage directed at two philanthropists who rescinded a three-million-dollar gift to a zoo because the plaque showing their names was too small.[6] These judgments are no small thing now that charitable institutions are increasingly charged with solving some of the world's most pressing problems, including hunger, disease, natural disasters, economic development, and political instability. Attitudes about the incentives for giving can determine how much good philanthropy can do. For instance, the entrepreneur Dan Pallotta organized fundraising events like AIDSRide and the Breast Cancer 3-Day that raised more than three hundred million dollars for charities. But his organizations collapsed after complaints that they earned a profit. Pallotta said, wistfully, "People continue to die as a result. . . . This we call morality."[7]

As philanthropy scales up to the gigadollar potential of tech moguls, the scrutiny intensifies. Bill Gates, perhaps following the

Rashba, has not been shy about the massive resources he has put into the Bill & Melinda Gates Foundation. But the Foundation is laser-focused on the measurable benefits it delivers in reducing global poverty and disease, and the publicity is itself a part of this effort: Gates has leveraged it to inspire his fellow billionaires to sign the Giving Pledge, a promise to bequeath the majority of their wealth to philanthropy. In contrast, his opposite number in the Windows–Mac war, Steve Jobs, was excoriated by the *New York Times* because he had not signed the Giving Pledge, and "there is no public record of Mr. Jobs giving money to charity. . . . Nor is there a hospital wing or an academic building with his name on it."[8] This led to suggestions that Jobs was in effect a follower of the Rambam, keeping his largesse anonymous.[9] And the final laugh must go to Rabbi Larry ben David, because after the *Times* takedown, examples of Jobs's quiet philanthropy were outed by his family and friends, including the musician Bono, whose (RED) charitable project, he suggested, had been a beneficiary.[10] ("I'm proud to know him; he's a poetic fellow, an artist and a businessman. . . . You don't have to be a friend of his to know what a private person he is or that he doesn't do things by halves.") As with Ted Danson, the revealed anonymity burnished Jobs's reputation as a philanthropist (in his case posthumously), despite his having given away at most a thousandth of what Gates did.

Why do people care so much about a donor's anonymity, recognition, and ulterior benefits? None of this has anything to do with how much a donation improves the lives of the beneficiaries. Why not embrace donors' desires for recognition as a win–win opportunity to incentivize charitable giving?

One of the perquisites of being a professor is getting to turn a lifelong intellectual curiosity into a publication. Maimonides' Ladder had puzzled me since I debated it with my Sunday school teacher. A half-century later, its moralization of the contrast between private and common knowledge made it fit right into the research I had been doing with De Freitas, DeScioli, and Thomas. So we endeavored to figure out why levels of mutual knowledge should have such a potent effect on attributions of charitability.[11]

Charitable giving is altruism *par excellence*: a donor confers a benefit to others at a cost to himself. (To keep the prose simple, I'll use masculine pronouns for a generic donor and beneficiary, and feminine ones for an observer.) As we saw in chapter 1, the evolution of human altruism is commonly explained by reciprocity, in which a generous act may pay off in the long run if the beneficiary returns the favor, or if a third party catches wind of the good deed and infers that the donor has favors to spare. Unfortunately for making sense of Maimonides, this predicts that donors should strive to make their gifts public, and that beneficiaries and observers should appreciate the transparency—the exact opposite of the esteem that people bestow on anonymous givers.

The missing piece of the puzzle comes from a corollary of the theory of reciprocal altruism called partner choice.[12] Though it pays both sides in a reciprocal partnership to trade favors as long as each one gains more than he gives, people differ in how much advantage they'll try to squeeze out of an exchange while leaving it just profitable enough for the partner that he won't walk away. That's why not everyone evolves into a rapacious scalper: potential partners can shun them, preferring to deal with someone who offers more generous terms. Just as a store with a reputation for fair prices and good service can attract a loyal clientele and earn a bigger profit in the long run than a store that tries to wring every cent out of its customers only to drive them away a person who is inherently generous can be a more attractive friend, ally, or teammate than one who dribbles out favors only to the extent that he expects them to be repaid with a bonus. The advantage in attracting partners makes up for the disadvantage in forgoing the biggest profit in each transaction.

Now, those prospective partners will need to spot the more generous counterparts despite the inevitability that both generous and stingy partners will advertise themselves as generous. So people hone their radar for in-the-bone altruists. They want to spot partners who, deep down, are more magnanimous than they have to be. And that's where a reputation for charitability comes in handy. In addition to trying to help the poor, a donor may be signaling that he is a generous partner, which unfortunately undermines his case that he *is* a generous partner, because a truly generous partner would not be in it for the brownie points. None of this need be conscious; indeed, it's more effective when it is not.

Maimonides' Ladder, then, may be seen as an assay for the dispositional generosity of a donor. In that way its ethos is different from Effective Altruism, the ethical movement inspired by utilitarianism, which valorizes only the benefit to recipients.[13] This is clear enough in Maimonides' own rationale for his ladder: "We are obligated to be more scrupulous in fulfilling the commandment of charity than any other positive commandment, because charity is the sign of a righteous man." It's also apparent in the name for the ladder in the original Hebrew: *tzedakah* means not so much "charity" as "righteousness." We see it in the differences among the bottommost four rungs, each with common knowledge but differing in direct indicators of the donor's kindheartedness. And to return to the point of this chapter, we see it in the arrangement of Rungs 2 through 5, which differ in the levels of knowledge accompanying the act of giving. Here's how.

Rung 2: A double-blind gift, in which neither the donor nor the beneficiary knows the identity of the other, is a dead giveaway of a generous disposition, because the donor has forfeited any possibility of receiving favors in return. No baksheesh, tit for tat, or quid pro quo.

Rung 3: When a donor knows the beneficiary but not vice versa, as with a gift left on a doorstep, it obviates any possibility that the beneficiary could reciprocate directly. The donor, moreover, forgoes any boost to his reputation. But unlike on Rung 2 the donor *could* reveal himself to the beneficiary at some later date to call in the favor, so there could be something in it for him.

Rung 4: A public donor to a private beneficiary, like a sage with an open backpack filled with coins, can't obligate the beneficiary to reciprocate directly, but the beneficiary could choose to do so. Moreover, he could tell others about the donor's good deed and burnish the donor's reputation, granting him kudos with others. The open possibility that the donor could benefit from payback and reputation makes him seem less charitable than the donor one rung up, who can benefit only from payback.

Rungs 5–8: When the donor places money into the beneficiary's hand, each knowing the other, it creates common knowledge of the altruistic act and of an implicit relationship of reciprocity, obligating the beneficiary to repay the favor should the donor want it in the future (as in the opening scene of *The Godfather,* in which Vito Corleone says to a supplicant, "Someday, and that day may never come, I'll call upon you to do a service for me. But until that day, accept this justice as a gift on my daughter's wedding day"). A common-knowledge gift, then, may be far from selfless: the donor is in a position to call in the favor, and he enhances his reputation as a patron, sugar daddy, or godfather.

In sum, the more that donors are in a position to be paid back or admired, the less righteous they will appear, because the gift becomes less diagnostic of an underlying disposition for pure altruism. When charitable gifts are judged as windows into the giver's soul, the welfare of the beneficiary can slip out of sight.

In a modern context, this is a big reason why the Effective Altruism movement has not taken off. EA advocates have shown that different charities for a given cause—saving lives, educating girls, furnishing clean water—vary wildly in their efficacy, and recommend that donors exercise due diligence in selecting the most effective ones. But research into the efficacy of charities is private knowledge, and no one gets plaudits for selecting the charity that saves the most lives per dollar donated.[14] (To be fair to Maimonides, he did say about Rung 2, "A person should not give to a charity fund unless he knows that the person managing it is faithful, wise, and capable of administering it in a proper manner.")

Social scientists have come to appreciate that before they commit too much effort to explaining a phenomenon, they should make sure it's replicable, so De Freitas, DeScioli, Thomas, and I began by seeing whether Maimonides' Ladder captures people's intuitions today. Of course, Maimonides was doing normative ethics, not social science: he was laying out what is *inherently* righteous, not surveying what people *feel* is righteous. But in the absence of divine revelation, he may have been tapping into intuitions that most people would converge on when faced with these comparisons. We wanted to see whether the intuitions held up eight hundred years later. Try it yourself: go back to the ladder at the beginning of the chapter and see whether you agree with the ranking.

In an internet survey, we asked respondents to consider a charity that solicited funds for helping poor families in a small community who were victims of a hurricane and flood. The charity offered donors the choice of donating anonymously (Rung 2), receiving a photo of the family they helped (Rung 3), authorizing the charity to send a photo of them to the family they helped (Rung 4), or authorizing it to send the donor and beneficiary photos of each other and informing them of the exchange (Rung 5, Common Knowledge). We asked the respondents to consider donors who chose each of these options and rate how genuinely charitable they thought each one was, together with several other questions. The results were consistent across several studies with minor variations in their cover stories.

First, Maimonides got the ordering of the rungs mostly right: states of mutual knowledge do affect judgments of charitability. A double-blind donor was judged to be more charitable than a private donor who knew his beneficiaries, who was in turn judged as more charitable than self-revealing and common-knowledge donors. But our raters disagreed with Maimonides about the order of the lower two rungs. They gave a slight edge to common-knowledge donors over the ones who revealed their identities but didn't care to know whom they helped. I'll return to this surprise momentarily.

Second, when people assess other people's charitability, they are not just bestowing haloes but making predictions about their likelihood of giving in other circumstances. We asked the respondents whether they thought the donors would give to charities again in the future, and their predictions tracked their judgments of charitability almost perfectly.

Third, the reason that states of knowledge affect judgments of charitability is that they are seen as providing different opportunities to indulge ulterior motives. We asked the responders how much the donors were motivated by a desire to improve their reputations with the family they helped, and also how much they were motivated by a desire to improve their reputations in the community. Their judgments climbed Maimonides' Ladder exactly: double-blind donors were seen as least concerned with their reputations, followed by private donors, known donors, and common-knowledge donors.

Fourth, it really was *common* knowledge that downgraded the perceived charitability of donors, not just *reciprocal* knowledge. To appreciate the difference, let's go back to Maimonides' examples of Rungs 3 and 4. Suppose a neighborhood busybody had tipped off the poor family as to who had left the money on their doorstep, or had tipped off the sage as to who had picked money out of his backpack, without informing those they had outed. In those cases, the donor and the beneficiary would each know who the other was, but would not know that he knew that: the pairs would have reciprocal knowledge but not common knowledge. In a variant of the study, we asked respondents to consider a case in which the charity allowed the donor to confidentially request a photo of the beneficiary family, and vice versa, and asked them to judge a donor who exercised that option while the beneficiary did too (each unbeknownst to the other). That reciprocal-knowledge donor was judged as less charitable than a double-blind donor, but more charitable than a common-knowledge donor (where the exchange of photos was known to both).

Fifth, the virtue of the donors (as determined by states of knowledge) loomed larger in the judges' minds than the benefits they delivered to the needy. (Our respondents, in other words, were not Effective Altruists.) In one study we asked the respondents to compare a donor who anonymously gave $10,000 to help ten unknown families with a second donor who gave more money (ranging from $12,000 to $1,000,000) to help even more families—but either revealed his identity, agreed to allow photos to be exchanged (reciprocal knowledge), or handed the checks to the families in person (common knowledge). Our judges treated self-disclosure as a moral stain that tainted the good that a larger donation would bestow. A donor who gave with common knowledge had to give twice as much, and a donor with reciprocal knowledge five times as much, to earn the same kudos as a fully private donor. Astonishingly, when it came to the donor who simply made himself known, there was *no amount of money* he could give—not even a hundred times as much—that would make him as charitable in the eyes of our respondents as the anonymous giver.

Sixth, the beneficiaries of the donations, unsurprisingly, didn't see it that way. They just wanted the cash, righteousness be damned. Respondents imagined themselves in the shoes of the flooded families and were asked to choose whether they'd prefer $10,000 from an anonymous donor or $20,000 from a donor who also sent his photo. They took the larger gift—and, unlike the high-minded judges with no skin in the game, deemed the larger, known donor to be the more charitable one. And when the respondents imagined themselves as *donors*, they said they'd opt to reveal their identities, even though in the role of observers they judge such signaling to be uncharitable. But social psychologists have long known that people are moral hypocrites: they disapprove of acts by others that they commit themselves.[15]

Now, what about the flip of the two low rungs? Why, contra Maimonides, do people judge a known donor with an anonymous beneficiary to be a bit *less* charitable than a common-knowledge donor, even though it's the latter who's better positioned to call in the favor? Your own reaction to his example may suggest a reason. The sage with the open backpack seems a bit, well, lordly and haughty, while the pauper who scampers after him to pick through his backpack seems abased, degraded, demeaned. It's not that Maimonides was oblivious to the beneficiary's pride—he actually thought that the coin-pickers, their identities hidden from the donor, "would not be embarrassed." But his social instincts may have failed him here, not anticipating the unfortunate symbolism of a needy nobody tagging along behind a lavish big shot. Our respondents, when asked to judge whether the various donors in the story felt equal to or higher than their beneficiaries in status, deemed the one-way identity revealer as the most imperious. Judgments of righteousness, then, seem to incorporate whether a donor appears to care about status, not just reciprocity.

Turning now to the lowermost rung, there may even be a

redeeming quality to a donor who symmetrically exchanges identities with a beneficiary. He gives off vibes that the relationship is between equals, one of whom may just have hit a bad stretch and needs a hand, rather than a relationship between a rich patron and a poor supplicant. This concession to the beneficiary's feelings could have lifted the common-knowledge donor upward in charitability, at the same time that the known donor's high-handedness pushed him downward, explaining the reversal of Rungs 4 and 5. We confirmed this explanation by asking our respondents to rate how much the donors seemed interested in getting to know the family they helped. Sure enough, the common-knowledge photo exchanger was judged the most caring, which presumably spilled over into the ratings of charitability he earned. This may explain why even a charity famously driven by hardheaded evaluations of efficacy, the Bill & Melinda Gates Foundation, publishes annual reports with photographs of the eponymous donors mingling with beneficiaries in the poor countries they help.

What we have here is a third kind of relationship (together with reciprocity and status) that can tug judgments of charitability upward or downward: the warm bath of friendship. Like reciprocity, it sets the stage for favors given and received. But the economics are different: the favors are freely granted, and no one keeps score. And the common-knowledge signals that cement such a relationship are different, including convivial meals and fictive kinship rather than acts recorded in a mental balance sheet. Vito Corleone, tormenting his beseecher before agreeing to the favor, explains:

> We've known each other for many years, but this is the first time you came to me for counsel, for help. I can't remember the last time that you invited me to your house for a cup of coffee, even though my wife is godmother to your only child. But let's be frank here: you

never wanted my friendship. And you were afraid to be in my debt.
. . . But now you come to me and you say, "Don Corleone, give me
justice." But you don't ask with respect. You don't offer friendship.
You don't even think to call me Godfather.[16]

In sum, the Ladder of Charity, or at least the rungs separated by
levels of mutual knowledge, captures many of modern people's intuitions about righteousness. It distinguishes gifts by the opportunities
for payback, and thereby identifies anyone who willingly forgoes such
opportunities as constitutionally generous and a desirable partner.
Where it just misses the mark is in neglecting the signals of relationships other than exchange, namely status and communal warmth. And
that three-way distinction takes us into the rest of this chapter, where
we will see how levels of mutual knowledge govern the coordination
games that underpin our social relations.[17]

The incongruity of anonymous donors earning esteem for their anonymity is just one example of a social paradox, a term suggested by
the psychologist David Pinsof for phenomena like these:[18]

  1. We try to gain status by not caring about status.[19]

  2. We rebel against conformity in the same way as everyone
     else.[20]

  3. We show humility to prove we're better than other people.[21]

  4. We don't care what people think, and we want them to think
     this.[22]

5. We make anonymous donations to get credit for not caring about getting credit.[23]

6. We bravely defy social norms so that people will praise us.[24]

7. We avoid being manipulative to get people to do what we want them to do.[25]

8. We compete to be less competitive than our rivals.[26]

9. We help those in need, regardless of self-interest, because being seen as the type of person who helps those in need, regardless of self-interest, is in our self-interest.[27]

10. We make subversive art that only high-status people appreciate.[28]

11. We make fun of ourselves for being uncool to prove we're cool.[29]

12. We self-righteously defend false beliefs to prove we care more about the truth than virtue-signaling.[30]

13. We help our friends without expecting anything in return, because we know they would do the same for us.[31]

14. We show everyone our true, authentic self—not who society wants us to be—because that is who society wants us to be.[32]

How can we make sense of these everyday oxymorons? Pinsof suggests they arise from a back-and-forth between our social judgment and our recursive mentalizing. We're all attuned to behavioral giveaways of valued traits like honesty, generosity, competence, fairness, and trustworthiness. Knowing this, we try to curry the admiration of our fellows by displaying those signs and signals. But knowing that the people we judge also know this, we discount any apparent attempts at virtue signaling, since they indicate only social cunning, not the virtues themselves. And knowing that those who judge us know that we know they will discount our attempts to signal our virtue, we try to keep our signaling subtle enough that they won't think we're trying to signal at all—or at least subtle enough that it's not common knowledge, so we can all keep up the pretense that the behavior is authentic. (In the *Curb Your Enthusiasm* episode, the admiration for Danson depended on his identity being widely known, even universally known, but not *commonly* known.) As we shall see, it can be in the interests of the observers, not just the actors, to keep the virtue signaling out of common knowledge, in order to avoid an uncomfortable challenge to the assumption of mutual trust that makes social interaction possible.

What are we all trying to signal? That's what the rest of this chapter is about. In a nutshell: Social relationships are coordination games, which we solve with common salience and common knowledge. But unlike the one-shot encounters in chapter 3, a social relationship is a long game: it defines the players, the payoffs, and the strategies for an indefinite number of day-to-day games we might play in the future (opera or hockey, swerve or proceed, stag or hare). Social relationships are cemented by symbols and rituals that signpost the mutually beneficial coordination equilibria. People compete to be selected for these relationships by cultivating a reputation and saving face, both ratified by common knowledge. With the choice of partners and the terms of the relationship at stake, people become performers, drawing attention to events they want to become common knowledge, and hypocrites, diverting attention from events they want to keep out.

Let's start with the simplest coordination game, Rendezvous, where James and Charlotte are trying to find their way into one of the mutually enjoyable cells of a coffee date. In a Rendezvous game the payoffs are highest when the two players rendezvous, but where did the payoffs of enjoying each other's company come from in the first place? It's no fun to dine in close quarters with a randomly selected stranger, as any airline passenger in economy seating can attest. And James and Charlotte were not just thrown together in a round of speed dating—they wanted to meet because they had an ongoing friendship. That's what put the big payoff numbers into the two cells in which they rendezvous.

But what *is* a friendship, or any other relationship? It's not as if friends sign a contract. A relationship is a matter of common knowledge. If two people are friends, it means that each one knows that the other one knows that the first one knows that the second one knows . . . that they are friends. By now we've become used to the idea that common knowledge is needed to solve coordination dilemmas, and that it is usually generated by public or salient events. Let's see how that applies to relationships.

The matrix on the left below is a stylized conception of the long game of a relationship, embracing many interactions. A friendship begins with one party reaching out and the other reciprocating (or not). And because a friendship entails that each of you is there for the other whenever support may be needed, it must be periodically reaffirmed.[33] Let's call the overarching strategy of maintaining a friendship—calling, exchanging cards, sending birthday greetings—"Warm," and the strategy of ignoring, rebuffing, or drifting apart "Cool." The top left cell of the matrix shows the prospect of mutual satisfaction for a reciprocated friendship (500), and the bottom right cell shows that nothing is gained or lost with pairs that keep a cordial distance (0). There are costs to mismatches, when one makes an unwanted overture that the other must awkwardly rebuff, or when one is a false or fair-weather friend who exploits the friendship. The matrix thus has two Nash equilibria, making it a coordination game, because James and Charlotte are better off either as good buddies or ships passing in the night than as resentful or awkward acquaintances (let's average out those costs at −50). The large payoff in the consummated-friendship cell comes not just from the warm glow of becoming and staying friends but from the open-ended stream of positive-sum coordination games it enables in the future. Each of these can be shown as one of the matrices familiar from chapter 3, such as a coffee date (the right-hand matrix below), or an opportunity to take in a hockey game or a night at the opera.

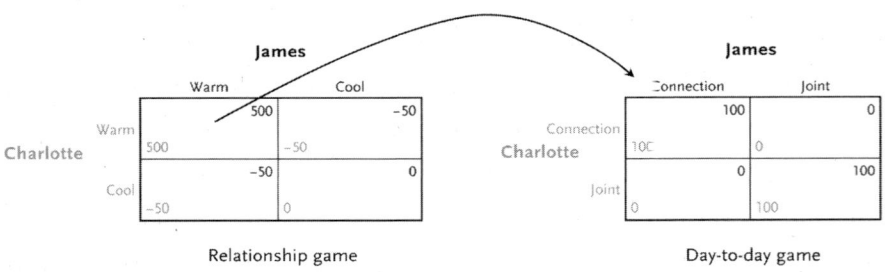

Relationship game   Day-to-day game

Other kinds of ongoing relationship also set the terms for day-to-day coordination games. The player who stands his ground in a first round of a Hawk–Dove or Chicken game may establish a reputation for dominance that emboldens him to play Hawk in every subsequent round, thereafter incentivizing his opposite number to play Dove to avoid the cost of conflict. Someone who shows himself to be an altruist in the early rounds of a reciprocity game, or a cooperator in an iterated Prisoners' Dilemma, or a stag hunter in a Stag Hunt, could bind himself and his partner in happy mutual cooperation every time they come together in rematches.

✂

Relationship games are fragile, with constant opportunities to mis-coordinate and defect, and they are sustainable only when they have focal points or common-knowledge generators to attract and keep the parties in the fruitful equilibria. This is how I interpret a sweeping theory of social relations proposed by the anthropologist Alan Fiske, based on his observations of universality and diversity in human cultures.[34]

Fiske proposed that all human social relationships fall into just four kinds (in traditional cultures, just three kinds), which he calls relational models. Each originated as an evolutionary adaptation, and applies by default to certain kinds of partners. Each embodies a coordination game which prescribes a distribution of payoffs. Each is cued by distinctive focal points and conventions. And since the human brain is adept at turning constants into variables, each of these primal models can be repurposed to apply to new combinations of players, resources, and situations.

The most basic relational model is Communal Sharing, Commu-nality for short. This is the natural way of relating in intimate part-nerships like families, couples, and friends, though it may be grafted onto more provisional groups which try to replicate their solidarity, like guilds, teams, cliques, bands, unions, brigades, communes, and kibbutzim. The primal examples of communality evolved from the mutualism provided by shared genes (for kin), offspring (for couples), interests (for friends), and enemies (for tribes). These overlapping interests yoke their fates and naturally place them in games where the equilibrium payoffs for both are positive (like Rendezvous and the Battle of the Sexes). They share resources freely under principles like

"What's mine is thine" and "From each according to his ability, to each according to his needs," with no one keeping track of who gives and who gets. (That's the basis for the joke about the dinner guest who says to the hostess, "The cookies were delicious; I ate four," to which she replies, "You ate five, but who's counting?")

Blood is thicker than water, so while Communal Sharing comes naturally to families, it's more tenuous for other groups. Even within families the genetic interests of kin are only partly aligned. These discrepancies can tempt people out of the mutually beneficial equilibria into cells where they can prosper at the expense of the others. Though in a communal relationship no one keeps a ledger, if an imbalance of taking and giving becomes extreme the person with the short end of the stick is bound to notice. ("When she was down, I was there for her, but in my moment of need, where was she?") Another vulnerability of a communal relationship is that one or both parties can simply lose sight of the opportunities for mutual benefit (as in "I can't remember the last time that you invited me to your house for a cup of coffee").

The fragility of communal relationships leads people to take care in choosing communal partners, seeking those who are constitutionally warm, generous, noncompetitive, and nonmanipulative. If these qualities seem to overlap with those that commend someone as a better reciprocation partner on the Ladder of Charity, that's no coincidence. Reciprocators who grant generous offers and terms of repayment can blur into friends who don't exploit the friendship by taking more than they give.

In addition to choosing congenial members, communal groups need to attract and retain them with focal points that steer them into the happy equilibrium of mutual benefit. Fiske observes that people all over the world coordinate their communal relationships with rituals that draw from a few conceptual metaphors.

The human mind naturally thinks that SOLIDARITY IS PHYSICAL CLOSENESS, and so we bond with meetings, hugs, kisses, handshakes, and, in intimate relationships, cuddling, caressing, and sex. It senses that SOLIDARITY IS KINSHIP, and so it labels its coalitions as *brethren, brotherhoods, bands of brothers, fraternities, sisterhoods, sororities, soul sisters, the fatherland, the mother country,* and *the family of man.*

Most creatively, our species finds focal points in the metaphor SOLIDARITY IS BEING MADE OF THE SAME FLESH. We bond by eating together in family meals, dinner dates, luncheons, feasts, and ceremonial banquets. It's as if you are what you eat, so if you eat the same stuff you are the same stuff. Conversely, we impose food taboos to differentiate our ethnic group (with all its proprietary coordination equilibria) from neighboring ones. We refashion our bodies by hairstyling, piercing, scarring, tattooing, circumcision, and more gruesome genital mutilations. We synchronize our movements in dancing, bowing, waving, fist-pumping, chanting, marching, and rising and sitting together, creating the illusion that we are part of one big superorganism.

And we coordinate with the metaphor SOLIDARITY IS HAVING THE SAME MIND. This can take the form of shared emotional experiences, like ecstatic raves and concerts, thrilling victories and agonizing defeats in sports, or ritual ordeals of terror, hunger, or pain. It also may take the form of shared beliefs. The content of the belief may reinforce the same-family or same-flesh metaphor by asserting that members of the group all descended from a patriarch or primeval couple, or came into being in the same act of creation, or are connected to a natal land. The beliefs may glorify the virtue, purity, and bravery of the group itself, or of the noble heroes and martyrs that founded it.[35] Or they may be a costly signal, a preposterous belief in miracles, dogmas, contradictions, or other affronts to common sense that only the truly committed would affirm.[36]

Conspicuous by its absence is language. Children may come right out and say, "Do you want to be friends?" or "I don't want to be friends anymore," but grownups seldom talk about their communal bonds in so many words. That's because the very act of negotiating the perquisites and obligations of a communal relationship would undermine the emotional and physical fusion that encourages them to share instinctively. The exception that proves the rule is ritualized language: boilerplate strings of words that are recited in unison or in call-and-response, like *I pledge allegiance*, *Our father who art in heaven*, *Let's go Red Sox!*, or the big matzo ball *I love you*.

⊰⊱

A very different relational model is the one Fiske calls Authority Ranking: hierarchies of power, status, prestige, deference, dominance, preeminence, or autonomy. In the minds of the people who respect an authority ranking, the hierarchy is legitimate and natural, and it entails reciprocal obligations for those lower down to defer and to those higher up to protect. But its evolutionary origin is in the dominance contest, a clear example of a coordination game solved by common-knowledge focal points. It's simply Hawk–Dove. When contestants both want a resource that cannot be divided and is not worth fighting over, they may tacitly agree that it should be ceded to one of them. The winner is decided on by some convention that could be arbitrary, but typically is correlated with, or calls to mind, the ability to prevail should they ever come to blows. Among other species, this may be who got there first, who outlasts the other, or who is bigger, brighter, or louder.

The ever-ingenious *Homo sapiens* has come up with countless symbols to remind people of who outranks whom, generally tapping into the common salience of size, elevation, or precedence. Dominant individuals such as bosses, chiefs, presidents, and generals look bigger (with the help of hats, helmets, and headdresses), *are* bigger (on average), are depicted as bigger (in outsize images and statues), stand higher (on platforms and balconies), and have bigger and higher offices, palaces, and monuments. They strut ahead of their subordinates, and enter and exit first. (Remember Maimonides' inadvertently demeaning image of the pauper trailing the sage.) According to a common idiom, they even urinate farther. The logic of commonly knowable authority markers was recognized in 1670 by Blaise Pascal: "How rightly do we distinguish men by external differences rather than by internal qualities. Which of us two shall have precedence? Who will give place to the other? The least clever? But I am as clever as he. We should have to fight over this. He has four lackeys, and I have only one. This can be seen; we have only to count. It falls to me to yield, and I am a fool if I contest the matter."[37]

Big shots and strongmen with formal authority can preserve their stations with conventional symbols of dominance. But in the informal struggles of everyday life, people have to set up their own deference-inducing focal points. They may consciously flaunt the trappings of dominance, like loud motorcycles, muscle cars, or an overbearing demeanor, but that can turn into a social paradox. A self-conscious display of dominance will be seen as its opposite, a sign of weakness: as bluster, bravado, bombast, braggadocio, being a blowhard, or as they say in Texas, "all hat and no cattle."

Within social networks, the common knowledge that coordinates Hawk–Dove games generally comes not from perceptible focal points but from a shared understanding of who will stand his ground (because he expects others to give way, because they expect him to stand his ground, because he expects them to give way, and so on), and who will give way (because he expects the others to stand their ground, because they expect him to give way, and so on). Over the long term, this goes into a person's reputation or "honor." Over the short term, it's calibrated by incidents in which a person saves or loses "face." Face is an obvious metaphor for common knowledge: it's the part of you that sees while being seen (more on this in the next chapter). The metaphor refers to common knowledge of the deference and sympathy that a person expects to be granted.

Facework is the sociologist Erving Goffman's term for our everyday efforts to preserve our standing—but also the standing of our friends and friendly acquaintances, since a challenge to a settled understanding of sympathy and deference has costs for everyone.[38] Facework includes the countless moves and responses that are recognizable enough to have earned idioms in the English lexicon:

> affronts, apologies, bitchiness, cool, dignity, digs, diplomacy, false pride, faux pas, fig leaves, flimsy excuses, gaffes, grumblings, huffs, kid gloves, knowing where you really stand, letting it pass, lip service, open secrets, poise, pretexts, remorse, righteous indignation, savoir faire, self-respect, shamelessness, slaps in the face, snubs, standing on ceremony, sugarcoating, tact, thin skin, walking on eggshells

These little shows are often efforts to prevent some fact that would challenge a person's dominance or status from becoming common knowledge when the stakes for everyone are small. When an embattled politician resigns to "spend more time with his family," the pretext needn't fool anyone. It just has to be plausible enough that listeners are open to the possibility that *other* people might believe it.[39] In their landmark book *Politeness,* the anthropologists Penelope Brown and Stephen Levinson argue that facework is the motive behind the formulas of verbal courtesy found in cultures all over the world, a theory we will return to in chapter 7.[40]

The stakes are not always small. Since common knowledge of dominance may determine the outcome of social contests for the indefinite future, sometimes the airy nothingness of face, honor, and reputation really are worth fighting over. That explains a long-standing puzzle in criminology: why the single largest motive for homicide is "altercations of relatively trivial origin; insult, curse, jostling, etc."[41] Loose acquaintances, usually young men, come to blows over a small gambling debt or a pool table or a parking spot, or they avenge a humiliation by returning to the bar with a gun or by ambushing their heckler with a knife. Violent retaliation for insults and affronts is a sacred value in traditional cultures of honor, and it was elevated to a performance art in those with formal dueling.[42]

As the evolutionary psychologists Martin Daly and Margo Wilson remark in their book *Homicide*, "The participants in these 'trivial altercations' behave as if a great deal more is at issue than small change or access to a pool table, and their evaluations of what is at stake deserve our respectful consideration."[43] What's at stake is common knowledge that they will stand their ground in a confrontation. Daly and Wilson explain: "Men are known by their fellows as 'the sort who can be pushed around' and 'the sort who won't take any shit,' as people whose word means action or people who are full of hot air, as guys whose girlfriends you can chat up with impunity or guys you don't want to mess with." In laboratory studies in which participants are given the opportunity to punish someone who has insulted or cheated them (by shocking him, blasting him with an air horn, or spiking his snack with hot sauce), they retaliate more harshly when they think others are watching.[44] Real-life studies have found that the presence of an audience doubles the likelihood that an argument between two men will escalate to violence.[45]

In more civilized settings, social hierarchies are ordered not by dominance but by status: publicly acknowledged assets like looks, smarts, skills, wealth, and clout.[46] If dominance is backstopped up by the implicit threat "I could hurt you," status is backstopped by the implicit promise "I could help you." Admired traits can be converted into soft power because the traits that confer status are also, according to surveys, the traits that go into leadership, particularly initiative, intelligence, competence, and generosity.[47] The leaders of collective endeavors are rewarded by voluntary deference, which makes leadership and the status that feeds it worth competing over, even while it differs from the brute force behind dominance.

The overlapping but distinct logics of leadership and dominance can be laid bare in a game devised by the mathematical psychologist Anatol Rapoport called Leader–Follower.[48] Consider a coordination dilemma in which a group of people can accomplish either of two tasks if their activities are coordinated by a leader, but they accomplish nothing if they all do their own thing, or if multiple leaders try to pull the group in different directions, leading to wasteful confusion and squabbling. A leader who succeeds in getting everyone to pull together, should one emerge, is rewarded with extra influence or benefits. Consider, say, a band of hunters who can set out eastward to hunt kudu, conveniently near the home of one potential leader, or westward to hunt bushbuck, near the home of another. Or suppose that Alphonse and Gaston can pass through a narrow doorway, that each prefers to go first (unlike in the old comic strip), that they'd collide if they tried to squeeze through at the same time, and that they would waste time if each kept deferring to the other (as they actually do in the comic).

Gaston

	Follow	Lead
Follow	0 / 0	200 / 100
Lead	100 / 200	-100 / -100

Alphonse

There are two Nash equilibria, the diagonal cells in which one leads and the other follows.[49] But it's not easy for the players to find their way into them, because each prefers to lead, but if they both try to lead they end up worse off. As with Hawk–Dove, they'd both do better (albeit unequally) if there were a focal point that allowed them to agree on who defers to whom. It could be an arbitrary focal point, like who arrived or spoke first, or a convention that picks the same one every time. But it's likelier to be whoever has the greater reputation for initiative, skill, and generosity—in the case of the hunting party, the better tracker and more generous carcass-divider. That's because leadership qualities tilt the payoffs, making one coordination cell more attractive than the other. The perquisites of leadership in turn set up a prior competition to accrue a greater reputation for qualities like initiative, skill, and generosity. And the benefits of coordination over chaos can make it worthwhile for people to accede to status hierarchies even when they are not at the top.

The dark side of a hierarchy is structural inequality. Richard McAdams, citing the work of the economist Gillian Hadfield, notes that in games like the Battle of the Sexes, Hawk–Dove, and Leader–Follower, it's easy for everyone to settle on a focal point that gives the edge to a sex, race, or ethnic group, locking the other one into second-class status indefinitely.[50] He explains:

> If everyone expects women or a racial minority to ' settle for less" in a bargaining situation, then women or minority members will find that refusing to settle for less will, by preventing agreement, leave them worse off. In [Battle of the Sexes] situations between a man and woman, if the man expects the woman to settle for her less favored outcome, then the man will play the strategy associated with his most preferred outcome. If the woman, counter to expectations, also attempts to claim the larger share, they will fail to coordinate and she will be worse off than if she did what was expected.[51]

The "Battle of the Sexes," originally just a conventional mnemonic, can become a battle of the sexes in reality, where one sex always prevails (or one race, or religion, or ethnicity). It needn't be men—the convention "Ladies first" solves the doorway game—but in most contexts it is, and an individual woman defies it to her disadvantage. The same would be true for an African American during the era of Jim Crow. This is the game-theoretic basis of the commonplace that many forms of entrenched inequality are arbitrary, and that they cannot be undermined by individuals renegotiating their relationships but only by a collective effort to overturn the norm.

McAdams notes that this puts the subordinate group into a second game, Assurance (or a Stag Hunt). If they coordinate among themselves to challenge the norm (hunt stag), they can prevail, but until they do, each may be nervous about suffering the day-to-day consequences of discoordination with the dominant group and stick with the status quo (hunt rabbit).[52] In chapter 1 we saw the importance of common knowledge in coordinating protest movements, and I'll return to them at the end of this one. And to link back to the beginning of the chapter, it's also worth noting that whenever people have a choice of partners, they can escape a game that consistently puts them on the losing side by seeking new ones.

꘎

Though a focal point that solves a coordination game need not be fair, it's obviously better in the long run if it is. This sets the stage for the third relational model, which Fiske calls Equality Matching, though it could also be called Equity or Fairness. People enter into arrangements in which they divvy up resources equally, or take turns, or barter goods and services for equivalent goods and services, or trade favors in a tit-for-tat exchange. They flip a coin, draw straws, line things up in rows, weigh them in balances, play scissors-paper-rock, or count out rhymes like "eeny-meeny-miny-moe." The even-steven, fair-and-square symbolism of these operations serves as a focal point in the long relationship game, and the operation itself apportions the resources in each day-to-day game. The emotions accompanying these transactional relationships are cool and cordial, and the reputation that people cultivate to be chosen for them is trustworthiness: being a straight shooter, a plain dealer, a stand-up guy, the salt of the earth.

If you can stand one more game, here's one that captures the essence of Equality Matching, called Divide the Dollar.[53] Suppose that two people are offered a dollar to divide between them, and have to submit sealed bids on their share of the split, with the rub that if their combined offers exceed a dollar, no one gets anything. The game has ninety-nine mutually profitable Nash equilibria: 1 cent for me, 99 cents for you; 2 cents for me, 98 cents for you; all the way up to 99 cents for me, 1 cent for you. No matter what the other player's bid is, I would do no better by offering less than the difference between that bid and a dollar (because I'd be leaving money on the table), nor by offering more than that difference (because that would blow up the deal). The matrix is on the following page, with three of the possible moves shown

	25¢	50¢	75¢
25¢	25¢ / 25¢	50¢ / 25¢	75¢ / 25¢
50¢	25¢ / 50¢	50¢ / 50¢	0 / 0
75¢	25¢ / 75¢	0 / 0	0 / 0

Though all the splits along the lower-left-to-upper-right diagonal are Nash equilibria, one of them pops out as a focal point: 50:50. It's in fact close to the solution that real people arrive at when they actually play the game (including a sequential version called the Ultimatum Game, which I'll return to in the next chapter).[54] And it's the evolutionarily stable strategy that players settle on when the game is played over multiple generations and the payoff is reckoned in descendants—giving us an explanation for the evolution of fairness.[55]

People play a version of Divide the Dollar whenever they haggle over a price; the equivalent of the dollar is the difference between what the item is worth to one and what it's worth to the other. They also play a version when they play repeated rounds of the Battle of the Sexes, where the couple may agree to take turns in their activities. The game is also played in the follow-up to a Hawk–Dove confrontation in which both antagonists play Dove and they have to divide the territory, or a Stag Hunt in which both hunters hunt stag and they have to divide the carcass. Similar compromises emerge in reciprocal relationships, which can be seen as a repeated Prisoners' Dilemma (equivalent to a Stag Hunt), where the stable strategy is trading favors tit for tat.

In all these cases, an equitable split may be a condition for staying in the partnership. And the negotiations have a twist that brings us back to Maimonides' Ladder and the social paradox of revealed anonymity. When people playing any of these games find themselves in a competitive market for partners, they may seek an edge by being known as the kind of person who divides the dollar more generously than he has to.

⊸⦇⊷

Relational models, by default, provide certain kinds of focal points for certain sets of people. It's natural for families to share food communally, for bosses to wield the trappings of authority, and for neighbors to trade favors. But the assignments are not rigid, and different cultures can mix and match the components in different ways. A culture is composed of many social norms that link a relational model, a role (parent, child, teacher, student, husband, wife, supervisor, employee, customer, neighbor, stranger), a context (home, school, workplace, store), and a resource (food, money, land, housing, time, advice, sex, labor).

Good friends, as we have seen, mainly operate with the model of Communal Sharing. They share food in communal meals and do each other favors without keeping score. But they may also work together on a task in which one is an expert and gives orders to the other (Authority Ranking) or split the cost of gas on a trip (Equality Matching). But the exceptions have limits: a guest at a dinner party may not pull out his wallet at the end of the evening to pay his hosts for the meal, nor should he reciprocate with an ostentatious invitation for dinner the very next night. But in many cultures such reciprocity is calculated openly, the way people in our culture privately keep track of the annual exchange of Christmas cards. A boss in a corporation can control an employee's salary and office space but may not help himself to the employee's possessions. In Western cultures we buy, sell, and trade our land but don't do so with brides; in some cultures it's the other way around.

To be a competent member of a culture means to internalize dozens of these packages. People who violate the terms of a relational model—say, by not sharing with their kin or by failing to return a favor—may be seen as parasites or cheaters and become a target of anger. But when a person applies one relational model in circumstances ordinarily governed by another, the reaction is not so much that he has violated the norm as that he "doesn't get it." The reaction can range from confusion and awkwardness, if the breach is accidental or one-shot, to shock and outrage, if it is deliberate and sustained.[56]

For example, there can be awkward moments in a workplace or university when an employee or student makes a transition from a subordinate (dominance) to a friend (communality) and isn't sure whether she can call her boss by her first name or invite her out for a drink after work. Good friends (communality) are advised not to engage in a business transaction (fairness), like the sale of a car or a house, which everyone knows "can put a strain on the friendship." The ambiguity between dominance and sex (a kind of communal relationship) is the battleground of sexual harassment. And the ambiguity between friendship and sex gives rise to the frisson of dating.

The embarrassment of breaching a social norm is no small matter.

Inspired by Goffman, the sociologist Harold Garfinkel and the psychologist Stanley Milgram each conducted "breaching experiments" in the 1970s in which they had their graduate student collaborators go out into the world and deliberately flout the customary relational model and observe people's reactions. They might be tasked with going home to their families and behaving as if they were lodgers, or bargaining for a lower price for merchandise at a department store, or cutting into a line to purchase theater tickets, or asking a subway passenger to give up his seat. A major discovery of these studies, before the first data point was recorded, was the reaction of the experimenters themselves: they dreaded their assignments, and when they carried them out they were overcome with apprehension, embarrassment, and nausea. The next two chapters will return to these self-conscious emotions.

Alongside all these informal relationships, people in modern societies coordinate many of their affairs with rule-governed institutions. In particular, they subject the exchange of goods and services to a fourth relational model, which Fiske calls Market Pricing. This embraces the apparatus of modern economies, including currency, prices, salaries, benefits, rents, interest, credit, bonds, and shares. The exchanges are reckoned in hard numbers and regulated by legal contracts. As with the other relational models, people in a culture are touchy about which resources may fall in its purview. Most things are openly for sale in modern Western societies, though not organs, votes, babies, or sex. Applying a Market Pricing mindset to commodities that conventionally fall under Communal Sharing is taboo, and anyone who violates it can be a target of outrage.[57]

Market Pricing is the implementation in the economic sphere of a more general mode of social organization which the sociologist Max Weber called "rational-legal." In a Rational-Legal model, a system of transactions is worked out by reason and implemented by formal rules.[58] Other examples are corporations, universities, nonprofits, scientific and scholarly institutions, constitutional governments, and international organizations.

These institutions are consciously engineered to optimize goals like peace, security, prosperity, truth, or justice. And far from encouraging their members to interact in natural ways, they regulate the relationships by explicitly stipulated rules. Government power in a democracy is not claimed by a dominant strongman, as in Authority Ranking, but granted to representatives who are picked by elections and whose prerogatives are delineated by checks and balances written into a constitution. Supervisors may not dole out jobs to their friends and relations, as in Communal Sharing, nor proffer them as favors to be called in later, as in Equality Matching, but are boxed in by regulations and fiduciary duties. And in knowledge-seeking institutions like universities and the press, beliefs are not avowed as uplifting communal creeds but evaluated for their truth by empirical testing and fact-checking. In chapter 8 I will suggest that the friction between the two grounds for belief, propriety versus truth, has sparked today's cancel culture and free speech wars. More generally, the tension between intuitively natural human relationships and the impersonal demands of our formal institutions may underlie much of the discontent of modernity.

◦⚬◦

It's not just individual people who fall into stable relationships. Collectives such as classes, races, religions, ethnic groups, and nations can have common interests that make them behave as coherent agents. And each collective may coordinate its interactions with other collectives using displays of communality, dominance, status, or reciprocity writ large.[59]

A groupwide analogue to the public insult that sparks a lethal brawl is the communal outrage. This is a recurring plotline in human history, first identified by Schelling and later analyzed by the evolutionary psychologist John Tooby.[60] One or more people are attacked in a public setting, apparently because of their membership in some group. The victim becomes a symbol of the group, and the incident is perceived as an intolerable insult that may not be allowed to pass unchallenged. Rumors about the atrocity go viral and may be embellished, if not fabricated outright, to make it seem more intentional and horrific. The affront is cherished as a morbid sacred myth, with skeptics ostracized or silenced. The victim's group lashes out ferociously and indiscriminately at members of the aggressor's group, far out of proportion to the original harm. The result may be a riot, pogrom, revolution, war, or social movement.[61]

The annals of history are filled with examples. In 1739 a British ship captain was the victim of a malicious wounding by Spanish coast guards searching for contraband, setting off the nine-year War of Jenkins' Ear. The USS *Maine* exploded in Havana Harbor in 1889, and the rallying cry "Remember the *Maine*!" egged the US government into the Spanish-American War. Rumors that Jews had murdered a Christian boy to make matzo with his blood sparked the Kishinev pogroms of 1903–1905 (my grandmother's earliest memory). The sinking of the RMS *Lusitania* in 1915 tipped the United States toward entering World War I. The Reichstag fire of 1933 enabled the consolidation of the Nazi regime. Pearl Harbor in 1941 sent America into World War II.

The dynamic has continued to shape history in this century. In 2000, a stroll by the Israeli politician Ariel Sharon on the holy ground that Jews call the Temple Mount and Muslims call Al-Haram al-Sharif sparked the Second Intifada, a five-year campaign of terrorism. The attacks on September 11, 2001, licensed the invasions of Afghanistan and Iraq. The self-immolation of a produce pedder who had been harassed by Tunisian authorities in 2010 set off the Tunisian Revolution and the Arab Spring. The fatal choking of George Floyd in 2020 by a white police officer led to nationwide protests, many of them violent. And the murder of twelve hundred Israelis by Hamas terrorists in 2023 touched off a massively destructive invasion of Gaza.

The responses to communal outrages are not acts of revenge, which, to be effective, must be targeted at the perpetrators and proportional to the harm. They are better understood as solutions to two coordination games. One is Hawk–Dove between the groups. A group that acquiesces to a conspicuous attack has conceded that in the future it will back down in an unlimited series of confrontations. Striking back while the whole world is watching is a way for the group to recalibrate self-fulfilling expectations of how it is to be treated.

The other is a Stag Hunt within the group. A group can contest its collective subordination only when its members are united in the struggle. But each of its members, even if they all have been seething with resentment against the dominant group, may be skittish about standing up and exposing themselves to reprisals, if only out of fear that others are skittish about exposing themselves, and so on. The focal point of a communal outrage can signal to all of them that the time to take up the struggle is now. As we saw in chapter 1, a public demonstration can create common knowledge that the protesters are numerous and united. A communal outrage may be necessary to create the common knowledge that emboldens them to turn out for the demonstration in the first place.

Countries, with their organized governments and human leaders, are likely to call to mind the conceptual metaphors A COUNTRY IS A

PERSON and INTERNATIONAL RELATIONS ARE SOCIAL RELATIONS. As a result, countries are not always rational actors that maximize their material interests. Instead they are social creatures who worry about saving and losing face as they make friends, compete for status and dominance, and demand fair treatment. In his prizewinning 1999 book *Honor, Symbols, and War,* the political scientist Barry O'Neill invokes game theory and recursive mentalizing to explain the social scene of nation-states.[62]

In one analysis, O'Neill found that countries' main exports are not just commodities like maize or bauxite but focal points. Every year there are around forty-five incidents in which a government engages in some purely symbolic act of the kind that individual people perform to ratify their relationships. Leaders embrace, stay at each other's mansions, shake or hold hands, give gifts, break bread, cross or gaze at borders, lay wreaths, send vice presidents to funerals, and exchange athletes, students, or zoo animals. They declare ceasefires after the shooting has stopped, renounce nuclear weapons they have no intention of building, and apologize for the crimes of their long-dead ancestors.

O'Neill also confirmed a conclusion that is a commonplace among historians of war but a surprise to the many people who think countries fight over resources. The sequence in the Marx Brothers' movie *Duck Soup* in which Rufus T. Firefly, leader of Freedonia, provokes a war with Sylvania because he imagines its ambassador refusing to shake his hand, is all too close to the historical record. In *The Origins of War*, Donald Kagan wrote, "The reader may be surprised by how small a role . . . considerations of practical utility and material gain, and even ambition for power itself, play in bringing on wars, and how often some aspect of honor is decisive."[63] In *Why Nations Fight*, Richard Ned Lebow came to the same conclusion. In an analysis of all the major interstate wars between 1648 and 2008, he found that "contrary to conventional wisdom, only a minority of these were motivated by security or material interest. Instead, the majority [were] the result of a quest for standing, and for revenge."[64] Vladimir Putin's pointless invasion of Ukraine in 2022 to restore the greatness of Russian civilization and rebuke its humiliation in the eyes of the West is only the most recent example.

The most perilous feature of the world today, its armory of nuclear weapons, is also, according to O'Neill and others, the legacy of contests for status, dominance, and equality matching.[65] The only sane rationale for possessing nuclear weapons is deterrence against an all-out attack, and many strategic analysts have concluded that a country could accomplish that with a few dozen missiles in concealed submarines. No one can explain why the world needs more than twelve thousand nuclear warheads—as an American admiral put it, "You seldom see a cowboy, even in the movies, wearing three guns. Two is enough."[66] But during the eighty years that nuclear weapons have been around, nine countries have accumulated these threats to humanity's existence because they served as status symbols, or displays of resolve, or gestures of reassurance to allies, or moves of tit-for-tat matching or gap-closing or besting or keeping up with the Joneses.

So why aren't we all dead? In chapter 3 we saw that since 1945 the incidence of interstate wars has been reduced by adherence to a norm, the respect for existing borders. The avoidance of Armageddon during this era may be the dividend of another focal point, the nuclear taboo. Responsible leaders developed a shared understanding that the detonation of any nuclear weapon in war (even a low-yield battlefield weapon) would cross a dreadful line, bringing eternal opprobrium to the country that launched the world into an unimaginable new era.[67] Like all taboos, it is ringed with hypocrisy, but so far the common understanding that the use of nuclear weapons is unthinkable because everyone knows it is unthinkable may literally have saved the world.

Human social life can seem baffling. It is played out with rituals and symbols and ceremonies, rife with social paradoxes and strategic absurdities. This gives us the conceptual metaphor SOCIAL LIFE IS THEATER. All the world's a stage, and the men and women merely players, acting out arbitrarily assigned roles.

But the logic of coordination and common knowledge reveals intelligible motives behind the strutting and fretting. Life provides people with opportunities to flourish if they coordinate their actions with others. They can pool their caregiving and resources and risk; they can preempt costly disputes; they can exchange benefits and divide the fruits of their cooperation. But they can realize these opportunities only if they know which one they are pursuing, if they choose and are chosen as partners, and if they harmonize their actions as they pursue them. The logic of these enmeshments often upends our expectations, assigning a meaningful role to meaningless symbols. Many of the odder spectacles of social life—the rituals, the hypocrisies, the affronts and embarrassments—may be explained as efforts to generate or avoid the common knowledge that allows people to coordinate their actions in these games.

6

Laughing, Crying, Blushing, Staring, Glaring

Conspicuous emotional expressions as common-knowledge generators

The human face is a fabulously expressive organ. Its forty-odd muscles are controlled by the voluntary division of the motor nervous system, and they are effortlessly choreographed into configurations that signal joy, sadness, fear, anger, surprise, disgust, interest, contentment, and pain.[1] These expressions are displayed beginning in infancy and recognizable all over the world. They can be dialed up or down to convey the intensity of the emotion (concern → anxiety → fear → terror; sternness → indignation → anger → rage), and they can be blended to display other distinctive feelings (anger + joy = cruelty; fear + sadness = devastation; disgust + joy = "Eeww!").[2] Most of them have homologues in our primate cousins.[3] In his 1872 "forgotten masterpiece," *The Expression of the Emotions in Man and Animals*, Charles Darwin touted these facts as proof that the human mind, not just the body, was a product of evolution.[4]

These emotional displays, in all their strengths and blends, don't exhaust the combinatorial potential of the human facial musculature. Other expressions, like a concerned furrowed brow or a quizzical raised one, enrich spoken languages and are essential in signed ones. We wink and leer and grimace, we bite our lips, we puff out our cheeks. And we come up with new configurations when we make faces to amuse babies.

But in addition to endowing us with this copious repertoire of silent, voluntary signals, the process of evolution saw fit to equip our species with other channels with a very different character. In a 1579 treatise the French physician Laurent Joubert described one of them:

> Everybody sees clearly that in laughter the face is moving, the mouth widens, the eyes sparkle and tear, the cheeks redden, the breast heaves, the voice becomes interrupted; and when it goes on for a long time the veins in the throat become enlarged, the arms shake, and the legs dance about, the belly pulls in and feels considerable pain; we cough, perspire, piss, and besmirch ourselves by dint of laughing, and sometimes we even faint away because of it. This need not be proven.
>
> Some men, when they laugh, sound like geese hissing, others like grumbling goslings; some recall the sigh of woodland pigeons, or doves in their widowhood; others the hoot-owl one an Indian rooster, another a peacock; others give out a peep-peep, like chicks; for others it is like horse neighing, or an ass heehawing, or a dog that yaps or is chocking, some people call to mind the sound of dry-axled carts, others, gravel in a pail, others yet a boiling pot of cabbage; and some have still another resonance, aside from the look on their face and the grimacing, so variedly diverse that nothing parallels it.
>
> These are among the great marvels of laughter, how it escapes so quickly that it seems to come without our knowing it, almost sneaking out, and how sometimes, letting ourselves be overcome with

laughter, we cannot stop or suppress it. For when we laugh until we split, carried away by cachinnation, it is not in our power to close our mouth or to have breath at our bidding, so that with the air lacking, sometimes one almost suffocates.[5]

Joubert's description rings true almost half a millennium later. Laughter, far more than any facial expression, is involuntary, unignorable to a perceiver, and all-possessing of the expresser. It takes over the laugher's face, voice, diaphragm, and with extreme merriment, the rest of the body.

There are other vehicles of expression that bypass the facial musculature. Our lachrymal glands can secrete more fluid than can be contained in our eye sockets, overflowing as tears. The blood vessels in our face can dilate, reddening and heating our cheeks in a blush. The whites of our almond-shaped eyes make the direction of our gaze obvious, especially when they lock onto their counterparts in someone else's face.

Laughing, crying, blushing, eye contact. Each is conspicuous both to perceiver and expresser, emotionally evocative, unique to humans, and, with the first three, involuntary. The point of this chapter is that these distinctive expressions may be explained by a key idea: they generate common knowledge. In this way they differ from facial expressions, which we're often unaware of, as when people say, "You should have seen the look on your face," or "Wipe that smirk off your face."[6] No one can be unaware that they're laughing, crying, blushing, or making eye contact, nor that those around them are aware, and aware of the emoter's awareness. This common knowledge, I'll suggest, is well-suited to tuning and tweaking the coordination equilibria that underlie our social relationships. I'll conclude by turning to an expression that *is* displayed by the muscles of the face, but which also may be explained as a coordination signal: the glower.

The academic study of humor has a well-deserved reputation for obtuseness, as in this cartoon about "The Cognitive Institute for Advanced Humor Research":

ROBOTMAN by Jim Meddick

It's not just the humorlessness of humor research that makes it so grim. It's also that the theories always seem to miss the point. They single out as the essence of humor things that are not really funny: engaging in play, signaling safety, violating expectations, breaching norms, blending concepts, flaunting intelligence, asserting superiority, encouraging affiliation, encrypting messages, resolving inconsistencies, releasing tension. All these experiences, to be sure, are sometimes associated with humor, but most often they happen without a trace of mirth.[7] There must be some distinctive combination of mental events that causes the breast to heave and the voice to be interrupted rather than just shaping our faces with a look of surprise or puzzlement or relief.

At the risk of giving the world yet another humorless take on humor, I tried to identify that combination in *How the Mind Works*. Though I didn't use the term, common knowledge was the essential component. Laughter generates common knowledge that challenges a convention of dominance, status, or prestige. The authority may be challenged aggressively, with the aim of leveling or reinforcing a dominance hierarchy, or it may be challenged convivially, to make it common knowledge that the basis of a relationship is not dominance at all but rather communality. Let me step through the facts that led to these conclusions.

Joubert identified the first two. Laughter disrupts the comportment of the laugher, perturbing his breathing, vocalization, and facial composure. And it intrudes on the consciousness of the perceivers, forcing them to register the hissing and neighing and hee-hawing. (As Joubert said, these need not be proven.) And since, as we saw in chapter 4, mutual conspicuity creates common knowledge, all this implies that public laughter is common knowledge: when you laugh, you know you're laughing, and those with you know it, and you know that they know it, and they know that you know that they know it.

But much else about laughter does need to be proven, and the person who has proven the most is the neuroscientist Robert Provine, author of *Laughter: A Scientific Investigation*.[8] More accurately, he has *discovered* the most, because in the tradition of the medieval upstart who interrupted a scholastic debate on the number of teeth in a horse's mouth by finding a horse, opening his mouth, and counting, Provine has recorded and analyzed more than a thousand instances of laughter in natural settings.[9]

One discovery is that laughter usually *is* public, the signature of common knowledge. People seldom laugh when they're alone. (The email abbreviation *LOL*, "laughing out loud," is almost always false.) Even when a solitary person does laugh, the laugher is usually in the presence of virtual people on television or radio or in their reading material. Another discovery is that laughter is contagious. That's why situation comedies used to have laugh tracks, and the jokes of vaudeville comedians were punctuated by a laughlike rim shot (*bada bing!*).[10]

The contagiousness of laughter reveals another prominent feature: it's involuntary. We don't decide to laugh, and sometimes have to stifle the urge. Indeed, laughter is hard to produce at will. Provine recounts, "Ask people to laugh and about half of them will claim that they can't laugh on command. The other half gamely honks out an obviously fake 'ha-ha,' proving the point."[11]

How, then, did Provine get a sample of real laughs to analyze? He visited colleagues, or intercepted passersby, microphone in hand, and announced, "I'm studying laughter. Will you laugh for me?" The request itself elicited a burst of genuine laughter, even though carrying out the request yielded a useless fake "ha-ha." And this fit with Provine's most striking discovery: most laugh lines are not particularly funny, but rather are comments on minor indignities, incongruities, or interruptions of everyday decorum. Typical laugh lines in real life are "Are you sure?" "What is that supposed to mean?!" and "It was nice meeting you too!" Fewer than a fifth of the comments provoking a laugh in Provine's sample were remotely humorous. He writes:

> Even our "greatest hits," the funniest of the twelve hundred pre-laugh comments, were not necessarily howlers: "You don't have to drink, just buy us drinks," "She's got a sex disorder—she doesn't like sex," and "Do you date within your species?" Your life is filled with a laugh track to what must be the world's worst situation comedy.[12]

Try it yourself: the next time you're in a social gathering, pay attention to the triggers of laughter. You'll be surprised by their witlessness. I suspect this is universal. A search for "laugh" in the citizen scientist Louis Liebenberg's book on the San hunter-gatherers of the Kalahari turned up times when one had misidentified an animal they were tracking, or when they were trying to scare away a lion by shouting insults at it (like "You big penis!").[13] The anthropologist

Napoleon Chagnon reported that the Yanomamö of the Amazon rainforest had a hearty laugh at his expense when they nimbly strode across a slippery log bridging a stream and he inched his way across, clinging precariously.[14]

Provine also compared human laughter to its closest homologue in primates. It's a form of panting accompanied by a play face—mouth open, upper teeth covered, lower teeth exposed—which they emit when they are tickled or engage in rough-and-tumble play. Physiologically and acoustically it's different from the rhythmic ha-ha syllables of human laughter. Playful chimps vocalize when they inhale as well as exhale, and they make a sound that is noisy rather than harmonic. (Listeners describe it as "panting," "asthma attack," "hyperventilation," "sawing," "sanding," and "having sex.") Laughter as we know it is uniquely human, though it may have evolved from these play vocalizations in tandem with the controlled exhalation and vowel-centered syllables of language.

Tickling, play fighting, and rough-and-tumble play are practice for real fighting, and the laughlike sounds signal that the roughhousing is all in fun, ensuring that it doesn't escalate into real aggression. Feigned, and sometimes veiled, aggression also underlies a lot of human laughter. Almost always there is a butt to a joke, a target of the teasing or mocking or ridicule. Often it is someone who has staked a claim to prestige or dominance, and the jibe punctures the aura of dignity that signals it. People enjoy taking down royalty, clergy, bosses, and teachers, together with the neighborhood blowhard, bully, gasbag, goody-goody, or know-it-all. George Santayana observed that "to knock a thing down, especially if it is cocked at an arrogant angle, is a deep delight of the blood." And because even the highest and mightiest of us is incarnate, with a body that ignominiously obeys the laws of physics, excretes waste, and accedes to biological imperatives, opportunities to humble us abound, and we are target-rich areas for slapstick, scatological, and sexual humor. As G. K. Chesterton noted, "Every man is important if he loses his life; and every man is funny if he loses his hat and has to run after it."

As in play fighting, sometimes laughter signals that any harm is unintended. This is the basis for nervous laughter, like in the famous experiments by Stanley Milgram in which participants had been pressured into shocking an actor playing a fellow participant, and many reacted to his screams with a mirthless laugh.[15]

But often the assault on dignity that drives laughter is neither in fun nor unintentional but deliberately hurtful. Children are miserable when they feel laughed at, and every teacher or boss in command of a room knows that they must try not to become a target of laughter. Starting in 2011, Barack Obama would roast Donald Trump at the annual White House Correspondents' Association dinner, where the butts of the jokes are expected to be good sports. That year, having just released his birth certificate to refute Trump's charge that he was born in Africa, Obama announced that he would now release his actual birth video. He proceeded to play the opening scene from *The Lion King* with the presentation of the newborn cub Simba (adding, "I want to make clear to the Fox News table: that was a joke").[16] On another occasion he quipped about Trump's presidential aspirations: "There's one area where Donald's experience could be invaluable, and that's closing Guantanamo [the American prison camp in Cuba]. Because Trump knows a thing or two about running waterfront properties into the ground." Amid the merriment Trump visibly seethed, and some analysts speculate that the humiliation tipped him into running for president as revenge and redemption.

The barbs drew blood because of a feature of humor pointed out by James Joyce: "*In risu veritas.* In laughter there is truth." More accurately, in laughter there is common knowledge. Obama's playing of the Disney clip was funny because everyone knew that

Trump's "birther" theory was little more than a cartoonish stereotype. His add-on jibe presupposed a common understanding that Fox News was credulous about anything that disparaged liberals. The unkindest cut of all was the wisecrack that called to mind Trump's bankruptcies, since it undermined Trump's proudest boast, that he was a successful businessman.

With every punch line, all the audience members who "got the joke" must have tacitly known the compromising premise, which was automatically supplied by the brain's power to connect the dots in conversation.[17] If people laughed, it showed that they knew the hidden premise without anyone having to say it aloud. And their conspicuous, involuntary, and contagious laughter made it apparent that everyone else knew the premise, and knew that everyone else knew it, and so on—that the damaging fact, which may have been widely distributed private knowledge, was now common knowledge. And this new common knowledge exploded the equilibrium of mutual acceptance of dominance that had prevailed until that moment. This is the basis for aphorisms like Mark Twain's "Against the assault of laughter, nothing can stand" and the activist Saul Alinsky's Rule #5: "Ridicule is man's most potent weapon."

And this brings us to an explanation of the function of laughter. Like many social species, humans have hierarchies of dominance, which are equilibria cemented by common knowledge or common salience of the likely outcomes of Hawk–Dove contests. We humans also form hierarchies of prestige and status, governed by Leader–Follower and similar games, which are settled by a common recognition of competence, confidence, and beneficence. Now, many species that recognize dominance also have instincts of *counter-dominance*, which allow subordinates to coordinate their efforts and unseat an alpha.[18] Laughter may be seen as our organ of counter-dominance—more generally, of counter-authority, including counter-status and counter-prestige. By making some infirmity of a superior common knowledge, something that laughter is well-engineered to do, subordinates can undermine the reigning hierarchy to their advantage. The unstatedness of the derogatory premise provides cover, the involuntariness of the laughter signals that the premise was already privately known (rather than opportunistically adopted for the occasion to join a coalition), and the contagion ensures safety in numbers.

The logic of relational models from the previous chapter also explains the benign side of laughter—the convivial badinage among friends and family that is one of life's greatest pleasures. It's not about climbing up a hierarchy; it's about climbing off the hierarchy. It's about opting for a relational model of Communal Sharing rather than Authority Ranking. Most people don't want to clamber up the ranks of every social milieu they inhabit. It's nice to be on top, but it's no fun to be constantly watching your back or to fear that your allies will ditch you the moment someone else's star shines brighter than yours. Friendship doesn't work that way. Friends accept you for who you are, and are there for you in thick and thin.[19]

But this leaves you with a signaling problem: which game are you playing? As Samuel Johnson noted, "No two men can be half an hour together but one shall acquire an evident superiority over the other." How do you indicate that despite your superior looks or skill or intelligence or wealth or charm, or that of your counterpart, neither of you wants to lord it over the other? One answer is convivial teasing and self-deprecation. When someone creates common knowledge of an indignity that has befallen one of you, followed by common knowledge that neither of you is taking it as a face threat, it bespeaks a common understanding that the basis of the relationship is egalitarian friendship rather than hierarchical ranking. All the better if the two of you "get each other's jokes," that is, are able to fill in the unstated premises that make a joke funny. Sharing a sense of humor is a sensitive assay for a shared understanding of the world, and it's not surprising that it's one of the keys to romantic attraction.[20]

In sum, laughter generates common knowledge of an indignity that undermines a claim to dominance or status, and may be used either aggressively, to challenge a dominant figure, or convivially, to signal that dominant–subordinate competition doesn't apply. (Of course it can also be used aggressively, to keep a subordinate in his place.) But I need to add an amendment to deal with a challenge to the theory from a man who knows a thing or two about humor, Robert Mankoff, the former cartoon editor of the *New Yorker* and a witty cartoonist himself. When I explained my theory to him, noting that humor always has a target whose dignity has been docked, he came back with what he took to be a typical counterexample from his world: a cartoon with a smiling figure skater who had just traced "VIII" onto the ice. (Just in case: VIII is the Roman numeral for 8, and skaters often do a double-loop maneuver called a figure 8.)

Rather than forcing a strained interpretation in which the skater or reader had been humbled, I suggested broadening the theory by venturing that humor may be used to challenge any arbitrary convention, not just a convention that underlies dominance. A convention may lock in a design feature that is not particularly adaptive, like the QWERTY keyboard, but persists because everyone is stuck with it as the solution to a coordination problem. Perhaps we use humor to call attention to arbitrary features of a social convention that would otherwise be obscured by familiarity. In the case of the cartoon, it would be the convention that the numeral "8" is what we use to symbolize eightness, while also being a geometric shape. The extension also handles another challenge to the dignity-reduction theory, the pun, as in Oscar Wilde's *The Importance of Being Earnest*, or the musician Paul Desmond's comment on women who marry for money rather than romance, "This is the way the world ends, not with a whim but a banker." Words are conventions that pair a sound with a meaning, usually beneath our awareness, and puns call attention to the sound qua sound.

There are two ways to interpret this extension of the theory. In one, humor is an adaptation for undermining conventions, and one kind of convention is the aura of dignity that props up dominance or status. In the other, humor is a tool for undermining the aura of dignity that props up dominance or status, and people sometimes co-opt it to undermine more abstract conventions, like words and symbols. Since the arch drollery of *New Yorker* cartoons and literary in-jokes tends to elicit a wry smile (or, in the case of puns, a groan), rather than a hearty laugh, I'm inclined not to dilute the theory to accommodate them, and so favor the second interpretation. But either way, laughter may be understood as a common-knowledge challenge to a commonly held social convention.

The banality of laugh lines in everyday conversation reminds us that any theory of laughter shouldn't focus too much on jokes. Jokes, recall, are not the natural triggers of laughter. They are more like cheesecake: a pleasure technology created by human ingenuity when it sets itself the challenge of purifying and concentrating stimuli that in natural doses give us small doses of enjoyment. In this case, jokes are engineered to deliver the pleasure of day-to-day humor in a concentrated jolt. Still, just as cheesecake spotlights our craving for sugar and fat, jokes can spotlight our delight in the creation of common knowledge of an indignity. I won't resist the temptation to close this section with an analysis of a few, notwithstanding E. B. and Katharine White's warning that "humor can be dissected, as a frog can, but the thing dies in the process and the innards are discouraging to any but the purely scientific mind."[21]

The best theory of jokes comes from the writer Arthur Koestler in his 1964 magnum opus *The Act of Creation*, and it lays out three steps.[22] A punch line to a joke presents the listener with an incongruity; the listener resolves it by mentally jumping into a different frame of reference in which the punch line makes sense; in the new frame of reference, someone suffers a descent in dignity. "My wife likes to talk during sex. She calls me up and says, 'Nathan, I'm having sex.'" (*Bada bing!*) Nathan's explanation is incongruous because we expect "talking during sex" to refer to intimate and mutually arousing exclamations. It's resolved by switching to an understanding of a spiteful taunt in a bad marriage. And being cuckolded is the ultimate indignity (and a common butt of jokes; Freud spent much time dissecting a rather unfunny one in *Jokes and Their Relation to the Unconscious*).[23] I will spare more frogs and let you ponder for yourself how the theory might apply to these ones.

DON: Oh Bill, it must be hard to lose a relative.
W. C. FIELDS: It's almost impossible.

A waiter takes the order from two men at a Lower East Side restaurant. "I'll have a glass of tea," says one. The other says, "I'd also like some tea. And make sure the glass is clean." The waiter returns with a tray. "Two teas. And which of you asked for the clean glass?"

DOCTOR: What seems to be the trouble, Mrs. Shapiro?
PATIENT: I can't pee.
DOCTOR: How old are you, Mrs. Shapiro?
PATIENT: Eighty-seven years old.
DOCTOR: You've peed enough.

❦

The first word that people associate with *laugh* is *cry*, and that tells us something.[24] In word associations, the two words usually belong to the same semantic category but are set off by a salient contrast (*night–day*, *girl–boy*, *dog–cat*).[25] Like laughter, tears express an emotional state by means other than the muscles of the face. They are involuntary, conspicuous to a perceiver, and unique to *Homo sapiens* (a conclusion flaunted in the title of the most comprehensive book on the subject, the psychologist Ad Vingerhoets's *Why Only Humans Weep*). And they seem engineered to generate common knowledge. A weeping person feels the welling in his sockets and the trickle on his cheeks and sees a blurry world through his own tears, a world that contains other people seeing the same tears from the outside.

The contrast between laughing and crying is obvious: tears convey sadness, not enjoyment. The sadness comes from a loss, defeat, or humiliation, and is accompanied by a feeling of helplessness and self-pity.[26] The obvious coordination game resolved by common knowledge of a loss is Hawk–Dove. Like the white flag of surrender or throwing a towel into a boxing ring, crying signals that a person acknowledges defeat and can no longer put up a fight, sparing both sides in a conflict from the costs of further fighting when the outcome is a foregone conclusion. Koestler, whose analysis of weeping is as insightful as his analysis of laughter, describes a prototypical instance in a contest between boys:

> A little boy is beaten up by a gang of bullies. For a while he tries to fight back, to hit, scratch, and kick, but his tormenters immobilize him, and at last he begins to cry in "impotent rage."
>
> But the expression is misleading. Anybody who has watched children fight knows that weeping will start only after the victim

has given up struggling and wriggling and accepted defeat. After a while new outbursts of rage may renew the struggle, but, each time this happens, weeping is interrupted. It is not an expression of rage (although the two may overlap) but an expression of helplessness after rage has been exhausted and a feeling of being abandoned has set in—a yearning for love, sympathy, consolation.[27]

In a similar way, a bickering couple can sense that one of them has "gone too far" in pressing an argument when the other starts to cry.

As Koestler observes, crying is a signal not just of surrender but of neediness, designed to elicit succor and comfort from sympathizers. This function is consistent with the developmental origin of crying in the infants' need for nurturance, and its evolutionary origin in the separation call of juvenile mammals. A critical shift in both sequences is from the noisy demanding wail of crying to the teary pathetic whimper of weeping. No one knows why the processes of evolution recruited the lachrymal glands to convey this helplessness. Perhaps tearing originally grew out of a physiological reflex that restored moisture to the eyes and nasal passages after they had been dried out by the pressure of wincing or the hyperventilation of arousal.[28] More likely it's that humans both see the world through their eyes and fixate on the eyes of others (more on this soon), and a scrim of tears was the best way to capture the attention of the expresser and beholder simultaneously.

The idea that crying is a conspicuous signal of surrender in a conflict is a satisfying theory of the prototypical scenario. But as you read the explanation, I'm sure counterexamples surged into mind. Far from signaling misery, crying can be a source of pleasure, as when people pay good money to read a tearjerker or watch a three-hankie movie. People cry for joy at weddings. They cry when they are crowned Miss America, or win the NBA championship. They may cry in the presence of the sublime, like a closeup sighting of a whale, or, in the case of one of my colleagues, reading a brilliant PhD thesis in cognitive neuroscience.

And people may cry when they apprehend love and compassion in others. The closest words in English for this emotion are *touched* and *moved*.[29] It's the most common trigger for me, and many memories can make tears well up. The sight of a soldier in an airport returning from Iraq, locked in an embrace with his wife, neither able to let go. My parents' toasts to each other on their sixtieth wedding anniversary. Ray Charles performing "Georgia on My Mind" in a joint session of the Georgia legislature in 1979 when they adopted his rendition as the official song of the state, which in his lifetime had been a bastion of segregation and oppression.[30] My great-aunt Sabena, who lost her husband and children in the Holocaust, standing up at the end of each seder and delivering a short speech in Yiddish thanking the family for giving her a new life in Canada. A young scientist discussing her research with me over coffee at a conference, who during a lull in the conversation got a faraway look and murmured, "I miss my son." A *Peanuts* strip in which Linus describes a last-second upset victory by the home team in a football game—"Thousands of people ran out onto the field laughing and screaming! The fans and the players were so happy they were rolling on the ground and hugging each other and dancing!"—and Charlie Brown replies, "How did the other team feel?"

How do we make sense of tears of joy, tears of sublimity, tears of compassion? One of the apparent counterexamples is easy to explain, the tearjerker. People take pleasure in self-administering safe, controlled doses of harmful stimuli, presumably a motive to calibrate and control their emotional reactions. And so they enjoy hot chili peppers, roller coasters, thrillers, saunas, strong cheese, water-skiing, bungie jumping, and other borderline or illusory dangers. A simulated tragedy in the comfort of a theater seat may be another example of this benign masochism.[31]

The others are more puzzling. With weddings and victories, the joy may be mixed with a dollop of poignant sadness. Perhaps a bride walking down the aisle brings to mind a daughter lost forever to her parents, or a history of loneliness and heartbreak now put behind her. Weeping victors sometimes invoke the obstacles they had to overcome to reach their moment of triumph, or a deceased parent who would be proud. Koestler suggests that a stroke of good fortune, or a vision of the sublime, may evoke a sense of powerlessness—of being rapt, overwhelmed, enraptured, entranced—which overlaps with the helplessness of loss and defeat, and which evokes a similar surrender. All these are plausible as far as they go, but they don't add up to a satisfying explanation. Let me suggest a different direction.

In his forgotten masterpiece Darwin explained the evolution of emotional expressions with three principles.[32] The first is "serviceable habits." Animals configure their faces and bodies in certain postures for practical reasons—for example, unsheathing their teeth before biting, widening their eyes for a panoramic view of danger, flattening their ears to protect them in a fight. These preparatory movements then become habits that are carried out in a weaker form even when the action is suppressed. So we bare our teeth in anger and become headlight-stricken in fear.

It's Darwin's second principle that's relevant here, "antithesis." When an animal is in a state opposite to one that triggers a certain posture, it produces the physically opposite posture. When a dog is hostile, it stiffens its body, retracts its lips, raises its head and shoulders, and holds its tail erect and rigid, all in preparation for attack. When a dog feels affection, it does not have to prepare for action, but it assumes a posture that is part-for-part the antithesis of the attack pose: it crouches, wriggles, slackens its ears and lips, and rocks a limp tail from side to side—the mystery of tail-wagging solved. In a similar way, a man who is defiant stiffens his neck, squares his shoulders, lowers his brows, and clenches his fists with his knuckles forward. What does a man do when he feels resigned or impotent? He slackens his neck, raises his shoulders and brows, and opens his hands with palms outward. We have the evolution of the shrug.

Though Koestler appeared unaware of Darwin's work on emotional expression (one of the signs that the book had been forgotten), he made a strong case that weeping is the antithesis of laughing. The two facial expressions are literally inversions of each other—as the song says, a smile is just a frown turned upside down. When we weep, we inhale in the short, deep gasps of a sob, then exhale in a long sigh. When we laugh, we exhale in the short bursts of a ha-ha-ha, a sob in reverse, followed by a long, deep inhalation, a sigh in reverse. When we laugh, we throw our head back. When we weep, we lower our head into our hands, onto the table, or on someone's shoulder. When we laugh, our muscles contract and our bodies flail, banging the table, slapping our knees. When we weep, our muscles go flaccid, our shoulders droop, and we slump into our chair. Even the musical reminders are opposite. The comedian uses the staccato rim shot of a drum; the cinematic tearjerker uses legato strains of violins.

Now let's work backwards, from the diametrical outward displays to diametrical internal states. Suppose the mental triggers for weeping are the antithesis of the triggers for laughter. This is obvious enough in the contrast between the aggressive takedown in humor and the helpless surrender in tears. But the less obvious stimuli for weeping can also be seen as the diametrical opposites of the things that make a joke funny.

Humor savors an infirmity—a foible, a failing, a venality, a flaw. Weeping savors a virtue—compassion, tenderness, pity, love. Humor responds to a misfortune with sadism and schadenfreude. Weeping responds to good fortune with empathy and shared joy. Humor delights in the degraded, the debased, the sordid—puking and farting, shitting and pissing, fornicating and cuckolding, pratfalls and pies in the face. Weeping delights in the exalted, the sublime, the magnificent—a symphony, a vista, megafauna, even a brilliant dissertation.

So there is, after all, a common denominator beneath the diverse things that make us weep: they're the diametric opposite of the things that make us laugh. Now the question becomes why we have a conspicuous bodily display for the unlaughworthy (above and beyond the core of surrender and helplessness). Darwin thought there was no good reason for displays to come in opposites: once an organism has evolved an emotional expression, its antithesis just falls out of the mechanical pushes and pulls of the nervous system. And perhaps there is no reason we weep in response to joy or compassion or sublimity, other than that we laugh at the ridiculous, and human emotional responses come in opponent pairs.[33]

Alternatively, perhaps we have reason to signal that we are sensitive to tenderness and magnificence and joy—and for others to know that we know that they know we are sensitive. Perhaps it commends us in the market for good communal partners, or coordinates like-feeling people in some as-yet-unanalyzed game. I'm not prepared to make this argument just yet. But I hope that it's true, because it's comforting to think that we are physically designed to share our appreciation of the best that life can offer.

⌗

Blushing, wrote Darwin, is "the most peculiar and most human of all expressions." His contemporary, Mark Twain, agreed: "Man is the only animal that blushes—or needs to."[34] As with laughter and tears, blushing is a conspicuous and involuntary physical response to a cognitive, social, and moral trigger. And like those expressions, it is a generator of common knowledge. When you blush, you feel the heat in your cheeks, which reminds you that others can see you reddening, which makes you redden even deeper, and so on—intensifying all the more when someone points out, gratuitously, "You're blushing!" Indeed, telling people that they're blushing, even if they're not blushing, can make them blush.[35]

People blush in their cheeks, ears, and necks, the most exposed parts of the body (though not, Darwin noted, in their hands, which don't attract others' gaze). A blush is an internally undeniable way in which we display embarrassment and shame, and it's accompanied by other postures. Darwin describes them:

> Under a keen sense of shame there is a strong desire for concealment. We turn away the whole body, more especially the face, which we endeavour in some manner to hide. An ashamed person can hardly endure to meet the gaze of those present, so that he almost invariably casts down his eyes or looks askant. As there generally exists at the same time a strong wish to avoid the appearance of shame, a vain attempt is made to look direct at the person who causes this feeling; and the antagonism between these opposite tendencies leads to various restless movements in the eyes.

Darwin captured the experience, down to the shifty eyes. Looking downward, making oneself small, and touching oneself are chimpanzee submission postures, sometimes accompanied by a silent bared-teeth display, the evolutionary precursor of our "sheepish," "silly," or "shit-eating" grin.[36]

Darwin also took up what is still a frequently asked question: do dark-skinned people blush, and can anyone tell? His answer from

1872 remains correct today: yes and yes.[37] Darwin had furnished questionnaires to missionaries, explorers, and colonial officers, asking about the emotional expressions of the diverse peoples with whom they had firsthand contact. The universality of the expressions and their triggers led him to conclude that "the several races [are] descended from a single parent-stock, which must have been almost completely human in structure, and to a large extent in mind, before the period at which the races diverged from each other."[38] It was a rebuke to the theory, congenial to the racism of his day, that peoples with different continental ancestry had each evolved separately from apes, and that those with dark skin had underdeveloped moral sentiments—they were literally shameless. In reality, people with dark skin feel the heat of a blush, and their audiences see it in a darkening or color shift. Lest you be surprised that this could be as salient as the reddening of pale skin, remember that people look very, very carefully at each other's faces, and the years of scrutinizing can magnify small differences. That's why members of every race feel that the others "all look alike," and why mothers of identical twins often think they're fraternal, so different do the two offspring look to them. The Ghanaian physician and geneticist Felix Konotey-Ahulu notes that even in ebony-skinned people, blushing is discernible "by very close relatives (as in my case by my mother)."[39]

The obvious triggers for blushing are embarrassment and shame, which are two of the three negative self-conscious emotions. The third one, guilt, doesn't do it. A blush is not a lie detector or a telltale heart, and it works on the opposite principle from "innocent until proven guilty." Darwin nailed it again, quoting Thomas Henry Burgess, the author of the 1865 treatise *The Physiology or Mechanism of Blushing*:

"I blush," says Dr. Burgess, "in the presence of my accusers." It is not the sense of guilt, but the thought that others think or know us to be guilty which crimsons the face. . . . Many a person has blushed intensely when accused of some crime, though completely innocent of it. Even the thought . . . that others think that we have made an unkind or stupid remark, is amply sufficient to cause a blush, although we know all the time that we have been completely misunderstood.

This became clear to Kyle Thomas and me when we ran a study with our psychophysiologist colleague Wendy Berry Mendes to see if a touchy proposition couched in an innuendo would be less physiologically stressful than the same proposition expressed in plain language (the topic of the next chapter). Participants pretended to be actors reading lines from scripts expressing bribes, threats, and sexual come-ons, either stated overtly or veiled as a hint, while we measured subtle changes in their heart rate, breathing, and skin conductance. The first line recited by the first participant happened to be an overt sexual invitation, and her physiological reaction was anything but subtle: though presumably innocent of any lascivious desire, she flushed ruby red.

So guilt is not the trigger for blushing. What's the difference between the two self-conscious emotions that do trigger blushing, shame and embarrassment? Embarrassment is the response to the public breach of a social norm (a faux pas), like a pratfall, blunder, or lapse of bodily control. Shame is the response to the public breach of a moral norm, like lying, cheating, being derelict in one's duties, or hurting or neglecting a loved one.[40] Some affective scientists argue that shame must be triggered by a perceived failing in one's enduring self, as opposed to a momentary lapse in behavior of the kind that triggers embarrassment. But others have shown that people can feel ashamed, just as they can blush, at the mere awareness that they have been publicly discredited, whether or not they feel it is deserved.[41]

What's the point of blushing? The slip-up is obvious; why signal that you know it's obvious? Darwin thought it had no point. But then he didn't admit that *any* emotional expression had a point. He was irked by claims by Burgess and others that facial expressions were proof of divine creation: God had endowed humans with a means of expressing moral sentiments. Darwin was damned if he was going to let this argument hang out there unopposed, and so he insisted that expressions were either vestiges, antitheses of vestiges, or overflows of nervous energy.[42] Blushing was the result of blood rushing to whichever part of the body a person was thinking hard about.

Almost no one agrees with this part of Darwin's analysis today.[43] Blushing has an obvious function: it's a nonverbal apology, more credible than cheap talk because it emanates from the involuntary autonomic nervous system, the part that controls blood flow and other physiological necessities. Blushing acknowledges that you realize you have erred in others' eyes, that if you are guilty you willingly accept a punishment (at the very least the agony of blushing itself), and that you plan to do better in the future. Even holding constant the crime, credible remorse matters in everyday life, just as it matters in the courtroom. Blushing indicates, "Yes, I screwed up, but I *know* I screwed up, according to standards I understand and share." No one's perfect, and a person who slips up but acknowledges it may still be a viable social partner rather than a weirdo, psychopath, lone wolf, or loose cannon.

Though blushing is agonizing to the blusher—some people seek surgical treatment to stop it—it can endear them to an observer. Blushing works. Studies have shown that it can obviate an apology, make an actual apology seem more sincere, and earn the blusher forgiveness and trust.[44]

Now, if you've been recalling blush-worthy episodes in your own life, you may protest that many are not remotely breaches of morality or even etiquette. Being in the spotlight is enough. People blush when they're praised or congratulated in a group, or even when they're just stared at. (Darwin quotes Samuel Taylor Coleridge: "Account for that he who can.") In surveys, one of the most common incidents in which people remember blushing was when a group sang Happy Birthday to them![45]

Let me try to account for that. People who blush when all eyes are on them say they worry that they may appear smug or immodest, or that they may not respond graciously, or that scrutiny will reveal that they don't truly deserve the accolades being showered upon them.[46] This looks like another version of the need for self-deprecation that drives convivial humor. It's the desire to be a good buddy in a relationship of communal sharing rather than a contestant in a relationship of authority. Through no fault of one's own one has been thrust into the spotlight, *as if* one were a social-climbing, status-seeking, fame-grubbing pooh-bah. Blushing disavows any such ambition.

Though we have seen why blushing generates common knowledge, so far I have not explained why it should be *triggered* by common knowledge rather than by mere reciprocal knowledge. In reciprocal knowledge, the transgressor knows he has slipped up, and that onlookers know that, and the onlookers know he has slipped up, and that he knows that. But to be embarrassed or ashamed, is it necessary, in addition, that the transgressor knows that the onlookers *know* he knows?

That's not as convoluted as it may first appear. Imagine that you've just spilled gravy on yourself, or passed gas, or got caught with your hands in the cookie jar. As Darwin noted, you'd probably make a considerable effort to avoid meeting the eye of a witness, even though each of you knows the other knows of the gaffe. (As we'll see, eye contact is a potent common-knowledge generator.) Yet another Victorian, the poet Coventry Patmore (1823–1896), observes in his poem

"The Kiss" that even four embedded levels of recursive mentalizing may spare a person from embarrassment when the breach falls short of common knowledge:

> "I saw you take his kiss!" "'Tis true."
> "O, modesty!" "'Twas strictly kept:
> He thought me asleep; at least, I knew
> He thought I thought he thought I slept."

(To understand the poem in its historical context, we must engage in two more layers of recursive mentalizing and appreciate that Victorian readers would have been thinking about the woman's propriety and the mutual embarrassment if it had been breached, rather than her consent.[47])

In the following century, Thomas Schelling presented another vignette in which embarrassment would be triggered by nothing short of common knowledge. He and a friend were engaged in one of academics' favorite pastimes, complaining about the unfairness of peer review, in this case a scathing review of a journal submission that the friend had just received. Schelling soon realized that he was the anonymous and blind reviewer.

> I had a choice. I could confess at once, guaranteeing mutual embarrassment, or I could feign sympathy and risk a worse embarrassment if he discovered that I not only was the referee but had deceived him during his diatribe. I took the chance; he never knew; we were not embarrassed.
>
> Suppose he had caught on. He might, for example, have been quoting something from the referee's report that he had not thought to associate with me, but with me beside him the attribution to me had become inescapable. He might have turned to me in shock as he discovered my

dirty secret. . . . As we looked in each other's faces, and he knew that I knew that he knew that I knew that he knew I was the referee, our "common knowledge" of my role would have allowed me no escape from an embarrassment that might have afflicted us both forever.

Suppose instead—and conceivably this is what happened—that he had caught on, just while complaining to me, to who the referee was and appreciated the mutual embarrassment that would ensue if he let on; he might have kept secret that he knew my secret and spared us both. If it had become apparent to me that he had caught on and was not letting on that he had caught on, I should have cooperated in disguising my awareness of his awareness. The important thing was to avoid "ratification," mutual acknowledgment of the mortifying fact that I was the referee.[48]

Thomas, DeScioli, and I decided to verify that common knowledge was indeed the surest trigger for embarrassment, guilt, and shame.[49] We theorized that an unrepentant transgressor with mere reciprocal knowledge leaves it open that he is aware of the norm but feels no obligation to atone for it there and then, because as far as he is concerned, any observer may not know that he is aware of their knowledge. He's still compromised by whatever incompetence or lapse allowed him to slip up, and he knows it. But acting insouciantly avoids signaling that he is, in addition, contemptuous of the reigning norm, and it can spare both him and his partners the need to question the relationship, which could disadvantage both if it led to the relationship unraveling. In contrast, if he proceeded as if nothing untoward had happened even if others knew that he knew that they knew he had messed up, he would, in effect, be flipping the bird to the norms that had been allowing them all to coordinate. In the arena of common knowledge, a public breach must be repaired by a public acknowledgment.

In one study we asked people to read embarrassing vignettes, imagining themselves as the naughty protagonist. They imagined that they had passed gas in a lecture hall, or that they had made fun of a friend by imitating her speech impediment to a mutual friend, or that they had inflated an expense reimbursement report to compensate themselves for a missing receipt from a previous report. Two other vignettes were fillers, designed to elicit other emotions.

The key contrast we focused on was their level of mutual knowledge with an observer who caught them in the act. Here are the variants in the flatulence scenario, ordered by the state of knowledge of the earwitness:

> **No knowledge:** The room is noisy, so the person next to you hasn't heard it.
>
> **Private knowledge:** The person next to you notices. But because the room is noisy, you don't realize she's noticed.
>
> **Detected knowledge:** The person next to you is visibly startled by the sound and glances over at you. You secretly notice this, but you don't react and you keep on taking notes. The person cannot tell that you noticed, and she goes back to her own note-taking.
>
> **Reciprocal knowledge:** The person next to you is visibly startled by the sound and glances over at you. You notice this, and you reflexively flinch in response. She notices you flinching. But you don't look at her, so she can't tell that you noticed that she was startled. She goes back to taking notes.
>
> **Common knowledge:** The person next to you is visibly startled by the sound and glances over at you. You can't help but notice this, and can't help but look over and meet her gaze, making it obvious that she knows it was you.

The participants then rated how intensely they would experience each of six negative emotions if they were in the protagonist's shoes: anger, fear, sadness, and the three self-conscious emotions, embarrassment, guilt, and shame. We knew that people often confuse negative emotions, both in labeling them and in experiencing them. (A major goal of cognitive behavioral therapy is to get patients to learn to identify what's eating them.) We weren't surprised, then, that all the ratings were correlated, and so to capture a purer index of self-conscious emotion per se, we averaged the ratings for embarrassment, shame, and guilt and subtracted the average for the other three emotions.

Ideally, we would have measured their blushing and other physiological responses, but we ran this study on the internet rather than in person. So we settled for just asking the participants how intensely they thought they would exhibit each of sixteen physical reactions. The ones associated with the self-conscious emotions—blush, cover or touch face, hang head down, nervous laughter, sheepish grin, slump shoulders, and stammer—were intercorrelated, and we averaged them.

Now, everyone knows that we feel self-conscious emotions in the presence of our accusers, so it was no surprise that our participants imagined experiencing these emotions more intensely when they knew that their infraction had been witnessed (detected or reciprocal knowledge) than when it was private. Less obviously, and consistent with our prediction, we found that the most mortifying circumstance of all was when their awareness of the witness's discovery was ratified by eye contact, that is, when it was common knowledge. Their anticipation of blushing and cringing showed the same pattern: it was greater when the faux pas was detected, but greatest of all when it was common knowledge.

Experimental psychologists love the methodological revolution that allows them to test hundreds of subjects a day on internet crowdsourcing platforms like Amazon Mechanical Turk. But reveries about hypothetical vignettes by gig workers sitting at a keyboard in their pajamas can tell you only so much about real behavior, so we sought to corroborate the findings by actually embarrassing people in the lab. A standard humiliation technique, blessed by committees for the protection of human subjects in research, is to have participants sing a song aloud, such as "Old MacDonald Had a Farm," complete with animal noises (" . . . with a *quack! quack!* here and a *quack! quack!* there . . . ").[50] We opted instead to have them do a karaoke performance of Adele's "Rolling in the Deep," complete with soaring chorus.

The students' vocal stylings, they were told, were being rated in real time by a panel of their fellow students in another room, whose stony faces they could see on a live two-way video feed (in reality, a recording). The participants were told either that the judges were unaware it was a two-way feed and thought that they were judging the participant anonymously (reciprocal knowledge), or that the judges, like the participants, were fully aware that each was visible to the other (common knowledge). As predicted, the participants reported more embarrassment when their bad singing was common knowledge than when it was reciprocal knowledge. It's another bit of evidence that embarrassment, like the blushing it sets off, is triggered in the arena of common knowledge.

In the last two sections I provided a glimpse into what makes me laugh and cry, so I'll end this one with a true story. A few years ago, the invitation to the annual banquet of the American Academy of Arts and Sciences indicated in fine print, "Black Tie Optional." I mistakenly assumed it was the default, and on the designated evening found myself as the only man among the hundreds of luminaries decked out in a tuxedo. I knew I had done nothing wrong. I had nothing to be ashamed of. But until a fellow penguin showed up and put me out of my misery, I slunk around the hallowed halls the color of a ripe tomato.

⚜

Whether or not the eyes are a window to the soul, they certainly are a window to the mind. Our eyeballs are in constant motion to extract detail from the spot in the visual world most relevant to our current interests, so when people follow our gaze they are reading our mind. And when the gaze they follow is gazing back at them, they are reading the mind of a mind reader. Eye contact is the ultimate common-knowledge generator: we are seeing the part of the person that sees us seeing them seeing us.[51]

Eye contact is not uniquely human, but it must have been uniquely important in the evolution of our species, because we are designed to flaunt the direction of our gaze. Our black pupil and colorful iris are set off by a contrasting white sclera, unique among primates, and they are framed in an oblong window, also distinctively human.[52] It all fits: eye contact generates common knowledge; common knowledge is necessary for coordination; humans are consummate coordinators. Not surprisingly, eye contact is a major choreographer of human social life.

The anthropologist Irv DeVore used to tell his Harvard behavioral biology class, "If two people anywhere on earth look into each other's eyes for more than five seconds, then either they're going to have sex or one of them is going to kill the other." It's a bit of an exaggeration, but the potency of eye contact in sex and violence is undeniable.

In many species, a stare is a sign of malign intent.[53] (Some species of butterflies have taken advantage of these semiotics by evolving eye spots on their wings for self-defense.) The reasons are clear enough: a hunter draws a bead on his quarry; a sniper gets his target into the crosshairs. The targets, for their part, glance at the threat just long enough to know they're in danger, then turn their attention to where they can flee or hide. To stare at a rival is to play Hawk in a Hawk–Dove game; to avert one's gaze is to play Dove; to meet a stare with a stare is to join the battle. Hence the belligerent barroom taunt, "You lookin' at me?" (Before the main event at the Ultimate Fighting Championship, the fighters take part in a ceremonial "staredown." And one way to spook people out of their hiccups is to give them a cold, hard stare.) In professional settings, higher-ranked people look into the eyes of lower-ranked people far more often than the reverse, and when the subordinates are looked at, they look away.[54] After the resolution of the Cuban Missile Crisis, in which a standoff between the United States and the Soviet Union could have escalated into nuclear war, the US secretary of state Dean Rusk told a relieved nation, "We were eyeball to eyeball, and the other guy blinked."

Lovers gaze into each other's eyes, but before they reach that point, one may probe the other's interest by trying to catch their eye and seeing if the gaze is reciprocated. People forget this at their peril. The Safeway supermarket chain in California once instructed its cashiers to greet customers by looking into their eyes and giving them a friendly smile. They had to retract the policy when the female cashiers objected that the male customers were taking it as a come-on. More recently, Netflix banned their employees from looking at each other for more than five seconds, saying it was a form of sexual harassment.[55]

Now, all this talk of sex and violence may strike you as overwrought. Can't eye contact be more innocuous? Indeed, isn't it the essence of social grace? Skillful politicians are said to establish rapport with their constituents by looking them in the eye. And at the other end of the spectrum, awkward nerds are notoriously unable to make eye contact. If suave conversationalists are making eye contact all the time, why doesn't the conversation end in murder or intercourse?

It turns out that "eye contact" in everyday social interaction is a bit of a misnomer. It's not just the five-second rule. What people call "eye contact" in conversation is not a pupil-to-pupil straight line. Our eyes dart all over our interlocutors' faces, spending the most time on the bridge of the nose and often dipping down to read their lips.[56] Come to think of it, we *can't* look each other in the eye, because each of us has two of them. Parallel rays from eyeball to eyeball would mean that we were staring through each other into infinity, not peering into each other's souls. Meaningful, sustained eye contact means choosing one eye to stare into, then jumping to the other one, a switch we don't even notice. Try looking at one eye in your reflection in a mirror, then the other. It's as if nothing happened. You are blind during the eye movement, and looking into either eye feels like looking into both. Hollywood directors know this, and tell actors in a love scene to switch eyes every few seconds.[57]

In day-to-day life, significant eye contact falls between these extremes: long enough to pause the dance around the face, but not so long as to make a scene. This is the kind of eye contact that kept coming up in the section on blushing and self-conscious emotions—the kind we try to avoid by looking askant when caught in a compromising act. In these cases, the coordination equilibrium we try to stay out of is a new one in which we would lose face, having relinquished a presumption of competence and probity.

Eye contact in everyday human interactions is not restricted to a specific coordination game, like dominance, status, or sexual communion. It can mean "Something that has been plausibly private or reciprocal knowledge up to this point is hereby common knowledge." Hence the standard challenge to a flimsy pretext: "Can you say that while looking me in the eye?"

According to a joke told to me by my good-natured, nominally teetotaling hosts at an event in Utah, "Jews don't recognize Jesus. Protestants don't recognize the pope. Mormons don't recognize each other in the liquor store." What allows people to get away with compromising behavior merely by avoiding each other's glances? It's not as if they didn't see each other, or could plausibly deny that they had, though perhaps they could plausibly deny that they knew the other had seen them, or that the other one knew that they knew this. This "pretext," "mutual pretense," "open secret," or "elephant in the room" really does depend on common knowledge, but not of the compromising fact. The sociologist Morris Friedell, an early theorist of common knowledge in social life, suggested that with an open secret, what is common knowledge is that everyone is colluding to act as if the opposite of their private knowledge is true. He gave the example of people delicately acting as if a terminal patient in their midst were not dying.[58]

The need for open secrets can be an indicator of systemic prejudice. A bizarre American custom in the century after the Civil War was "passing for white," in which a light-skinned African American might be legally and social classified as white and enjoy freedom from discrimination and prejudice, though living in fear that malicious gossip might explode the common understanding. The concept disappeared with the civil rights movement of the 1960s. In an odd kind of progress, some white people now try to pass for black, like Rachel Dolezal, who headed the Spokane chapter of the National Association for the Advancement of Colored People before being outed in disgrace in 2015.

Soon to follow the demise of "passing as white" was the parallel custom of living "in the closet." Until he "came out" in 1989 at the age of sixty-six (note the metaphor for creating common knowledge), my graduate advisor, the social psychologist Roger Brown, never acknowledged that he was gay, nor did any of his colleagues or students, though it was obvious to each of us privately.[59] The euphemism everyone used was "bachelor."

Yet another prejudice may be the next to go. In 2023, the writer Lindy West was interviewed on National Public Radio about an article in which she had announced a recent decision:

> IRA GLASS: Coming out as fat is a strange idea, because, of course, people can see if you're fat. It's no secret. It's not like when you come out as gay or transgender. Nobody says to you, dude, I can't believe you're fat. Lindy says it was obvious how big she was.
>
> LINDY WEST: But I always felt like if I didn't mention it that maybe people wouldn't notice. Or it could just be this sort of polite secret, like, open secret that we didn t address, because it felt so shameful. It just felt impolite to talk about, like me not wanting to burden you with my failure.[60]

The "burden" of acknowledging an obvious, unobjectionable, and mostly involuntary condition is irrational, but emotionally real for all that. I recall a dinner party at which an execrable oaf remarked of the host, "We always knew that Ed likes fat women." Though it was undeniable that the hostess had an above-average body mass index, the conversation froze, and the urge to avoid eye contact was so overpowering that we all buried our gaze in our laps. I appreciated an idiom that speaks of making eye contact impossible: we wanted to fall through the floor.

The role of eye contact in human social life has implications for technology. In defiance of the usual narrative in which Silicon Valley announces an insanely great gadget and the world snaps it up, the big tech companies have all told us we would soon be living in a virtual reality metaverse, only to lay an egg each time. Meta hawked its Quest Pro, Microsoft its HoloLens, Google its Glass, Apple its Vision Pro, and people stayed away in droves. A postmortem in the tech chronicler *Wired* explained why:

> An Apple headset, no matter how nifty its specs, is still a big honking gizmo plonked between its wearer and the rest of the world, inherently a barrier more than a conduit. . . . People don't want to spend lots of time wearing this type of device, for aesthetic reasons (snorkel mask for dorks), practical reasons (cumbersome, activity-limiting), and for social reasons (it's an isolation chamber you slide over your eyes to experience an individualized simulacrum of the world instead of our shared reality).[61]

The other tech revolution that may never happen because of the natural human common-knowledge generator is the replacement of in-person meetings with videoconferencing. We all lived with Zoom and similar platforms during the Covid-19 pandemic, and the platforms have made inroads into meetings since then because they save time, hassle, and fossil fuels. Yet everyone finds the experience fatiguing and a bit awkward (they become *oysgezoomt,* "Zoomed out," a Yinglish neologism that made the rounds after the second year of online seders). A big reason is that the effigies in the rectangles, all of them looking at their own screens instead of the camera, cannot make eye contact.[62] One workaround never caught on: an AI module that generated a deepfake of each person's eyes looking straight out of the screen. It was too much: viewers ended up looking at each other more than they do in natural conversation, and they were cognitively taxed by constantly having to interpret what the pair of eyes gazing back at them meant.[63] Making, breaking, and interpreting eye contact is a nimble human performance, and it exploits an anatomical feature of the face that can't be duplicated by a camera and a screen: the image capture device and the image of interest are the same.

⚜

Though expressions conveyed with facial muscles don't have the mutual salience of those conveyed with noise, fluid, heat, or locked eyes, one of them is conspicuous to expresser and perceiver alike: the glare. Many idioms for glowering capture its conspicuousness: *the stink-eye, the hairy eyeball, looking daggers, if looks could kill.*

The psychologist Lawrence Ian Reed, DeScioli, and I reasoned that an angry expression was not just an overflow of bile but might have a communicative function: making our threats credible. Threats have a built-in limitation: they're rational only when they don't have to be carried out, when they have intimidated the target into capitulating. If the threatener has to make good on the threat, he might only be hurting himself, because meting out the harm requires energy and risk. The target can anticipate this and call his bluff by defying him. Maddeningly, a determination to be irrational—to carry out a threat regardless of the cost—is the only way to be rational; this is the idea behind Schelling's paradoxical tactics, like locking the steering wheel in a game of Chicken. Perhaps, the three of us reasoned, a determined glower is a credible signal that the threatener means business, registered by threatener and threatened alike. But how could we show this?

We used one of the most thought-provoking demos in experimental game theory, the Ultimatum Game. It's a sequential version of Divide the Dollar. A proposer is endowed with a dollar to split, and a responder can either take her share or leave it, in which case neither gets a cent. A rational proposer would seem to have a rational responder over a barrel: he can offer as little as one cent, and the rational responder must accept it, because a hundredth of a loaf is better than none. A minimal split would seem to be an offer she can't refuse.

But when the game is played by real people, refuse it they do. Responders spitefully blow up the deal by turning down offers that are too much less than fifty cents. Proposers, presumably anticipating this, preemptively offer an even split. The intuitive explanation is that responders don't want to look like patsies by accepting bare scraps, so they are willing to cut off their noses to spite their faces and turn down small offers out of self-respect and a concern for their reputation. It makes little sense in a laboratory study with strangers they'll never see again, and even less when the study is done in the anonymity of the internet. Gleeful critics of classical economics say that it refutes their beloved model of humans as rational actors. But it does make sense if we remember that in experimental games, people often act as if there is no such thing as an anonymous stranger (which was true in the small-scale societies in which humans spent most of their history).[64] They're acting as if they were playing in the real world, where people want it to be known that they demand to be treated fairly.

And this takes us to emotional expressions as common-knowledge generators. The game theorist Ken Binmore points out that if people treat an Ultimatum Game as if they might play it again with the same people, it is a kind of coordination dilemma.[65] A greedy, 99-percent-for-me proposer and a pragmatic, better-than-nothing responder are in a Nash equilibrium, since neither would do better by changing their choices. So are an equitable proposer and a self-respecting, spiteful-if-necessary responder. The multiple equilibria make it a coordination game. Obviously the second equilibrium is better for the responder, and perhaps for everyone in the long run, since roles can reverse, but how do they get there?[66] The equilibrium consisting of equitable proposers and indignant-at-not-being-treated-fairly responders may be thought of as a convention. Conventions are ratified by common knowledge, and one way to generate that common knowledge, we reasoned, is by a resolute countenance that announces, "Don't mess with me." And so we predicted that an angry glare would serve the interests of a responder by steering the pair into an advantageous equilibrium in an Ultimatum Game.

The experiment was straightforward.[67] We enrolled internet volunteers in a standard Ultimatum Game, with the twist that before the proposers proposed, they saw a video clip of the responder over a caption threatening that she would turn down an ungenerous offer. Of course, this is cheap talk: once the proposer made an offer, however stingy, there would be nothing the responder could do about it, and both of them know that. But half the time we put some mustard on the threat by having the responder—in reality a student we had trained in facial expressions—accompany her threat with a frown, a steely stare, and a glowering mouth. Sure enough, the tough-gal look cowed the proposers into sweetening their offers beyond what strict rationality demanded.

Admittedly, an Ultimatum Game, like all the toys in behavioral labs, is contrived. But it distills a critical feature of real life. People are vulnerable to other people imposing their wills on them. Stubborn self-respect can give them a modicum of bargaining power that encourages others to treat them fairly. The glower helps to ratify this equilibrium of self-respect and equity, just as our other conspicuous displays ratify our friendships, hierarchies, and norms.

7
Weasel Words

Why we don't just come out and say what we mean

In the film *Schindler's List*, after some of Schindler's Jewish workers have been deported to Auschwitz, he negotiates with an SS commandant for their release. The commandant says, "It is not my task to interfere with the processes that take place down here. What makes you think that I can help you?" Schindler replies, "Allow me to express the reason," and empties a satchel of diamonds onto the table. The commandant says, "I could have you arrested." Schindler's response: "I'm protected by powerful friends. You should know that." This leaves the commandant at a loss. Finally, he says, "I'm not saying that I am accepting them. All I say is that I am not comfortable with them on the table." The commandant scoops up the diamonds and stuffs them into his pocket.[1]

No one who watches this conversation can miss the bribes, threats, agreements, and denials that pass between these characters. Yet the terms of those transactions are never spelled out. Schindler does not say, "If you release my workers, I will give you these diamonds" or "If you have me arrested, I will see to it that you are punished." Nor does the commandant say, "If you let me have the diamonds, I will release the workers" or "I accept this exchange but will deny it to others."

When people negotiate in fraught areas of human life, they seldom blurt out their intentions in so many words. They hint, wink, sidestep, shilly-shally, and beat around the bush. They use innuendo, euphemism, and subtext, counting on their listeners to catch their drift, connect the dots, and read between the lines. Off-record indirect speech, as linguists call the phenomenon, is common in fictional dialogues, which challenge the recursive mentalizing powers of readers and viewers to discern how one character is trying to affect the beliefs of another.[2]

Many indirect propositions are so recognizable that they have become tropes of popular culture. The prototype of the veiled bribe is a motorist who is pulled over by a police office and asks him whether there is some way of settling the traffic ticket right there. This cartoon combines the scenario with another stereotype about the police:

"What Hershey bar? I don't see any Hershey bar."

A variant was played out in the television comedy *Silicon Valley*:

> JARED [in the passenger seat, as the officer approaches]:
> I heard on a podcast that patrolmen are actually a lot
> more tempted by bribes than you might think.
> DINESH [the driver]: Officer, hi! Is there anything I can do to
> make this all [smiles, rocks head] . . . "go away"?
> OFFICER: Sir, I would think very carefully about the next
> words that come out of your mouth.[3]

But Jared was right: the officer was bribed by an offer to take the wheel of the Tesla and try out the car's "Ludicrous" acceleration mode.

The veiled threat is typified by the musing of a mafioso to a store owner about the positive qualities of the store and how lamentable it would be if a mishap should befall it. This line, too, has become recognizable enough to inspire a cartoon:

Here again scriptwriters have updated the cliché. In an episode of *The Sopranos*, a member of the family accosts an old acquaintance in a store, pays for his candy bar, and says, "Listen, Danny, we just want you to know how glad we are a guy like you is on the jury [of the] Junior Soprano trial. . . . [You're a] hard-working guy. Wife and two kids. Performing a civic duty we should all take part in. We know you'll do the right thing."[4]

No one knows where the classic sexual come-on "Would you like to come up and see my etchings?" originated,[5] but according to one source, it is quite old:

"Won't you step in and look at my etchings?"

By the 1930s it had become familiar enough to figure in a *New Yorker* cartoon by James Thurber:

"You wait here and I'll bring the etchings down."

The twenty-first-century equivalent is the invitation to "Netflix and chill," now well enough known to have inspired an album title by Ariana Grande, a flavor of Ben & Jerry's ice cream, a brand of condoms, and its own Wikipedia entry.[6]

And then there are everyday polite requests: the non sequiturs, irrelevancies, apologies, musings on hypotheticals, and hyperbolic acknowledgments that we mutter to avoid bossing each other around: *Can you pass the salt? Do you think you could pass the salt? I was wondering if you could pass the salt. If you could pass the salt, that would be awesome.* The burbling and groveling reach a peak when the addressee is more powerful than the beseecher, as we see in the *Piled Higher and Deeper* cartoon on the following page. (The name of the strip comes from an old academic joke that *BS* stands for what it sounds like, *MS* means "more of the same," and *PhD* stands for "Piled Higher and Deeper.")

For all the cartoons and ironic allusions, indirect speech is no laughing matter. Instances are subjected to close exegesis in court cases on bribery, extortion, and sexual harassment (including one where a professor was investigated for showing a female colleague an article on fellatio in fruit bats).[7]

A recent example linked three of the world's most famous people: Donald Trump, Volodymyr Zelensky, and Joe Biden. The trio would go on to star in such world-shaking dramas in the 2020s that it's easy to forget the historic case that entangled them in 2019.[8] More than two years before Russia's invasion, Trump called Zelensky up for a chat in which he reminded the Ukrainian president what a good friend the United States had been to his country and complained that the relationship had not been reciprocal. Zelensky ventured that Ukraine's willingness to buy Javelin anti-tank weapons from the United States, approved by Congress but awaiting Trump's go-ahead, might even things up. Trump replied, "I would like you to do us a favor though," the favor being to investigate (bogus) corruption rumors involving Joe Biden and his son Hunter. When a transcript of the conversation was leaked, most readers interpreted the remark not as a request for a favor but as a veiled bribe: if Zelensky dug up dirt on the Bidens, Trump would hasten the sale of the missiles (or even a veiled threat: if he failed to dig around, Trump would delay the sale). The US House of Representatives charged Trump with abuse of power and impeached him, only the third impeachment of a president in American history (Trump would later become the defendant in the fourth). Trump denied that his words implied a quid pro quo. The Republican-majority Senate agreed and acquitted him.

⚬⦅⚬

Why don't people just come out and say what they mean? It would be quicker for the speaker, less work for the listener, and freer of the possibility of misunderstanding. Common sense says that innuendos provide *plausible deniability*: if challenged, the speaker could insist that he was only musing on hypotheticals, or really did have a collection of etchings he was dying to show. Trump's acquittal would seem to bear that out. But the Senate vote fell almost entirely along party lines, and was likelier a product of partisan loyalty than semantic analysis. And the jokes, memes, and cartoons would not have worked unless a denial of the intended meaning was in fact implausible, if not risible.

In this chapter I'll offer a refinement. Innuendo indeed works off plausible deniability, but what's plausibly denied is not the intended meaning but *common knowledge* of the intended meaning. As we have seen, common knowledge ratifies or nullifies social relationships, and people sometimes need to float a possibility without threatening a relationship. I proposed this idea in *The Stuff of Thought* in 2007, and since then I've been able to make it more precise and gather some evidence that it's true.

The first part of the theory nails down the logic of plausible deniability. To understand why people are tempted to use off-record indirect speech, let's start by imagining life without it. Consider a hypothetical speaker who follows the maxims of efficient communication and is succinct, truthful, direct, and relevant.[9] He is pulled over for speeding and is pondering whether to bribe the officer. His choice is whether to remain silent or to say "If you let me go without a ticket, I'll pay you fifty dollars." Unfortunately, he doesn't know whether the officer is corrupt and will accept the bribe or is honest and will arrest him for attempting to bribe a police officer.

This dilemma falls outside the kinds of games we've explored so far in the book. In the simplest cases in game theory, the players' rationality and payoffs are common knowledge: each knows what the possible outcomes are worth to the other (and know that they know, and so on). But our driver here is in a pickle: he knows the officer is rational, but he doesn't know his values (whether he's corrupt or honest) and hence doesn't know the payoffs. Schelling called this the Identification Problem; it's also known as a game of incomplete information.[10] The payoffs can still be illustrated by a little matrix, but in this case the columns don't represent different choices by the second player; they represent different types of player. (We'll assume for now that the player's values determine his choices.) Here's the driver's dilemma, showing only his payoffs:

	Corrupt officer	Honest officer
Don't bribe	Ticket	Ticket
Bribe	Go free	Arrest

Driver

If the driver doesn't try to bribe the officer (first row), either way he gets a ticket. If he does offer the bribe (second row), the stakes are much higher either way: going free with just the cost of the bribe if he is facing a corrupt cop, or an arrest for bribery if he is facing an honest one.

But now suppose the driver is verbally facile enough to proffer an ambiguous bribe, like "Is there anything I can do to make this all . . . 'go away'?" Suppose he knows that the officer can sniff out the bribe but couldn't make a bribery charge stick in court, because the ambiguous wording would prevent a prosecutor from proving his guilt beyond a reasonable doubt. The driver now has a third option:

	Corrupt officer	Honest officer
Don't bribe	Ticket	Ticket
Driver Bribe	Go free	Arrest
Veiled bribe	Go free	Ticket

The payoffs in this third row combine the large advantage of bribing a corrupt cop with the relatively small penalty of failing to bribe an honest one. Indirect speech is the rational choice.

Sounds plausible, but do the numbers add up? The mathematical biologist Martin Nowak, working with me and the psychologist James Lee, devised a simple mathematical model, which we called the Strategic Speaker theory.[11] The expected cost of a bribe—the sum of its good and bad outcomes, each weighted by its probability—can be calculated from five things: the proportion of officers who are honest, the cost of the bribe, the cost of the ticket (which must be greater than the cost of the bribe, or it would never pay to bribe), the cost of an arrest for bribery (which must be greater than the cost of the ticket, or it would always pay to bribe), and—the crucial psycholinguistic variable—the probability that an officer will treat an utterance with a given degree of directness as a bribe. This variable, "directness," runs from subtle to blunt, and corresponds to the plausibility of a denial: the proportion of readings of the utterance that are consistent with its being a bribe rather than an innocent remark. A generic remark like "I've learned my lesson; you don't have to worry about me doing this again" is least direct. A leading question like "Is there some way to take care of it here?" is in between. An *if–then* proposition like "If you let me go, I will give you fifty dollars" is most direct.

With these five numbers, figuring out the expected cost to the driver of a given wording is just high school algebra. But the algebra reveals a hitch in the logic of plausible deniability which is hidden when it's just described in words. The corrupt and honest cops both speak English, so presumably they interpret the utterance in the same way: the more direct the proposition, the higher the probability that a corrupt cop will accept it and that an honest cop will arrest the driver. But the surprise is that if they do interpret statements the same way, veiled bribes are pointless. The optimal response will depend only on the fraction of officers out there who are honest. If the proportion is above a certain threshold, the optimum strategy for the driver is not to try to bribe at all but just comment on the weather. If the fraction of honest officers is less than the critical value, the optimum strategy is to blurt it out: "If I give you a fifty, will you let me go?"

Where did the commonsense notion of plausible deniability go wrong? The missing piece is that the honest and corrupt officers have to react to the same statement in different ways. Even if they have identical gut feelings as to whether an invitation to "settle it here" is an attempted bribe, the honest cop must be more hesitant to arrest the driver than the dishonest cop is to accept it. If we imagine moving up a scale of possible bribes from subtle to blatant, the corrupt cop would take the payola with subtler bribes than an honest cop would arrest the driver for. With this extra assumption, the math works: a veiled bribe is the way to go.

How plausible is the crucial assumption that corrupt cops are more trigger-happy in accepting a bribe than honest cops are in blowing the whistle? The answer depends on the payoff from the *officer's* point of view. Take the honest officer. Why does he say "Sir, I would think very carefully about the next words that come out of your mouth" rather than arresting the driver for the words that already did come out of his mouth, words that would have been enough for a corrupt officer to have plucked the fifty (or the Hershey bar) out of the wallet? The reason is that even if all dishonest drivers offer remarks that can be interpreted (correctly) as veiled bribes, some honest drivers make those remarks too, as innocent observations, so any arrest might be unsuccessful. The charge might go to court, where it would have to meet the high standard of guilt beyond a reasonable doubt. If it doesn't, the unsuccessful arrest could be costly to the officer: he might be blamed for wasting the department's time, harming its reputation, or leaving it liable for damages. This means that the *officer's* identification matrix, with his choices as columns and the possible driver types as rows, looks like this:

Officer

	Arrest	Don't arrest
Honest driver	False arrest	Ticket
Dishonest driver	Conviction	Ticket

The cost to the honest officer of arresting the driver will thus depend on the proportion of dishonest and honest *drivers* who utter a remark with that level of directness, and on the professional rewards for successful arrests and the penalties for false ones. For a corrupt cop, the cost depends on the amount of the bribe, the consequences of making a false arrest, and the penalty for being convicted of accepting a bribe.

Putting these numbers all together, the decision rules for corrupt and honest cops regarding how naked a bribe has to be before they spring into action are not going to be the same. And if they're not the same, we have a plausible theory of plausible deniability.

The math works, but is the explanation right? Nowak likes to tell a joke at his own expense about his profession's reputation for caring more about mathematical elegance than details about the living world:

> A shepherd is tending his sheep, and a man comes by and says, "If I guess the correct number of your sheep, can I have one?"
>
> The shepherd says, "Please try."
>
> The man looks at the flock and says, "Eighty-three."
>
> The shepherd is amazed that he got the right number. The man picks up his prize and starts to walk away.
>
> The shepherd says, "Wait! If I guess your profession, can I have my sheep back?"
>
> The man says, "Sure."
>
> The shepherd says, "You must be a mathematical biologist."
>
> The man says, "How did you know?"
>
> "Because you picked up my dog."

Nowak was happy to leave it to Lee and me to test the theory of the Strategic Speaker with actual sheep, that is, people.[12] The point of our study was not to show that people know how to bribe officials with cash, only that when faced with this challenge (which, conveniently for us, has quantifiable costs, benefits, and risks), they apply conversational skills they have honed in everyday life.

We asked them to imagine themselves on a road trip through a fictitious former republic of the Soviet Union. A guidebook informs them that because bribery is rampant in this part of the world, a traveler must be prepared to know how to act in an encounter with a police officer. (The setup is not far-fetched: the anti-corruption organization Transparency International found that more than a third of the world's population feels that most of the police in their country are corrupt, and a quarter had paid a bribe to a government official in the preceding year.[13]) The participants were asked to imagine driving in each of several provinces and being pulled over by an officer who has falsely accused them of speeding, and they now have to consider what they would say to him. The provinces varied in the four variables that go into our model of optimal vagueness: the percentage of cops who are corrupt, the cost of a traffic ticket, the cost of a fine for bribery, and the customary size of a bribe. They were then asked how likely they would be to couch a bribe in each of four wordings:

"I'm very sorry, officer. If I give you a fifty, will you just let me go?"

"I'm very sorry, officer. But I'm actually in the middle of something right now, sort of an emergency. So maybe the best thing would be to take care of this here . . . without going to court or doing any paperwork."

"I'm very sorry, officer. I know that I'll have to pay for my mistake."

"I'm very sorry, officer. I've really learned my lesson."

Sure enough, our participants chose their words strategically: the larger the proportion of cops in the province who were honest and the lower the cost of the ticket, the mealier-mouthed the bribe. Across the sixteen provinces, the respondents chose a degree of bluntness that closely matched the predictions of our theoretical model.[14] But the critical test of the theory came from another question we asked our participants, namely how likely they thought the corrupt and honest officers were to act on the different wordings. With the blatant bribe, everyone thought that every last corrupt officer would take the bribe and every last honest officer would arrest the driver. But with the three veiled bribes, they judged that the corrupt cops would be quicker to leap into action than the honest ones. This was the make-or-break prediction of the theory that indirect speech is strategically optimal in a typical identification problem, and it gives some heft to the intuition that weasel words buy the speaker plausible deniability.

So it looks like we succeeded both in counting the sheep and in knowing what kind of animal we were dealing with—almost. One finding revealed a way in which people are not so optimal. When all the factors pile up on the side of bluntness, in particular when *all* the cops in the province are corrupt, then blurting out a quid pro quo is a no-brainer: there's nothing to lose, while a vaguer proposition would run the risk of going over the officer's head, leaving him unaware that he was being bribed at all. Yet our raters were squeamish about going all the way to a barefaced bribe: they opted for an unnecessary modicum of indirectness.

People are reluctant to let drop a direct proposition even when the cold, hard payoffs indicate it's perfectly safe. This brings us to the related question of why we use indirect speech in daily life, when we aren't being faced down by a man with a badge. No one has to worry about being arrested for offering a bribe in day-to-day life. So why do we habitually watch our words?

A bribe in day-to-day life? When, you might ask, would a law-abiding citizen such as yourself ever be tempted to offer a bribe?

How about this: You want to go to a popular restaurant on a Saturday night. You have no reservation. Why not try to grease the palm of the maître d' to jump the queue and be seated right away? That was the assignment given to the writer Bruce Feiler by *Gourmet* magazine a few years back, and his report shines a light on the imperative of indirect speech in social life.[15]

As you might imagine, the assignment filled him with dread. Though he didn't have to worry about being frog-marched out of the restaurant in handcuffs, he "kept imagining the possible retorts of some incensed maître d'":

> "What kind of establishment do you think this is?"
> "How dare you insult me?"
> "You think you can get in with *that*?"

Still, it was an assignment, so he screwed up the courage and tried it in a series of tony Manhattan restaurants. Each time, he looked the maître d' in the eye, taking care not to glance down at the fifty in his hand, and came up with a line such as one of these:

> "I hope you can fit us in."
> "I was wondering if you might have a cancellation."
> "Is there any way you could speed up my wait?
> "We were wondering if you had a table for two."
> "This is a really important night for me."

To his astonishment, it worked every time—he was seated within two to four minutes.

Why did he think the maîtres d' would be so incensed? And why did the innuendo make things so much easier on both sides? The previous pair of chapters answers the first question. Recall that social situations are governed by relational models—communality, authority, or equity—that stipulate who is entitled to what and under which terms. A mismatch of models between two people—one thinks she's the boss, the other treats her as a friend; one thinks they're friends, the other drives a hard bargain in a transaction—can lead to hard feelings.[16]

This is the driver of politeness, as with the diner who wonders whether his companion could pass the salt instead of just telling her to pass the salt. Issuing a command is the kind of thing a superior does to a subordinate, an impression that friends and strangers want to avoid. So they take advantage of the way that conversationalists are habitually cooperative, filling in the missing links needed to keep the conversation coherent. A genteel hint usually consists of some prerequisite to the favor. It makes no sense to ask someone to pass the salt if you already have the salt, if you don't like salt, or if the hearer is incapable of passing the salt. So by airing a thought like "There's no salt shaker at this end," "I could use some salt," or "Can you pass the salt?" a polite diner can plant the desired next step into the head of his tablemate and get what he wants without seeming to treat her like a flunky.[17]

Getting back to our restaurant lobby, the maître d' is in an authority relationship with patrons: he has the right to seat them where and when he pleases. A patron tendering a bribe is insolently treating him as if they were in an equity relationship, governed by the norms of quid pro quo, in which he would be obligated to seat the patron as a condition of accepting the bribe. As we saw in chapter 5, applying the wrong relational model to a social interaction can lead to unpleasant emotions ranging from awkwardness to outrage. Hence the terrifying anticipation of the incensed retort, "How dare you insult me!"

The emotional cost is as onerous as a monetary fine, and it makes the game of bribing a maître d' isomorphic to the game of bribing a cop. The matrix is the same, but the payoffs are reckoned as the sum of the practical cost (the pleasure of a quick table at the price of the bribe, or the nuisance of a long wait) and the emotional cost (the comfort of a mutual understanding of the relationship, or the awkwardness of a clash).

		Corrupt maître d'	Honest maître d'
Diner	Bribe	Quick table (equity – **equity**)	Awkwardness (equity – **authority**)
	Don't bribe	Long wait (authority – **authority**)	Long wait (authority – **authority**)
	Veiled bribe	Quick table (equity – **equity**)	Long wait (authority – **authority**)

Here again a literal-minded patron would be taking a chance if he tendered an overt bribe (first row), because he could end up with either a quick table or an ugly scene, and that gamble could be either better or worse than the sure nuisance of a long wait from being silent (second row). But a silver-tongued patron who came up with a veiled bribe (third row) could hedge his bet: a corrupt maître d' could sniff out the bribe and consummate the transaction, while an honest one could let it pass and pretend nothing had happened. A veiled bribe combines the large benefit of bribing a corrupt maître d' with the relatively small cost of failing to bribe an honest one. It is the optimal strategy with a maître d' of unknown values, as it is with an inscrutable cop.

(A personal anecdote: on the eve of the book tour for *The Stuff of Thought*, my wife and I were strolling along the Brooklyn waterfront without a dinner reservation when we passed the River Café, a chic restaurant with a gorgeous view. She noted that if I had the courage of my conjectures, now would be the time to apply my theories and bribe our way in. I mustered up the moxie but was defeated by the sight that greeted me at the hostess station: *two* maître d's, either of whom would see through a veiled proposition tendered to the other, making it deal-killing common knowledge.)

Threats follow a similar logic. A plain-speaking extortionist would be incriminating himself with his very words and risk legal penalties, just like a briber. He faces the additional risk that the target will call his bluff by defying the threat. To maintain the reputation on which his livelihood depends, the extortionist would have to carry out the threat, which can be risky and expensive and yet is pointless after it has failed in its purpose of coercing the target. A veiled threat solves both problems. If he's reported, it's hard to find him guilty of extortion beyond a reasonable doubt for merely encouraging a juror to "do the right thing." And if he's defied, he can choose not to carry out the threat without literally going back on his word and forfeiting his credibility.

Sexual come-ons face the identification problem big-time. People (at least, people of one of the sexes) are highly selective in who they sleep with, so a proposition is a gamble with a high payoff if the interest is reciprocated and a high cost if it is rebuffed. The cost is in the awkwardness of a relationship mismatch between, on one side, carnal and romantic communality and, on the other, platonic communality (among friends), equality (among coworkers), or authority (when it's a student or supervisee—in which case there is legal jeopardy as well). As with the driver and the cop, or the diner and the maître d', the verbal art is in landing on the optimal level of vagueness: subtle enough that an uninterested partner can choose to let it slide, but not so subtle that it goes over the head of an interested partner. In an oft-quoted *Seinfeld* episode, George Costanza, recounting a date to Jerry and Elaine, illustrates the second risk:

> GEORGE: She invites me up at twelve o'clock at night, for "coffee." And I don't go up. "No thank you. It keeps me up. Too late for me to drink coffee." I said this to her. People this stupid shouldn't be allowed to live. I can't imagine what she must think of me.
>
> JERRY: She thinks you're a guy that doesn't like coffee.
>
> GEORGE: She invited me up! Coffee's not coffee! Coffee is sex!
>
> ELAINE: Maybe coffee *was* coffee.
>
> GEORGE: Coffee's coffee in the morning. It's not coffee at twelve o'clock at night.
>
> ELAINE: Some people drink coffee that late.
>
> GEORGE: Yeah, people who work at NORAD on twenty-four-hour missile watch.[18]

And now we get to what's missing from the plausible-deniability theory, even after we have added emotional costs to the financial and legal ones. The problems are not small. One is the deniability: people use indirect speech even when there's no need for it. Recall that when the participants in our study were told that *all* the cops in the province were corrupt, so there was no cost to being direct and some cost in being indirect (a Costanza-like cop), they *still* opted for a veiled bribe. And as we learned from *Gourmet* magazine, all the maître d's in Manhattan are bribable—yet diners still resort to innuendo.

The other problem is the plausibility. Could any maître d' really be in doubt as to what "speeding up my wait" means? Or a jury foreman about "doing the right thing," or a grown woman about "etchings" or, these days, "Netflix and chill"? How about a cop interpreting the meaning of "taking care of this here without going to court or doing any paperwork"? In the last case, we have an answer. When our respondents were asked to estimate the probability that it was intended as a bribe, the average guess was 99 percent.

Thinly veiled propositions don't pass the giggle test, but people are still more comfortable with them. Why? What would have been so terrible for a New York maître d' if the customer had just stated the bargain in black and white? Why is a rebuffed sexual overture more uncomfortable when it is proffered as a bald proposition than when it is conveyed by unmistakable innuendo, even in the most extreme circumstances?

"I know it's late, but you wanna come up for a coconut or something?"

When all is said and done, there's something special about direct language. Couching an intention in a literal sentence—barefaced, on the record, in so many words—makes a difference. Some things once said can never be unsaid.

What's special is that language generates common knowledge. That's the way it works. Saying something to an understanding hearer is a self-evident event (the kind discussed in chapter 4), one that can't happen without the two parties knowing that it happened, and knowing that the other one knows.[19] It's not that the *content* of each sentence is automatically believed—that would make hearers sitting ducks for lies and manipulation. But for comprehension to take place, the *intention* to share that content must be common knowledge. Recognizing that intention is necessary for the hearer to draw on their common ground to resolve the countless ambiguities that permeate a sentence, and to interpolate the unstated assumptions that link one sentence to the next.[20] When the plain meaning of a speaker's message is unambiguous in context, given the common ground they share, the hearer may conclude that that is what the speaker intends her to believe, and the speaker knows this.

Direct speech generates common knowledge. Common knowledge steers people into social relationships. When people are leery about consummating such a relationship, they want to avoid that common knowledge, and so they resort to indirect speech. To keep up the understanding that the maître d' is an authority in his domain while broaching the possibility of switching to a transactional relationship, or that the man and woman are just friends while broaching the possibility of switching to sexual communion, they stick with literal wording that is compatible with the status quo, avoiding wording that would signal a very different social reality which one of them may not want.

This raises a still deeper question. What makes common knowledge of a willingness to switch to a new relationship so scary? One reason is that the common knowledge is a Rubicon, a discrete shift that stands out as an unmistakable focal point. Relational models are qualitatively different modes of interaction, and for a pair of people to switch from one to another is no small matter. Since it takes two to tango, people must jointly recognize a policy about when to switch. Exactly how close can a man sit to a woman, how lavishly can he compliment her, how slim a pretext for inviting her to his apartment can he offer, before she concludes that his intentions are sexual? Her private assessment can track the hints in an analogue fashion, but her relationship with him must be one thing or the other. If she is unwilling, she might have to tolerate a considerable amount of ambiguity before blowing the whistle, because there are costs to switching the relationship and it's hard to know where to draw the line. A barefaced proposition that resolves all doubt certainly falls on the other side, and the difference between it and the continuum of innuendo may be the only clear place to draw that line. The plausibility of the denial may be small—one percent, or one-tenth of one percent—but as long as it isn't zero (as it would be for a blatant proposition), she may not be able to call him on it. With the lack of a focal point to trigger a change of relationship, the speaker is given "the benefit of the doubt," and the relationship can remain unchanged. The deniability, then, doesn't have to be plausible, only possible.

The other difference between direct speech and even the most suggestive innuendo is that direct speech shortcuts recursive mentalizing, granting common knowledge at a stroke. Imagine that James says, "Wanna come up for Neflix and chill?" and Charlotte demurs. There may be little uncertainty about James's intent, and none about Charlotte's: Charlotte knows that she has turned down an overture, and James knows that she has turned down an overture. But Charlotte doesn't necessarily know that *James* knows; she might think to herself, "Maybe James thinks I'm naïve." And James doesn't necessarily know that *Charlotte* knows that he knows; he might think to himself, "Maybe Charlotte thinks I'm dense." Though there is private knowledge, there is no common knowledge, and they can maintain the fiction of a purely platonic friendship without surrendering their claims to rationality and honesty. In contrast, if James were to have said, "Wanna come up and have sex?" then James instantly knows that Charlotte knows that James knows that Charlotte knows, and so on. With this common knowledge, they cannot maintain the fiction of a friendship. They would have the sense that "it's out there," that "he can't take it back." In other words, it's not deniability of the *intent* that has to be plausible; it's deniability of *common knowledge* of the intent.

The theory that indirect speech provides plausible deniability of common knowledge of relationship-threatening information seemed to put all the pieces together, but we still had to test it. Lee and I asked people to read three sets of vignettes, each ending with a fraught proposition tendered by one of the protagonists. In one scenario, the proposition was a bribe, similar to the driver-and-cop story. In another it was a threat: an unscrupulous professor threatens to torpedo a brilliant student's candidacy for a prestigious fellowship unless she agrees to apply her talents in his lab. The third was a sexual come-on: Michael and Lisa are coworkers and friends; they have dinner, and while he's driving her home, they pass his apartment building and he makes his verbal move. As before, we presented each vignette with four variations of the climactic proposition, from roundabout to in-your-face. For example:

> "Wow. I feel like we've been talking about so much, but it's only ten-thirty."

> "My friend just emailed me those pictures from our trip to Europe that I was telling you about. Do you want to come over and have a look?"

> "You know, I have a really terrific view from my balcony. You can see the whole city, the lights, the ocean . . . Would you like to come over and have a look?"

> "I find you really attractive, and I enjoyed being with you tonight a lot. Would you like to come over and have sex?"

In every story, the hearer declines. Then, in a dozen questions, we probed our respondents' understanding of what transpired.

As in the first experiment, the answers vindicated the commonsense idea that innuendo allows for plausible deniability. Indirect speech is not just a ritual, like saying *please* or *thank you*, but generates uncertainty about the speaker's intent. The respondents, putting themselves in the shoes of the hearer, indicated that they interpreted blunter propositions as furnishing more confidence that the speaker had the illicit intent in mind, and as likelier to bring him unfortunate consequences, such as a conviction for bribery or disciplinary action by the college.

We also wanted to confirm that indirect speech has emotional costs and benefits that are analogous to the legal and monetary costs in the clear-cut case of a driver bribing a cop. Not surprisingly, a speaker who took care to veil his proposition as an innuendo was seen as more respectful to the hearer, and as making it easier for the two to resume their day-to-day relationship.

Less obviously, we replicated the critical test of the Strategic Speaker model of optimal indirectness—that willing listeners are more trigger-happy in acting on an ambiguous offer than unwilling listeners—but this time with emotional rather than financial payoffs. A new sample of respondents judged how Lisa would react to a range of propositions in two different scenarios: the attraction was mutual and she intended to accept his offer, or it was one-sided and she intended to rebuff the advance and keep a chilly distance thereafter. As predicted, our readers thought that a willing Lisa would say yes with vaguer propositions than an unwilling Lisa would say no.

But our happiest finding was that blunt propositions, and only blunt propositions, were focal points, of the kind that generate common knowledge. First, we confirmed that the blunt propositions were seen as leaving no wiggle room for an innocent interpretation. In the bribe vignette, when our respondents took the vantage point of the officer, all but one gave a clean 100 percent estimate that the driver issuing a blunt offer really meant it. (That may seem obvious, but such unanimity is rare in behavioral experiments, which are usually subject to Lizardman's Constant: in any survey, 4 percent of the respondents will tick off an affirmative response to any question, no matter how bizarre, such as "Do you believe that the world is controlled by shape-shifting reptilians?"[21]) Almost as cleanly, a majority of our respondents were 99 percent sure that a driver uttering the most suggestive of the indirect propositions meant it as a bribe. The deniability of an innuendo may be implausible—in this case, one percent—but people distinguish it from certainty.[22]

The other test of common knowledge, that blunt propositions

bestow recursive understanding, presented us with a challenge that will be familiar by now. Suppose we asked people to rate their confidence that Lisa knows that Michael knows that Lisa knows that Michael knows that Lisa turned down his come-on. At best, our baffled respondents might think, "Yeah, whatever; it's turtles all the way down." If they thought this for the blatant proposition but not for the veiled ones, that would still tell us something (as in the study I did with Julian de Freitas on public events, described in chapter 4). But Lee and I wanted to give our respondents the best possible chance at taking apart the Russian doll.

As we saw in chapter 4, people *can* entertain several layers of thoughts nested in thoughts if the conditions are right. So we tried to set up those conditions and stretch our respondents' powers of mentalization as far as we could. We asked them to take a first-person perspective (removing one layer), introduced each thought in its own sentence, focused on one sentence at a time, and used a different verb in each so the sentences wouldn't mentally collapse into themselves.

Here's a test of two layers of mentalizing: the hearer thinks about what the speaker had in mind. After reading the potential come-on, our readers picked an interpretation:

Put yourself in Lisa's position. What is she thinking at this point?
   "I'm absolutely certain that Michael was not asking me to
      have sex (or at least as certain as anyone can ever be about
      someone's intentions)."
   "I'm virtually certain that Michael was not asking me to have
      sex."
   "I think that he probably wasn't asking me to have sex."
   "Did he just ask me to have sex? Or was he just asking me to
      stay out longer? I can't tell one way or another."
   "I think he probably was asking me to have sex."

"I'm virtually certain he was asking me to have sex."

"I'm absolutely certain he was asking me to have sex."

Not too hard. Let's encase it in a third layer—the speaker wonders about how the hearer interpreted what he had in mind:

> Lisa has politely said she wants to go home. Put yourself in Michael's position. Which of the following is he most likely thinking?
> "I'm absolutely certain that Lisa didn't understand that I was asking her for sex."
> . . . [five intermediate degrees of confidence, as in the list above] . . .
> "I'm absolutely certain that she understood I was asking her for sex."

Now let's try four layers: the hearer ponders that rumination by the speaker:

> Lisa knows that Michael was asking her to have sex. Put yourself in her position. What is she thinking?
> "Michael thinks that I didn't understand he was asking me to have sex. I'm absolutely certain of that."
> . . .
> "Michael knows that I understood that he was asking me to have sex. I'm absolutely certain of that."

Think you can handle a fifth layer, in which the speaker ponders the hearer's pondering?

> Suppose that Michael *does* realize that Lisa knowingly turned down his invitation to have sex. Put yourself in Michael's position. What is he thinking?

"Lisa thinks that I didn't understand that she turned me down
for sex. I'm absolutely certain of that."

. . .

"Lisa knows that I understood that she turned me down for
sex. I'm absolutely certain of that."

Now let's go for broke: six layers.

Suppose that Lisa *is* certain that Michael knows she turned down his invitation to have sex. Put yourself in Lisa's position. What is she thinking?

"Michael understands that I turned him down for sex. But he
doesn't realize that I know he understands that."

. . .

"Michael understands that I turned him down for sex. And he
realizes that I know he understands that."

In plotting the respondents' degree of confidence, we were interested in whether each additional layer of he-thinks-that-she-thinks
reduced their confidence in the entire thought. So before we plotted the
data, we conditioned the confidence rating for each item on how confident the participants were on the item one level down—for example,
how likely they indicated it was that Lisa thinks that Michael thinks
that Lisa thinks that Michael intended his invitation to be sexual
given that they indicated that she thought his invitation was sexual
in the first place (as revealed in their rating of the preceding item).

What we found was striking. With each of the veiled come-ons, the
more thoughts within thoughts they had to consider, the lower their
confidence sank. But with the blatant come-on, their confidence was
pretty much pinned at 100 percent: they were as sure that she thinks
that he thinks that she thinks that he thinks that she thinks it was a

come-on as they were that she thinks it was a come-on. This supports the notion that blunt speech generates common knowledge but innuendos don't. It's also the best evidence I know of that common knowledge in the sense of recursive mentalizing is tied to common knowledge in the sense of self-evidence.[23] In interpreting a self-evident direct proposition, people assented to however many layers of recursive thoughts they were challenged to think.

As you have been comparing blunt speech with innuendo in your own mind, another difference may have occurred to you. Innuendo has to be interpreted in context. Its exact interpretation depends on every scrap of information available to the hearer, including the lead-up to the proposition, the speaker's body language, and his tone of voice. Blatant propositions, in contrast, wear their interpretations on their sleeve. That means they can be interpreted by eavesdroppers and by the imaginary audience that we always play to (another insight of Erving Goffman). On top of all this, direct propositions are relatively lossless: if someone did catch wind of the dialogue, by overhearing it or getting a firsthand report, she could pass it along to a chain of gossipers with high fidelity. The incriminating knowledge could become common not just with the hearer but in wider circles.

So another reason that we may veil our intentions in innuendos is that their deniability might be plausible to the virtual audience, even if it is not plausible to the hearer, and people always act as if spectators are lurking and eager to pass any juicy gossip through the grapevine. We asked our raters to suppose that Lisa told her friend Emily what Michael had said. How certain is *Emily* that Michael was asking Lisa for sex? And suppose Michael learns about Lisa's blabbing; how certain does *he* think Emily was? According to our raters, the less direct the speech, the less likely a third party would interpret it with the fraught meaning, and speakers anticipated this. But with direct speech, you didn't have to be there: the confidante was as sure as the hearer, and the speaker worried about this.

DeScioli, Thomas, the economist Maxim Massenkoff, and I recently replicated the main findings in an experimental game that involved thrusting people into a situation in which they could *produce* innuendos, not just judge them. They took the role of a schemer or an accomplice who could agree to steal some of the payment owed to a third player. When a fourth player, a monitor with the power to fine them, could eavesdrop on their conniving, they switched to innuendos, like "Some things are better left unsaid" or "Hopefully this works out for both of us."[24]

I've suggested in this chapter that off-record indirect speech is a rational strategy to make common knowledge of relationship-threatening propositions plausibly deniable. The theory survived a number of empirical tests of how people interpret utterances, and of how they perceive the relationship between a speaker and a hearer, depending on the bluntness of the speaker's words.

The plausible-deniability claim successfully predicts that the bluntness of speakers' wording is not an arbitrary social ritual but is predictable from strategic considerations, in particular the proportion of sympathetic and unsympathetic hearers and the costs and benefits of either one catching the speaker's drift. The relationship-threat claim predicts that innuendo should be judged as generating less awkwardness, conveying more respect, and allowing the conversationalists to resume their relationship should the offer be rebuffed. And the common-knowledge claim predicts that blatant speech stands out as a focal point because people are certain about its intention, and that it grants recursive embeddings of belief: the speaker and hearer are as confident in their interpretation of the other's interpretation of their interpretation as they are in the interpretation itself. A related claim was that direct speech is perceived as lossless in chains of gossip: the last link in a chain may be as confident in the speaker's intent as the first.

⋈

Euphemism, politeness, genteel circumlocution, and other forms of indirect speech make social life possible, but they have a dark side. Several historians and social psychologists, inspired by George Orwell's classic essay "Politics and the English Language," have noted that the use of euphemisms (like *pacification* and *collateral damage*) may enable people to perpetrate atrocities while protecting their commonly acknowledged identity as moral beings.[25]

When hearing the dialogue from *Schindler's List*, one is struck by the euphemisms used to refer to the slaughter taking place in the concentration camps, like "special treatment" and "the processes that take place down here." It's a historically accurate rendition of how officials cloaked atrocities in face-saving vagueness.

In one of the film's final scenes, after the announcement of the German surrender, Schindler addresses the SS guards. The time for euphemism has passed. He challenges them to carry out their orders to kill the thousand Jews assembled before them. "Or," he says, "you could leave. And return to your families as men instead of murderers." A long silence follows Schindler's direct language. Finally one of the guards breaks ranks and leaves. And then another. And then another.

8

The Canceling Instinct

The urge to prevent ideas from becoming common knowledge, even in the knowledge profession

Do women, on average, have a different profile of aptitudes and emotions than men? Did indigenous peoples frequently engage in war and genocide? Are recovered memories of childhood sexual abuse really implanted by suggestive questioning by psychotherapists? Is morality an evolutionary adaptation of our brains, with no divine mandate or inherent reality? Does racial diversity benefit neighborhoods, academic departments, and companies? Are there two sexes in animals, including humans?

Do men have an innate motive to rape? Do violent riots reduce support for liberal political candidates? Would a rapid reduction in fossil fuel consumption do more harm than good? Is average intelligence declining because duller people have more children than smarter people? Is belief in an afterlife harmful, because it makes people less concerned with life on earth? Do racial preferences harm their beneficiaries by putting qualified individuals under a cloud of suspicion and mismatching students with the academic demands of their universities?

Is the maternal instinct adjustable, so that a woman who gives birth in difficult circumstance might be indifferent to her newborn? Do the Muslim doctrines of jihad and martyrdom encourage suicide terrorism? Is sudden-onset gender dysphoria in adolescent girls an effect of social contagion? Are polar bears thriving? Are female scientists with female mentors less successful than those with male mentors? Would people be likelier to stay out of poverty if they adopted bourgeois norms like completing high school and not having children out of wedlock?

Are differences in intelligence between individuals partly heritable? What about average differences between ethnic groups? Do parents have any lasting effect on the personality or intelligence of their children? Do police shoot a larger proportion of unarmed African Americans than whites when differences in crime rates among neighborhoods are taken into account? Did European colonialism bring any benefits to colonized peoples, in addition to its harms? If people have the right to change their gender, should they have the right to change their race?

Perhaps you felt your blood pressure rise as you read those questions. Perhaps you are appalled that people are so much as allowed to ask them. Perhaps you are not reading this sentence because you threw the book across the room.

But these questions were not raised by cranks or shock jocks seeking to offend, nor by militants for some malevolent cause. They were raised by serious scholars, scientists, and writers, most of whom were unprepared for what hit them. They were not just criticized, as advocates of any strong position ought to be, but censored, punished, fired, threatened, harassed, demonized, libeled, and in some cases physically assaulted.[1]

Freedom of speech is protected in all democracies. Yet the repression of controversial ideas is no longer a hallmark of theocracies and dictatorships but increasingly a fixture of universities, the very institutions most committed to exploring ideas. According to the Foundation for Individual Rights and Expression (FIRE), between 2000 and mid-2024 there were more than thirteen hundred attempts to punish scholars for constitutionally protected speech in American colleges and universities. These included 243 incidents of censorship and 273 firings, 62 of them of tenured professors, a regime of intellectual repression more severe than during the McCarthy era.[2] Worse, for every scholar who is sanctioned, many more self-censor, knowing they could be next. It's no better for the students, a majority of whom say that the campus climate prevents them from saying things they believe.[3]

Academic freedom, once a narrow concern of academics, was thrust into the national spotlight in late 2023 because of a widely viewed congressional hearing on antisemitism on American campuses, in which legislators grilled the presidents of three of America's eminent universities, including Harvard, my employer.[4] In response to the hypothetical question of whether students calling for the genocide of Jews violated university policies, Harvard's president, Claudine Gay, gave the inadvertently *Bartlett's*-worthy answer, "It depends on the context." The fury, from both the right and the left, was white-hot.

Gay was technically correct in saying that students' political slogans are not punishable by Harvard's rules unless they cross over into intimidation or incitement of violence, just as they are not punishable by American law under the First Amendment. But her testimony was excoriated because Harvard had just come in at last place in FIRE's Free Speech ranking of 248 colleges, with a perfect score of zero.[5] Among other things, the university had effectively driven out a biologist who said there are two sexes, persecuted an epidemiologist who had signed a conservative amicus brief on gay marriage eight years earlier, and disinvited a feminist scholar who questioned the policy of housing violent men who identify as transgender in women's prisons.[6] So for the president of Harvard to suddenly come out as a born-again free-speech absolutist, disapproving of what genocidaires say but defending to the death their right to say it, struck onlookers as disingenuous.

The debacle added another millstone to the sinking reputation of American higher education, a descent more precipitous than for any other institution.[7] A major reason was the impression that universities were enforcing orthodoxies and repressing disagreement, like the inquisitions, purges, and fatwas of more benighted times and places. The impression had already been stoked by viral videos of professors being mobbed, cursed, and heckled into silence.

I have a stake in this issue, having cofounded the Council on Academic Freedom at Harvard in 2023, a faculty-led organization dedicated to academic freedom, viewpoint diversity, and civil discourse.[8] But I raise the issue in this chapter because of its relevance to the theme of the book. I will suggest that the ever-present threat to freedom of speech emerges from two features of our psychology. One is that people hold many factual beliefs not because the beliefs have been shown to be true but because they are felt to uphold a moral order. The other is that upholding a moral order takes place in the arena of common knowledge. As we saw in chapter 1, norms exist to the extent that everyone knows that everyone knows they exist. A moral norm may be endangered if a threat to it becomes commonly known, and so defenders of the norm feel they must prevent the threat from becoming common knowledge, and if they fail, to punish the threatener as a commonly known example to all.

First, a few words on why academic freedom should matter to people outside academia. It's not a matter of the privileges of professors. Societies entrust universities, at fantastic expense, with a mandate to discover and transmit knowledge. This cannot be accomplished without intellectual freedom. No one is infallible or omniscient. Mortal humans begin in ignorance of everything and are saddled with cognitive biases that make the search for knowledge arduous.[9] These include overconfidence in their own rectitude, a preference for confirmatory over disconfirmatory evidence, and a drive to prove that their own tribe is wiser and nobler than their rivals. The only way that our species has managed to learn anything about the nature of things, and to claw increments of progress out of an indifferent universe, is by a process of conjecture and refutation. Some people venture ideas, others probe whether they are sound, and in the long run the better ideas prevail.

Any institution that disables this cycle by repressing disagreement is doomed to chain itself to error, as we are reminded by the many historical episodes in which authorities enforced dogmas that turned out to be flat wrong.[10] An academic establishment that stifles debate betrays the privileges that the nation grants it and is bound to provide erroneous guidance on vital issues like pandemics, violence, gender, and inequality. Even when the academic consensus is almost certainly correct, as with vaccines and climate change, skeptics can understandably ask, "Why should we trust the consensus, if it comes out of a clique that brooks no dissent?"

To take a recent example, by 2024 it had become clear that many early policies for combatting the Covid-19 pandemic—social distancing, cloth masks, disinfecting surfaces, Plexiglas barriers, draconian lockdowns, closure of beaches, parks, and schools—were based on no scientific evidence and were imposed by demonizing or suppressing what turned out to be reasonable criticisms.[11] The costs to the economy, mental health, and children's education were substantial, and the hit to people's trust in science and public health catastrophic.

To be sure, not even the staunchest advocate of free speech believes that speech should never be regulated.[12] The First Amendment to the American Constitution, which binds public universities and serves as a baseline for many private ones, is famously protective of freedom of expression, including crude, offensive, and hateful speech. But as it has been interpreted by the courts, even this bulwark admits of carefully justified exceptions. They include crimes that by their very nature are committed with speech, such as extortion, bribery, libel, fraud, and threats, together with incitement of imminent lawless action. Also justifiable are restraints on the time, place, and manner of expression. The First Amendment does not entitle you to blare your manifesto from a sound truck in a residential neighborhood at 3 a.m. or to set up your soapbox in the middle of a busy freeway.

Since universities are institutions with a mission of research and education, they are entitled to additional controls that are necessary to fulfill that mission.[13] These include vetting the quality and relevance of research and teaching, and ensuring an environment conducive to learning. Universities also have a legitimate interest in regulating protest that crosses a line from speech to coercion, such as heckling speakers into silence, forcibly occupying public spaces, and intimidating other students.

But the incidents of censorship and punishment on college campuses, as tallied by FIRE and other free-speech watchdogs, don't fit into any of these exceptions. The cancelers aim to suppress claims about empirical reality, or arguments about the implications of ideas, that were calmly expressed in interviews and essays, in social media posts, and in boring peer-reviewed articles in scholarly journals or monographs by university presses.

Often the sanctioners seem desperate for offenses to sanction, veering into farce. In that way, academic censoriousness blends into the social media shaming mobs discussed in chapter 1, in which an innocent quip deliberately taken the wrong way incites a horde of townsfolk to surround the newfound sinner, stones in hand. In a crowded elevator at an academic conference, the doors slid open and a political scientist made the dad joke "Ladies' lingerie" (showing his age by imitating an elevator operator in a department store); he was censured for sexual harassment.[14] An eminent psychiatrist tweeted of an ebony-skinned model, "Whether a work of art or freak of nature she's a beautiful sight to behold," and was suspended by his university and forced to resign from his hospital and professional institute.[15] A professor mentioned the Chinese filler word *nega* in class, and was suspended from teaching duties because it reminded some students of the racial slur.[16]

Of course, governments, corporations, and the media can be even more punitive. Repression of speech is more the rule than the exception in human affairs.[17] Over the course of history, occasional defenses of free speech pop out from a backdrop of persecution for blasphemy, heresy, or *lèse majesté*. And censorship and punishment of speech remains the norm in vast swaths of the globe today, including Russia, China, and most of Africa and the Middle East. I'm focusing on the drive by academics to censor one another both because of its timeliness and because it stands in such stark contrast to the professed values of a university in a liberal democracy. Why does repressing speech come so naturally to people that it bleeds through even in institutions dedicated to the exchange of ideas?

꘎

Why do people cancel? The fictional accounts of punitive mobs in chapter 1 suggest that people simply take delight and relief in being among the mobbers rather than the mobbed. But the real-life examples from social media were triggered by at least a pretext of protecting a moral norm. Though we can never be sure of the true mixture of conscious and unconscious motives of cancelers, a recent study of censorship of scientists by scientists (conducted by Cory Clark and a team of scholars, including me) confirmed that the ostensible motivation is moral.[18] Like the Savonarolas, Mathers, and Comstocks in earlier centuries, censorious scientists are convinced that they are safeguarding the moral order, especially the prevention of harm against historically marginalized groups.

Indeed, lurking beneath each of the cancelable ideas with which I began the chapter one can find a laudable moral principle. Racism, sexism, homophobia, transphobia, and Islamophobia are evils which must be combatted. Children must be reared with love and respect for their best interests. Rape is a heinous crime. Colonialism brought great suffering to indigenous populations. Climate change is a serious problem that will cause severe damage unless mitigated. People should live lives guided by moral principles and not just self-interest.

The principles are unexceptionable, but none of the cancelees had challenged them. On the contrary, many took pains to endorse the principles, insisting that they were entirely compatible with the point they were making. A few moments of brainwork confirm that the dire entailments feared by the censors are non sequiturs.[19] Even if it turned out, for example, that groups of people differed in their average traits, the overlap is so great that it would be irrational and unfair to discriminate against individuals for that reason. More important, the ideal of equality is not the empirical dogma that all human groups are indistinguishable but a moral commitment to treat people as individuals and not prejudge or mistreat them based on their membership in a group. Likewise, even if it turns out that parents don't have the power to mold their children's personalities, it would be wrong on grounds of basic decency to neglect or abuse them. If currently popular ideas about how to mitigate climate change prove to be counterproductive, it only highlights the need to know what *would* be effective. People's intimate personal inclinations that don't harm others should be respected, whatever their origins. And so on with the other contentious ideas. Each is a claim of empirical fact or conceptual consistency, and compatible with moral values the censors share.

All this is just the distinction from Moral Philosophy 101 between fact and value. But the distinction is far from intuitive. People engineer their bundle of beliefs toward winning arguments rather than laying out logical entailments, so they stack the deck by jiggering their factual assumptions to make their moral arguments more compelling.[20]

The psychologists Brittany Liu and Peter Ditto demonstrated this cross-contamination by probing people's beliefs in some textbook cases of moral reasoning. They presented people with the classic thought experiment of whether it is justifiable to stop a runaway trolley hurtling toward five unaware workers on the track by pushing a fat man over a footbridge onto its path, slowing the trolley and killing one to save five.[21] This preposterous scenario is, of course, purely hypothetical, engineered to probe whether people think that some acts are inherently immoral by their very nature even if they result in better outcomes, in this case more lives saved. But those respondents who did think it was intrinsically immoral to push the man also indicated, irrelevantly, that there's no way a human body could stop a runaway trolley!

Moving to a real-world case, Liu and Ditto noted that a principled opponent of capital punishment, one who believes it is inherently immoral for the government to take a life, should not care whether the death penalty deters murders. Yet in an amazing coincidence, these in-principle opponents of the death penalty *also* believed that it was, in practice, an ineffective deterrent. Moving in turn from correlation to causation, Liu and Ditto then presented people with purely moral arguments against the death penalty, and found that even in the absence of mentioning any facts, the arguments shifted the readers' factual beliefs about its deterrent value.

The human tendency to blur factuality with righteousness was part of the resolution of a paradox I took up in *Rationality*: how a species that was clever enough to have spread into every corner of the Earth and to develop sophisticated science and technology is also prone to believing zany conspiracy theories, fake news, and religious miracles.[22] I suggested that people naturally respect objective reality when it comes to their immediate experience: they have little choice if they want to keep food on the table and a roof over their heads. But they don't intuitively feel that it's possible to obtain objective answers to big, deep questions about history, society, and the hidden causes of natural phenomena. After all, before the development of a scientific and scholarly infrastructure with the Scientific Revolution and Enlightenment, there *were* no grounds for supposing that answers to big questions could be shown to be true or false. The questions were literally unanswerable, so you might as well believe the most edifying myths.

Universities aim to develop objective knowledge about big questions. But academics are only human, and despite their training in making conceptual distinctions, they are apt to avow whichever factual claims make their moral positions more compelling. Sexual discrimination and harassment are wrong, and anyway men and women are exactly the same. Rape is a vicious crime, and also men have no natural inclination to do it. War is horrific, and not only that, but our evolutionary ancestors never waged it. These empirical convictions can become communal beliefs, of the kind that bond a community or tribe (chapter 5), and they are particularly precious in an era of growing political polarization.[23]

Worse, many scholars blow off the distinction between facts and values not despite their academic training but because of it. The post-modern current in the humanities explicitly denies that there is any such thing as truth, fact, or objectivity, insisting that all such claims are pretexts to power. And in defiance of their universities' mission statements, many academics believe that the primary purpose of a university is not to discover and transmit knowledge but to pursue social justice, conceived as the wresting of power by victim groups from oppressor groups.[24]

So it's easy to blur the pursuit of objective knowledge with the upholding of moral norms, even in academia, *especially* in the sectors of academia that never signed on to the ideal of objective knowledge in the first place. And this brings us to the role of common knowledge in academic cancel culture.

According to an endlessly repeated story, in the late nineteenth century a woman (in various tellings a maiden, a spinster, or the wife of a bishop), upon learning of Darwin's theory, exclaimed, "My dear, descended from the apes! Let us hope it is not true, but if it is, let us pray that it will not become generally known."[25] Though the aghast woman almost certainly never existed, her reaction captures the attitude of many people about disconcerting ideas. They hope the

ideas are not true, but whether or not they are, they want them not
to become generally known—or, more accurately *commonly* known.
Our review and other surveys show that scientists are all too eager
to police common knowledge.[26]

In 2022 the editors of a major journal, *Nature Human Behaviour*,
announced that they would thenceforth reject or retract any article
they thought would cast some human group in an unflattering light,
even if it was scientifically sound.[27] Several journals have acted on
such policies, yanking peer-reviewed articles from their websites and
chucking them into the memory hole because some readers took
offense at their conclusions.[28]

Though a majority of surveyed academics say they are opposed to
hard censorship or dismissals for the airing of controversial opinions,
around a quarter are fine with it, and in an ominous sign for the future
of the academy, the younger the scholar, the stronger the urge to censor.[29] A majority of faculty under age thirty-five say they are in favor
of shutting down speakers with whom they disagree on a particular
issue, and a fifth support students who would use violence to prevent
a speaker from airing views they consider offensive.[30] The recent metaphor for this repression, *deplatforming*, is telling: being on a platform,
visible to all, is what allows a speaker to generate common knowledge.

What terrifies the censors and cancelers, it appears, is not that a
dangerous idea might be thought, or even expressed, but that it might
become common knowledge. As we have seen, people can privately
believe something with little effect on how they relate to one another.
But once something is not just known but known to be known, it can
rewrite the rules. It can change the collective understanding of how
to carry out one's affairs.

Let's spell out the fear. Suppose people harbor an opinion on
differences between sexes, races, or ethnic groups, and keep it to
themselves. Little may change. But now suppose the same opinion

is aired in public. People may be emboldened to act on the belief and use it to prejudge others, not just because it has been publicly ratified but because they anticipate that *everyone else* will act on the information. Some people might even discriminate against the members of an ethnic group despite having no pejorative opinion about them in the expectation that their customers or colleagues *will* have such opinions, and defying them would be costly. Now, all such discrimination would still be abhorrent under the principle that people should be judged by the content of their character and not by the color of their skin or the combination of their chromosomes. But when a difference is common knowledge, a person would have to avow this moral principle to treat people fairly.

The fear that common knowledge is what makes an idea dangerous helps explain the usual sequence in which a heretic who expresses an idea in a public arena must then be punished in a public arena. Pillories are passé, so in academia this takes the form of published manifestos and online petitions with hundreds of signatories (easy to gin up through social media). The heretics, for their part, are forced to grovel in public apologies and communal "restorative justice" sessions.

If this is right, we have a prediction: the speech police would not be particularly upset if a taboo idea were widely but privately known—expressed, say, in an email which everyone thought had been addressed to him or her alone because the recipient list had been suppressed or bcc'd. Even if everyone knew that everyone else got the email but thought that they were the only one who knew that, the outrage would be muted. But if the idea were commonly known by the same number of people—in an email with a lengthy cc list, say, or in a social media post—then I suspect hellfire would be loosed upon the sender.

Whenever the expression of an opinion is punished, the stage is set for people to falsify what they agree to in public, a phenomenon we saw in chapter 1 in connection with public demonstrations.[31] I can attest that this falsification of preferences is common in academia. Even politically correct professors who deny the reality of intelligence will privately gossip about the cognitive prowess, or lack thereof, of their peers and rivals. And those who deny sex differences will make mordant observations about the sex-typical concupiscence or dominance competition among the males.

When people falsify their public opinions, that in turn can create a "spiral of silence" resulting in pluralistic ignorance: the combination of private knowledge and common misconception in which everyone thinks that everyone else believes something, but no one believes it.[32] A documented example is policies of racial preferences in admissions and hiring. In today's universities, opposing these policies is a hanging offense, but every poll shows that they are unpopular with the majority of Americans (including African Americans).[33] Sure enough, students overestimate how many of their fellow students support the policy and underestimate how many oppose it.[34] I suspect this is true of many censored beliefs. Perhaps we will soon see an update of the joke about the Soviet dissident at the Moscow train station: a professor at an academic conference handing out blank sheets of paper.

⁓⁂⁓

Since the argument for academic freedom rests on the value of considering opposing ideas, it's only appropriate that I present the best case I can think of for limiting intellectual expression. This would also be in the spirit of the rationality community, which recommends "steel-manning" a view one opposes, the opposite of setting up a straw man to knock him down.[35]

Though I cannot muster an argument for censorship or punishment, I can envision the case for a different policy: Don't go there. Don't single out one side of a controversy for suppression, with all the distortions that would entail, but do deliberately leave the controversy unexplored, keeping the idea out of common knowledge. The model would be everyday social life, where we leave some observations unstated, sacrificing brutal candor for basic civility (an idea I'll return to in the closing chapter).

Any policy of deliberate agnosticism would have to be laser-focused on only the most dangerous ideas lest it condemn us to widespread ignorance. Let's consider the topic that Cory Clark and her collaborators discovered to be the most incendiary of the ten they examined in their survey of censorship in science, the possibility that average racial differences in measured intelligence have both genetic and environmental causes rather than environmental causes alone.[36] This issue has set the intellectual world ablaze every time it has been raised for more than half a century.[37] The case for not going there was first made in 1973 by Noam Chomsky, whose credentials both as a progressive and as a champion of free speech are unimpeachable. Chomsky invoked a tradeoff between scientific significance and social harm:

> Given the virtual certainty that even the undertaking of this inquiry will reinforce some of the most despicable features of our society, the seriousness of the presumed moral dilemma depends critically on the scientific significance of the issue that [the researcher] is choosing to investigate. Even if the scientific significance were immense, we should certainly question the seriousness of the dilemma, given the likely social consequences. But if the scientific interest of any finding is slight, then the dilemma vanishes.
>
> . . . A possible correlation between mean IQ and skin color

is of no greater scientific interest than a correlation between any two other arbitrarily selected traits, say, mean height and color of eyes. . . . In the present state of scientific understanding, there would appear to be little scientific interest in the discovery that one partly heritable trait correlates (or not) with another partly heritable trait. Such questions might be interesting if the results had some bearing, say, on some psychological theory, or on hypotheses about the physiological mechanisms involved, but this is not the case. . . . It would . . . be foolish to claim, in response, that "society should not be left in ignorance." Society is happily "in ignorance" of insignificant matters of all sorts.[38]

We have already seen the major possibility for harm. If differences in average intelligence are commonly known, especially if they are seen to be genetic and hard to eliminate, people might be tempted to use them as Bayesian priors in their treatment of individual African Americans, unjustly putting them at a disadvantage. It might embolden racists, make it easy to overlook systemic racism, shake the confidence of individual African Americans, and further divide the country along racial lines. For reasons like these, the French government avoids classifying its citizens by race or ethnicity at all, to the point of outlawing the collection of statistics on race and ethnicity. Perhaps we should adopt the French policy, if not by legislation (probably impossible in a country with the First Amendment), then at least by a gentleperson's agreement.[39]

But don't the demands of rationality always compel us to seek the complete truth? As Chomsky noted, not necessarily. Scientists accede to restrictions from committees for the protection of human subjects in research, and to regulations on keeping medical and other personal information confidential. In 1975 biologists imposed a moratorium on research on recombinant DNA pending the development of safeguards against the release of dangerous microorganisms. The more recent possibility that the SARS-CoV-2 virus had been genetically engineered and escaped a virology lab in Wuhan (originally suppressed as anti-Asian racism) has reinforced a call for regulating research and publication that could lead to accidental or bioterrorist pandemics. Perhaps a similar logic would call for keeping socially damaging information out of the public sphere.

Journalists, too, despite their ironclad commitment to freedom of the press, muzzle themselves in particular circumstances. They may, for example, choose not to identify confidential sources, juvenile suspects, the victims of sexual assault, or details surrounding prominent suicides. They may decline to publish the manifestos of rampage shooters, or train a camera on sports fans running onto the field.

Deciding to leave certain questions unanswered is not anti-intellectual, because it would itself be justified by reasoned argument. The quarantined topics would be highly circumscribed, and the benefits of limited agnosticism weighed against the costs of ignorance. Indeed, it could draw on the theory of common knowledge to pinpoint the harm of the idea becoming commonly known.

The case for not going there, to be sure, has many problems.[40] It's almost impossible to enforce. It faces the polar bear paradox: telling people not to think about an idea forces them to think about the idea. It may be hard to draw the line around the no-go zone so that it doesn't swallow up neighboring territories, like the study of intelligence or of continental ancestry. It forecloses the possibility of obtaining decisive evidence that racial differences are wholly environmental and eliminable, with all the social benefits that would bring.[41]

And it may be too late. Our era is obsessed with racial differences, attributing them unquestioningly to racism, which only invites curious people to wonder whether they might be attributed to other causes, intensifying the regime that criminalizes such curiosity. As the writer

Coleman Hughes has argued, there are good reasons for even the most open-minded people to want to keep the issue of race and intelligence out of mainstream conversation. But that tacit agreement should be a part of a larger commitment to color-blind policies in public and private life.[42]

Whether or not a viable case can be made for keeping a small number of particularly dangerous questions out of common knowledge, the default clearly must be intellectual freedom. As John Stuart Mill argued in his classic 1859 essay *On Liberty*, there are three reasons why an unwelcome opinion should not be suppressed.[43] For all we know, it might be true; even if it's false, it may contain a grain of truth; and even it's completely false, showing why it's false gives us a sounder understanding of what *is* true—"He who knows only his own side of the case, knows little of that." And if it turns out that an unwelcome idea is true, we had better accommodate our moral sensibilities to it, since no good can come from sanctifying a delusion.

This might be easier than speechophobes fear. The moral order did not collapse when people accepted that the Earth was not the center of the universe, nor that humans were descended from apes. The moral fervor that academics expend on demonizing heterodox ideas would be better directed to reinforcing the case that our cherished ethical convictions don't hang on tenuous empirical assumptions. It's wrong to mistreat or discriminate against people because of their race, sex, sexual orientation, or gender identity, regardless of where any differences between them originate. It's wrong to abuse or neglect children, to exploit vulnerable populations, to poison the environment, to wage offensive wars, to punish victimless personal choices, not because of some dogma that might be overturned if people were allowed to look too closely, but because they are inconsistent with deeply held and intellectually defensible moral commitments.

At the same time, we have seen that the urge to censor is a fear of common knowledge, and common knowledge is no small thing. The tension between aggressively expanding our knowledge to advance human understanding, and hypocritically keeping some knowledge private to preserve human harmony, is inherent to our condition, and a fitting subject for the final chapter.

9
Radical Honesty, Rational Hypocrisy

Why not everything should be common knowledge

The story of the Tower of Babel narrates the idea that when humans coordinate their actions though common knowledge, the sky's the limit on what they can accomplish. A shared language is the ultimate generator of common knowledge, but it's far from the only one. As we have seen in the preceding chapters, much of human social life consists in generating and partaking of the common knowledge necessary for coordination on scales large and small.

From the time we are small children, we follow the gaze of others and observe them observing what we are observing. We learn thousands of words, each of which conveys a meaning because we tacitly assume that others mean by it the same thing we do. We use these words to harmonize our activities: to rendezvous, to hunt, to attack, to divide the labor, to take turns or split a resource, to make complementary goods for a meal or a market. We exchange our beliefs and our confidence in them with other rational agents, expecting to converge on agreement. We signal communal feelings with prayers and pledges and declarations. We can promise, request, bribe, threaten, or proposition. We use metaphors of a conspicuous sound or object to express our awareness of our common awareness.

We are also outfitted with several nonverbal channels for generating common knowledge. We look each other in the eye to threaten, to seduce, or to make private knowledge common. We blush to acknowledge that we know others think we have flouted a norm. We laugh to lower someone's status or to make it known that we aren't competing for status. We shed tears to concede vulnerability or neediness, or to make it known that we appreciate the sublime. We glower to show we mean business.

We fill our lives with rituals and symbols that serve as focal points for coordination. Physical contact, collective meals, bodily adornment, shared creeds, and synchronized movement bind us in communal relations. Big, tall, high, first, bright, and loud advertise dominance or status. A public insult or challenge may threaten it, calling for public retaliation. Flipping coins, dividing in half, or taking turns can indicate fairness. Splitting the difference or settling on a round number clinches a deal. Dietary, sartorial, tonsorial, and diurnal practices broadcast our membership in groups with shared equilibria. Ceremonies of majority, marriage, investiture, confirmation, inauguration, and coronation broadcast the assignment of roles within a community. Public punishment of a public infraction serves to enforce a moral norm.

Our complex institutions, too, depend on displays of common knowledge. Formal laws, like informal norms, may be enforced by public punishments, but they may be self-enforcing when mere awareness commends them as focal points in settling disputes. Property consists of mutual recognition of the right to use, alter, and dispose of a resource, preempting costly disputes over who possesses it. Money functions as a medium of exchange, value, and accounting as long as everyone knows that everyone treats it in those ways, an agreement reassured by displays of solidity and solvency. Technologies depend on standards that may be suboptimal on engineering grounds but optimal on social and economic grounds once enough users get locked into them. Political leaders owe their power to laws, and establish their positions with ceremonies and symbols that align people in recognizing that power.

The dynamics of societal change are driven by the creation of new common knowledge. Currencies may hyperinflate, banks may collapse, securities may bubble and bust, or commodities may vanish from the shelves because of a self-fulfilling remark or news story. A novel technology, speculative asset, or status symbol that works only when popular may need the spark of conspicuous advertising. Politicians in democracies gain their power by clamoring for name recognition, accruing momentum, avoiding gaffes, and attracting voters afraid of wasting their votes. They may be deposed by a mass public demonstration, often triggered by a communal outrage. The authority of an emperor may even be challenged by an overheard remark of a child.

And in the international arena, nation-states exist because they are recognized to exist, and they belong to a league in which they are anointed as equals despite vast differences in land, might, wealth, and population. They open or arm their borders in response to displays of friendship or disrespect by their leaders. They accede to agreements brokered by toothless mediators, courts, and religious leaders. They go to war in response to insults and outrages, and in quests for honor and greatness on the world's stage and in the history books.

Yet for all the ingenuity that people expend in creating common knowledge, they also rack their brains in figuring how to prevent it. Misbehaving children avoid catching the glances of their parents, a strategy they never outgrow: adults, too, avoid eye contact with onlookers when they commit a faux pas. People may try not to notice a need for action when they sense that others might step in. They may fail to recognize each other in compromising circumstances, or pretend to be asleep to enjoy an illicit kiss. They may fail to disclose an inadvertent act of disloyalty. They may try to pass as white, or straight, or slim. They donate anonymously while hoping the gift leaks, and conceal their thirst for status, approval, and authenticity as they strive for all of them. They accept pretexts, open secrets, and flimsy excuses. They disguise their imperatives as idle questions and hypotheticals. They veil their bribes, threats, and sexual come-ons in innuendo. They conceal their complicity in evil acts using euphemism and circumlocution. We all are aware of efforts to stymie awareness, and exercise our talents at seeing through them in brainteasers, mysteries, and jokes.

And just as common knowledge may be generated at scale to enable our formal institutions, it may be squelched at scale to protect them. Central bankers avoid market-spooking words, and speak in platitudes like Delphic oracles. Scientific communities censor, self-censor, and retract research felt to threaten their ideal of social justice. Diplomats communicate to the public in an argot that conceals obvious conflict. The inner circle of a doddering leader may act as if all is normal. Leaders of countries may choose to neither confirm nor deny an assassination, an act of sabotage, or possession of weapons of mass destruction. The international community may sanctify fictitious sovereignty over a patch of land even when control of the territory encircled by the dotted lines on a map is aspirational.

So why don't we cut the crap? If common knowledge is necessary for coordination, and coordination is a win–win game, why do we keep so much knowledge private? Why the fig leaves, the white lies, the elephants in the room?

Certainly the historical trend has been toward transparency and openness—toward making private knowledge common. Though people probably have always harbored some skepticism about miracles and hero myths, for eons they have publicly affirmed them. But modern scientists have had no compunctions about disenchanting the world (as Max Weber put it) by unmasking comfortable illusions. Professional historians, too, no longer sanctify uplifting hero myths, but expose the crimes of the past and exalted leaders' feet of clay. Journalism prides itself on doing the same with the present. Democratic governments voluntarily open up their records in freedom-of-information acts and involuntarily suffer massive disclosures by whistleblowers and contributors to WikiLeaks, often to wide acclaim.

Alongside these changes, our social interactions have steadily drifted from the unspoken bonds of communal sharing and authority ranking to the explicit contracts of markets and other rational-legal institutions.[1] Our personal relationships all the while are being transformed by a tide of *informalization*: the erosion of titles, taboos, and trappings of hierarchy in favor of casualness, candor, and trappings of equality.[2] As Cole Porter wrote in 1934 in the midst of this process, "In olden days a glimpse of stocking was looked on as something shocking. Now heaven knows, anything goes." And Porter did not live to see oversharing on social media.

Many benefits have come from puncturing genteel hypocrisy and bringing taboos into the light of day. Cronyism and corruption in government have been exposed. Oppressive mores such as the subordination of women and the stigma against homosexuality have been deconstructed and decimated. Our understanding of the living world, including our own species, has expanded. And we have been relieved of many of the burdens of formality and pretense in everyday life.

How much can we continue to bring things into the open? Might we expect all knowledge to become common knowledge? Might we hope for it, since honesty is the best policy? Of course, honesty really is the best policy when it comes to our stated promises and duties. And in the other direction, some things, like passwords, must be private by design. But when it comes to the countless little rituals and pretenses of genteel social interaction, would we be better off if we were transparent about the knowledge that we know each other to have but discreetly keep to ourselves?

In reality, calling for complete honesty is the ultimate dishonesty. No one really wants it, sometimes for good reason. As we saw in the previous chapter, those disenchanting scientists are all too happy to censor ideas that threaten to disenchant their own vision of an ideal world. Editorialists condemn politicians for their dishonesty, and then report a "scandal" when they are too honest.

A historic example took place in the closing weeks of the 1976 presidential campaign, when Jimmy Carter agreed to a long-form interview with *Playboy*, a feature of the magazine that was highly regarded in its day. When he was asked whether his public image of straitlaced piety might turn off voters, he replied that he was in no position to claim moral superiority. Quoting the Sermon on the Mount, Carter explained that Jesus said having an impure desire in one's heart is tantamount to committing an actual sin, and confessed, "I've looked on a lot of women with lust. I've committed adultery in my heart many times."[3] Hardly a shocking revelation, especially from a notably monogamous politician. But his lead in the polls evaporated, and he barely eked out a victory over Gerald Ford that November.

Three decades later Hillary Clinton would not be so lucky. The political scientist John Mueller recounts the leak of frank emails among her strategists that may have doomed her presidential campaign:

> Hackers, apparently from Russia, . . . had fun getting into electronic mail connected with the Democratic National Committee. One dump of this information embarrassingly showed that Committee leaders, who were supposed to be neutral on who the party candidate for president would be, were decidedly in favor of Clinton—a revelation of almost stupefying banality to anyone who knows about American politics. Another dump showed that Clinton, like every other politician in the history of the planet, was capable of saying one thing to one group and another to another.[4]

Anyone who has nibbled on the clickbait at the bottom of a web page may have consumed a listicle like "The Most Embarrassing Instances of Famous People Forgetting Their Mic Was On." A typical hot-mic scandal was Barack Obama commiserating with French president Nicolas Sarkozy in 2011 about having to deal with a duplicitous Benjamin Netanyahu.[5] Hence the journalist Michael Kinsley's definition of a *gaffe* in Washington: when a politician says something that is true.

Political leaders, being human, bond with each other over gossip, candid remarks, and off-color humor, and they get things done through hardheaded deliberations about how to push their agenda over obstacles and opposition. Yet when their plans are made common knowledge, commentators will announce they are shocked, shocked, that politicians are so calculating and duplicitous. This has always been so: in 1792, Alexander Hamilton remarked of the Constitutional Convention:

> Had the deliberations been open while going on, the clamours of faction would have prevented any satisfactory result. Had they been afterwards disclosed, much food would have been afforded to inflammatory declamation. Propositions made without due reflection, and perhaps abandoned by the proposers themselves, on more mature reflection, would have been handles for a profusion of ill-natured accusation.[6]

The perils of making private deliberations common knowledge serves as a counterweight to the idea that all the dealings of democratic government must be public as they unfold in real time, and that leaking them is always heroic.

It also reminds us of the preciousness of privacy in the lives of individuals. Totalitarian states in fiction, like *Nineteen Eighty-Four*, and in reality, like communist East Germany and China, tolerate no zone of privacy, obliterating them with electronic surveillance and networks of anonymous informants. The rationale is, If you aren't doing anything wrong, what do you have to hide? But of course even the most innocent of us has a great deal to hide. We know our relationships and reputations would lie in smithereens if the convivial conversations we enjoy with friends and intimates, with all their mordant remarks and politically incorrect wisecracks, were ever made public. Again, this would appear to be a part of the human condition. As Blaise Pascal put it in 1670, "I lay it down as a fact that if all men knew what others say of them, there would not be four friends in the world."[7] I suspect that one of the reasons that Gen Zers (born in the mid-1990s or later) suffer from such acute anxiety and loneliness, despite unprecedented opportunities to connect with each other, is that they live in a surveillance regime where peers can snitch to "bias response hotlines" about their "microaggressions," and a corps of offense archeologists can dig through years of social media posts to unearth shards of bigotry.[8]

Authentic human relationships depend on the hypocrisy of keeping many kinds of private and reciprocal knowledge out of common knowledge. A popular T-shirt reads, "I'm not rude. I just say what everyone else is thinking." But of course that's often what rudeness *is*. This paradox is comic gold for the writers of mistaken-identity plots, whose characters entertainingly blurt out confidences not intended for their hearers. My favorite example adds a layer of recursive mentalizing to the plot and plays out our hypocrisy about our hypocrisy. In the comedy *Tootsie*, an unemployed actor, Michael (played by Dustin Hoffman), disguises himself as a middle-aged actress and wins a part in a soap opera, fooling everyone, including fellow actress Julie (played by Jessica Lange). They become close friends, even as Michael is besotted with her, and during a session of late-night girl talk Julie laments:

You know what I wish? That a guy could be honest enough just to walk right up to me and say, "Listen. You know, I'm confused about this, too. I could lay a big line on you, do a lot of role-playing. But the simple truth is: I find you very interesting. And I'd really like to make love with you." Simple as that. Wouldn't that be a relief?[9]

In a later scene her wish is granted when an undisguised and unrecognized Michael crosses paths with her and says exactly that. Before he can finish his candid come-on she throws a glass of wine in his face and storms away.

Writers of science fiction have the additional luxury of staging a thought experiment: through a stroke of supernatural intervention, a character is incapable of lying or even keeping his thoughts private.[10] Hilarity ensues as the character lets slip the tactless, insulting, or lewd thoughts that anyone might guess he is thinking but which socially competent adults keep to themselves (as in *Liar Liar*, when a lawyer played by Jim Carrey meets a buxom new employee who beams that everyone is really nice to her and he ventures an explanation as to why). Tellingly, the plots proceed from episodes of awkwardness and outrage to a denouement of relief all around as the gift of benign dishonesty is restored. (Perhaps just as tellingly, often a dysfunctional relationship, such as the marriage between an overbearing husband and his unappreciated wife, is repaired by the interlude of forced candor.)

Truth is stranger than fiction, and we are living through a real experiment in making private knowledge common. A movement called Radical Honesty, founded in 1997 by the psychotherapist Brad Blanton, advocates complete candor in all personal interactions, avoiding even white lies.[11] The rationale is not that lying is unethical but that it's "the primary cause of suffering," whose antidote is "living honestly." Since its founding it has gained adherents in Silicon Valley and in the rationality community, and has been featured in several films and TV series. The psychiatrist and rationalist Scott Alexander comments, "The advantage of radical honesty is that it provides a nice bright-line rule for when to tell the truth. The disadvantage of radical honesty is that it ruins your life for no benefit whatsoever."[12] As in the comedies, practitioners blab uncouth things like telling a boss that they are eyeing a new job or a girlfriend that she should lose some weight. Unlike in the comedies, there is no happy ending: they get fired or dumped.

A revealing interview in *Esquire* with Blanton by the journalist A. J. Jacobs (entitled "I Think You're Fat") makes it clear that practicing radical honesty is not baring one's authentic self but just another pretense—an act, a put-on, a shtick.[13] During the interview, Blanton insults Jacobs and *Esquire* while conspicuously belching, adjusting his crotch, picking his nose, and passing gas. It comes out that he enjoys the thrill of seeing how far he can go. And he discovered that it's an effective way to bed women, which stands to reason: if a player discounts the emotional costs of a rejection (the upper right cell in the innuendo game from chapter 7, page 247), the optimal level of directness soars. By charming women with lines like "I want to go to bed with you" or "Wanna fuck?" he gets many nos but enough yeses to have won him five hundred sexual partners (and since he's an advocate of radical honesty, we know he's telling the truth). Jacobs observes, "There's a fine line between radical honesty and creepiness. Or actually no line at all."

And then there's a famous recent experiment in radical honesty: the workplace culture of Bridgewater Associates, the world's largest hedge fund firm. Bridgewater was founded by the financier and business guru Ray Dalio, who calls his version Radical Transparency, and implemented it to avoid "office politics" and employees who "talk behind each other's backs." Instead they openly rate, and often berate, each other's performances, all the while surveilled by video cameras recording their interactions for future struggle sessions. The results could be material for another dark comedy. The company's "radical transparency" turned out to be "for thee but not for me." Its trading strategies are shrouded in mystery, hidden from everyone but an elect circle. Employees are muzzled by strict (and possibly illegal) nondisclosure agreements. And Dalio himself dismisses (and reportedly punishes) criticism of his policies.[14] The workplace has been described as a "hellscape" of bullying and paranoia, with employees reduced to tears at regular "public hangings" and an unusually high turnover rate.[15] When Dalio left in 2022, his successor promised to "rewire" the company.[16]

⁂

The historical trend toward openness has a natural limit, with radical honesty turning out to be the greatest hypocrisy of all. People need to keep many thoughts private, however illogical that might appear at first glance. It's easy to "explain" this diffidence by appealing to common sense: we're naturally sensitive and inhibited and polite, and want to avoid offending people or causing tension and embarrassment and awkwardness and bad feelings. All true, but too glib to be a satisfying explanation. *Why* did evolution equip us with these feelings, rather than a willingness to let it all hang out?

The logic of coordination and common knowledge applied to social relationships, as I have explained it in this book, provides an answer. Humans are not independent monads bouncing around like molecules in an ideal gas. The evolutionary niche of *Homo sapiens* is one of massive interdependence. Some of this working together is altruistic cooperation, where I'll scratch your back if you scratch mine, but much of it is mutualistic coordination, in which one hand washes the other. Life presents us with many stag hunts, coffee dates, dollars to divide, collisions to avoid, groups to organize, fights to avert, and other positive-sum games. All require common knowledge so that each player is sure the other opts for the same win–win equilibrium.

That includes our informal social relationships, which are held together by a compact of conventions.[17] The conventions are idealizations, verging on fictions. Yet in a strict logical sense they are necessary for the coordination equilibria we enjoy, and undermining them with contrary indications can poison that coordination. We often keep the knowledge that would undermine a social convention private, not because of some uptight fuddy-duddy inhibition, but for rational, indeed mathematically provable, reasons.

Take the communal sharing that grounds our relationships with family, lovers, friends, and colleagues. Communal sharing is based on the fiction that everyone is an equal member of a collective in which each unstintingly sacrifices toward the good of the whole. It's a lovely model, and it may be true as far as it goes, but it goes only so far. The overlap of interests that natural selection builds into families is only partial, with siblings competing over parental investment, parents pulled in different directions by their current and future children, and couples divided by loyalty toward blood kin and by opportunities for infidelity.[18] And when everyone contributes to a common pot, some have the opportunity to stint, hoard, or hog. These ever-present realities contradict the commonly held conventions that make the warmth of communality possible, and it's natural that they be kept out of common knowledge (while being understood privately so that people can protect themselves from exploitation).

The authority ranking that orders individuals in stable hierarchies also rests on useful fictions: that the hierarchy is legitimate, grounded in differences in talent, strength, generosity, initiative, and other valuable traits, and that the higher-ups have an interest in the well-being of the collective, including a paternalistic or pastoral responsibility to those below them. In reality, leaders may have assumed their station by brute force, undeserved inheritance, or sheer luck, and power inevitably corrupts. Everyone privately senses this. But both for self-protection and to preserve legitimate chains of command in complex organizations, people are sometimes best off not speaking their minds about the infirmities of their higher-ups.

Relationships based on equality matching, for their part, rest on mutually accepted informal conventions for apportioning goodies equitably. Yet individuals, never perfectly selfless, are ever tempted to bend the rules, game the system, fudge the numbers, cook the books, pull strings, or put a thumb on the scale. Now and again we entertain private suspicions that our acquaintances are not above these ploys. But if the suspicions were made common knowledge, then flouting the rules would be expected, and no one would agree to abide by them in the first place. Indeed, when the possibility of widespread cheating is common knowledge, we abandon the warm relational models based on trust and turn to cold formal markets and other rational-legal institutions, where every rule is common knowledge.

Even if overt cheating in social life is rare, the temptations may be abundant, as Jimmy Carter reminded us. The evolutionary anthropologist Donald Symons argued that the treacheries metaphorically desired by our selfish genes are seldom played out in overt behavior. That is because when we choose an action, we must compromise our wishes with those of other people and the constraints of the world. Our desires, though, have the run of our imaginations.[19] Consciousness, Symons suggests, is designed to scope out rare opportunities, particularly those with an outsize impact on fitness, such as sex, violence, and leaps of status. Routine calculations, in contrast, such as those that regulate our physiology or which direct a well-practiced skill like walking, are relegated to the boiler room of unconscious processing. So as we play the routine games of life, our imaginations seethe with wicked fantasies.

Symons, of course, was not the first to notice this. In 1651 Thomas Hobbes wrote, "The secret thoughts of a man run over all things, holy, prophane, clean, obscene, grave, and light, without shame, or blame."[20] James Fitzgerald Stephen, in his *History of the Criminal Law in England*, put it more pithily: "If criminal thoughts could be punished, all mankind would be criminals."[21] Modern surveys bear them out: substantial majorities of people report having fantasized about killing someone they resent (often with torture), about coercing someone into sex or being coerced, and about having sex with an inappropriate partner.[22]

We have private knowledge about our own minds: we know we have illicit desires. As soon as it dawns on us that we are not unique, we also have reciprocal knowledge: most people realize that most people have illicit desires. Yet voicing one of these desires aloud, generating the common knowledge in which each of us knows the other knows of the desire, and knows that, ad infinitum, is no small matter. You would be ill-advised to tell your boss that you have mused about killing him, or to inform either your spouse or a colleague that you daydream about sleeping with the latter, even if those possibilities may have been privately suspected. That is because the announcement would pollute the pool of assumptions that allow you to get along.

None of this implies that we should primly refrain from ever bringing up any private thought that makes people uncomfortable. Our tacit conventions can conceal many injustices and irrationalities, and social reform often begins with a loudmouth pointing to the pachyderm in the parlor or a juvenile remarking on the nudity of an imperial leader. Psychotherapy, too, may proceed by encouraging patients to see and challenge the unsaid norms in a relationship that may have locked them into dysfunction. Even the sci-fi and sitcom thought experiments on mandatory honesty usually depict some good that came out of the characters' ordeal. It's just that there's a logic to hypocrisy, and not every instance is a prudish anachronism.

꧁

A rational understanding of hypocrisy, grounded in the idea that common knowledge enables coordination, can stop us from ruining our personal lives with runaway candor. It can also prevent us from jettisoning some of the hypocrisies in public life that may seem obsolete but serve a real purpose.

The police often choose to look away from infractions that the offenders try to veil, however thinly, such as "escort services," drug paraphernalia advertised as tobacco accessories, and public drinking from a whiskey bottle in a paper bag. Enforcing the letter of every law would be exorbitant and intrusive, but allowing it to be common knowledge that laws may be openly flouted would signal that the legal system has forfeited its authority.[23]

In the 2022 Super Bowl commercial, when the framers of the American Constitution explain to Larry David's alter ego that the people shall have the right to vote, he asks incredulously "Even the stupid ones?" Democracies face the inherent problem that the most popular policies may not be the most beneficial or practicable ones, and have to quietly balance the need to respect the will of the people with the need to implement the knowledge of experts. Larry David could say it; politicians had better not.

Politicians and officials may also wish to avoid speaking too clearly about the laws of arithmetic. Resources are finite, and funds allocated to one goal must be subtracted from those allocated to another. Good things cost money, and there are an unlimited number of good things, so planners must make tradeoffs. Yet people are outraged when they are forced to consider trading off a secular value, like money, against a sacred one, like human life, children's welfare, or the environment. Politics is the art of keeping these tradeoffs out of common knowledge.[24] A politician would be ill-advised to say, "The government spends too much on the health of seniors," or "Our policy on traffic safety is that a human life is worth 9.6 million dollars and no more," though both may be privately known among decision-makers. The alternative, "We cannot put a price on human life" (or on the welfare of children, or of seniors), is nonsensical, yet it ratifies the fiction of unstinting mutual care that we demand of our communal relationships.

In the international arena, the fate of the world may depend on what is kept out of common knowledge. Israel's policy of "deliberate ambiguity," neither affirming nor denying that it has nuclear weapons, furnishes the deterrent value that makes possession worthwhile without provoking its Middle Eastern rivals to acquire their own to save face. Taiwan is patently a sovereign state, and the United States and the European Union unofficially treat it that way while officially denying that it exists. The reason for the duplicity is that publicly acknowledging the reality would be an affront to the People's Republic of China, which has staked its reputation on being the sole ruler of all of historic China. The history of violence sparked by communal outrages reminds us that symbolic affronts can have catastrophic consequences.

In all these cases, the people who maintain the hypocrisy could explain why they are maintaining it, but may choose not to undermine the rationale by stating the explanation in so many words. They may resort to euphemism and discreet omission, and in doing so they are far from being irrational. In a similar way, if scholars tacitly decide that the best way to handle a socially pernicious and intellectually minor topic is not to go there, they would not be surrendering to the ignorance of a dark age, but may be deploying a higher-order rationality which factors in the effects of making discoveries common knowledge. That could even be true if they reasoned that the best way of implementing such a policy is not to speak too long and loud about why they are implementing it.

All these trains of thought are exercises of recursive mentalizing, the cognitive talent that underlies common knowledge. The power of cognition to take its own outputs and feed them back into more cognition is a theme that has run through all my books, and it fills me with awe even after decades of pondering human intelligence. It underlies the vast expressive power of language, its ability to convey ideas from nursery rhymes to metaphysics.[25] It explains how human intelligence, having evolved to reason about survival and reproduction, can be extended to reason about science, philosophy, and mathematics.[26] It explains how human progress is possible, when people rethink their norms and institutions.[27] And it implies that rationality itself is limitless: even when an application of rationality is flawed, we can step back, rationally analyze how we are deploying our rationality, and devise a higher-order rationality that subsumes it.[28] It's what's most special about our kind: we not only have thoughts, but have thoughts about our thoughts, and thoughts about our thoughts about our thoughts.

NOTES

Chapter 1: The Emperor, the Elephant, and the Matzo Ball

1. Hans Christian Andersen's 1837 story "The Emperor's New Clothes" was inspired by earlier folktales and led to many adaptations. In Andersen's version, the sex of the child is unspecified; the child merely says to the father, "He hasn't got anything on"; the observation is spread in whispers from an overhearer to the rest of the onlookers; and the effect on the crowd is unspecified. The popular memory of the story, in which the child is a boy, he shouted his observation, and the crowd reacted with "ridicule and scorn," may have come from the 1952 song "The King's New Clothes," written by Frank Loesser and sung by Danny Kaye in the film *Hans Christian Andersen*.

2. Several scholars have been credited with originating the concept of common knowledge, including the political scientist Thomas Schelling (1960), the philosophers Robert Nozick (1963) and David Lewis (1969), the mathematician Robert John Aumann (1976), and the sociologist Morris Friedell (1969). Other seminal works include H. Clark & Carlson 1981; Monderer & Samet 1989; Rubinstein 1989; Schiffer 1972; Stalnaker 1978. For accessible explanations, see Aaronson 2015; Chwe 2001; De Freitas, Thomas, et al. 2019; Geanakoplos 1992; Pinker 2007 chap. 8; Thomas, De Freitas, et al. 2016; Vanderschraaf & Sillari 2023.

3. The most accessible previous book on common knowledge is the political scientist Michael Chwe's *Rational Ritual*, published in 2001. Common knowledge also figures prominently in *The Elephant in the Brain* by the economist Robin Hanson and the science writer Kevin Simler (2018) and in *Meeting at Grand Central* by the anthropologist Lee Cronk and the political scientist Beth Leech (2013). I know of no books on common knowledge written by psychologists.

4. *Mutual knowledge* in linguistics: H. Clark & Carlson 1981; Smith 1982. Previous usage: Pinker 2007, p. 457, note 57. The difference between the vernacular and technical meanings of *common knowledge*: Lederman 2018, notes 1 and 2.

5. For example, the entry "Common Knowledge" in the *Stanford Encyclopedia of Philosophy* (Vanderschraaf & Sillari 2023) defines mutual knowledge as universal private knowledge.

6. Pinker 1999/2011, chap. 1.

7. Chomsky 1972/2006; see Pinker 1994/2007 for an accessible explanation.

8. From "Like a Pebble in Space Is Like a Planet," *Typo Mag*, issue 10 (undated), https:// www.typomag.com/issue10/teicher.html. The passage quoted here is seven lines in the original poem; I have italicized "mouse."

9. Conventionality in children's word learning: E. Clark 1993.

10. Diesendruck & Markson 2001.

11. Reciprocal altruism: Dawkins 1976/2016; Trivers 1971.

12. For updates and elaborations, see Pinker 2011, pp. 532–37.

13. *How the Mind Works*, pp. 402–7; *The Blank Slate*, pp. 243–44, 255–61; *The Better Angels of Our Nature*, pp. 532–37; *Enlightenment Now*, p. 415; *Rationality*, pp. 238–42.

14. In Thomas, DeScioli, et al. 2014. Others came to this conclusion before me, including Cronk & Leech 2013; McAdams 2009; Skyrms 2004; Goldstein 2010.

15. The classic analysis of Rendezvous and focal points is Schelling 1960.

16. Lewis 1969; see also Chwe 2001.

17. From posts on X and Instagram, https://x.com/harari_yuval/status /1763230424682111367.

18. Y. N. Harari, "Humans are a post-truth species," *The Guardian*, Aug. 5, 2018.

19. For an elaboration on this point, see C. R. Hallpike, "A response to Yuval Harari's 'Sapiens: A brief history of humankind,'" *New English Review*, Dec. 2017, https:// www.newenglishreview.org/articles/a-response-to-yuval-hararis-sapiens-a-brief -history-of-humankind/.

20. S. Pinker, "Rock star psychologist Steven Pinker explains why #thedress looked white, not blue," *Forbes*, Feb. 28, 2015.

21. K. Chang, "A math problem from Singapore goes viral: When is Cheryl's birthday?" *New York Times*, April 14, 2015.

22. Dawkins 1976/2016, p. 372.

23. Chwe 2001.

24. https://www.youtube.com/watch?v=VtvjbmoDx-I.

25. https://www.youtube.com/watch?v=hWMnbJJpeZc.

26. Aaronson 2015.

27. Protests and common knowledge: Chwe 2001; Lohmann 1994.

28. Preference falsification in autocracies: Kuran 1989; Lohmann 1994. Spiral of silence: Noelle-Neumann 1974. Pluralistic ignorance: Centola, Willer, & Macy 2005; Willer, Kuwabara, & Macy 2009. See also the Wikipedia entry "Abilene Paradox."

29. *Gandhi* was directed by Richard Attenborough from a screenplay by John Briley.

30. Data and dynamics of nonviolent resistance: Chenoweth 2020; Chenoweth & Stephan 2011.

31. Nonviolent revolutions: Carnation (Portugal, 1974), Yellow (Philippines, 1986), Coconut (Papua New Guinea, 1988), Velvet (Czechoslovakia, 1989, and Armenia, 2018), Rose (Georgia, 2003 and 2004), Orange (Ukraine, 2004), Tulip (Kyrgystan, 2005), Cedar (Lebanon, 2005), Saffron (Myanmar, 2007), Melon (Kyrgystan, 2010), Jasmine (Tunisia, 2011).

32. Dobson 2012.

33. King, Pan, & Roberts 2014; Roberts 2018.

34. E. Barry, "Sound of post-Soviet protest: Claps and beeps." *New York Times,* July 14, 2011; A. Marantz, "How to stop a power grab," *New Yorker,* Nov. 16, 2020.

35. Radio Free Europe/Radio Liberty, "A Belarusian protester walks into a bar . . . ," *Transmission,* July 12, 2011, https://www.rferl.org/a/transmission_belarus_jokes /24263321.html.

36. Also attributed to the memoirist Elena Gorokhova in *A Mountain of Crumbs* (2010), though she may have been quoting a common saying.

37. J. Ronson, "How one stupid tweet blew up Justine Sacco's life," *New York Times,* Feb. 12, 2015.

38. The First Law, he explained, is: Always have something to print.

39. According to the Google Ngram Viewer, https://books.google.com/ngrams/; Michel, Shen, et al. 2010.

40. https://canceledpeople.org/cancellations/. Academic cancellations: Scholars Under Fire Database, Foundation for Individual Rights and Expression, https://www .thefire.org/research-learn/scholars-under-fire.

41. *The Atlantic,* April 11, 2022. See also Jesse Singal, "Social media is making us dumber. Here's Exhibit A," *New York Times,* Jan. 11, 2018. Exhibit A was an attack on me.

42. The online disinhibition effect: Suler 2004. Trolls and sadists: Buckels, Trapnell, & Paulhus 2014.

43. Chwe 2001; Cronk & Leech 2013; Lewis 1969.

44. Tooby 2017; Williams 2022.

45. Finkel, Bail, et al. 2020.

46. Humanitarian revolution: Pinker 2011, chap. 4.

47. Third-party punishment: Henrich 2006; Krasnow, Cosmides, et al. 2012.

48. From *Did I Ever Tell You How Lucky You Are?* (New York: Random House, 1973).

49. DeScioli & Kurzban 2009, 2018.

50. For experimental evidence and computer modeling that supports the idea that people in groups can become trapped into beliefs they individually reject when they join in punishment to avoid becoming the one punished, see Centola, Willer, & Macy 2005; Willer, Kuwabara, & Macy 2009.

51. Children ignore intentions: Cushman, Sheketoff, et al. 201?. Preliterate and small-scale societies ignore intentions: Henrich 2020; Posner 1980.

52. DeScioli & Kurzban 2009; Hoffman & Yoeli 2022.

53. A. Miller, "Why I wrote *The Crucible*," *New Yorker*, Oct. 13, 1996. The order of the two excerpts has been flipped.

54. Hoffman & Yoeli 2022; Pinker 2007; Pinker, Nowak, & Lee 2008; Smaldino, Flamson, & McElreath 2018.

55. Lakoff & Johnson 1980. For critiques of the idea when it is taken too far, see "The Metaphor Metaphor" in Pinker 2007 and "Block That Metaphor," in Pinker 2006.

56. *When Harry Met Sally* (1989) was directed by Rob Reiner and written by Nora Ephron.

57. Season 6, episode 22 (1995), "The Face Painter," written by Larry David and Fred Stoller.

Chapter 2: Common Knowledge and Common Sense

1. Aaronson 2015.

2. According to Geanakoplos 1992, the earliest known version appeared in 1953 in *Littlewood's Miscellania*, although "it was already well-known and had caused a sensation in Europe some years before." Other versions: Aaronson 2015; Gamow & Stern 1958; Gardner 1984; Geanakoplos 1992; Vanderschraaf & Sillari 2023.

3. By the cartoonist Randall Munroe (n.d.).

4. Cathcart & Klein 2007.

5. Binmore & Samuelson 2001; Geanakoplos 1992; Halpern & Moses 1990; Morris 2002; Rubinstein 1989.

6. Geanakoplos 1992.

7. Loopholes in the Electronic Mail game: Binmore & Samuelson 2001; Dulleck 1997; Monderer & Samet 1989.

8. Knowledge: Ichikawa & Steup 2018.

9. Possibly apocryphal, or a paraphrase of a saying by Josh Billings; see Kim A. McDonald, "Many of Mark Twain's famed humorous sayings are found to have been misattributed to him," *Chronicle of Higher Education*, Sept. 4, 1991, A8.

10. Monderer & Samet 1989.

11. Dalkiran, Hoffman, et al. 2012; Morris 2002.

12. Halpern & Moses 1990.

13. Fiske 1991; Lee & Pinker 2010; Pinker 2007.

14. The long goodbye and the Electronic Mail game: Binmore & Samuelson 2001.

15. The 2007 animated film, based on the TV sitcom created by Matt Groening, was directed by David Silverman and written by James L. Brooks.

16. Aumann 1976. Analyses: Aaronson 2015; Cowen & Hanson 2004; Geanakoplos 1992; Morris 2002.

17. Pinker 2021, chap. 5.

18. Conditional probability: Pinker 2021, chap. 4.

19. Pinker 2021, chap. 5; Tversky & Kahneman 1974.

20. The last aphorism is from the linguist Ann Farmer.

21. Aumann visualizes this dialogue at the end of his paper to make the theorem more intuitive (p. 1238). The theorem itself does not assume a dialogue between agents exchanging posteriors until they converge; it only shows that a state with different ones is impossible. As discussed below, Geanakoplos and Polemarchakis (1982) spell out how the dialogue would work; see also Aaronson 2015.

22. Geanakoplos & Polemarchakis 1982; see also Aaronson 2015; Hanson 2002.

23. Geanakoplos & Polemarchakis 1982, Proposition 2, p. 198.

24. Aaronson 2015; Cowen & Hanson 2004.

25. Probably his fellow economist Paul Samuelson said it: *Quote Investigator*, July 22, 2011, https://quoteinvestigator.com/2011/07/22/keynes-change-mind/.

26. Aaronson 2015; see also Milgrom & Stokey 1982.

27. For example, Geddes 2022.

28. Aaronson 2015; Cowen & Hanson 2004; Hanson 2006; Harsanyi 1983.

29. Trivers 2011.

30. Galef 2021; Raemon 2017; Tetlock & Gardner 2015. See also the blogs *Astral Codex Ten* by Scott Alexander, https://slatestarcodex.com/, *Shtetl-Optimized* by Scott Aaronson, and *Overcoming Bias* by Robin Hanson https://www.overcomingbias.com/.

31. Lakoff & Johnson 1980, p. 12.

Chapter 3: Fun and Games

1. The title has also been used for a book on game theory by Ken Binmore.

2. The rudiments are explained in chapter 8, "Self and Others," in my book *Rationality*. Other introductions: Binmore 1991, 2007; Hoffman & Yoeli 2022; Luce & Raiffa 1957; Rosenthal 2011.

3. Coordination games versus Prisoners' Dilemmas: Binmore 2007; Goldstein 2010; McAdams 2009.

4. The *noms de guerre* of some shady associates of my late uncle Johnny.

5. Importance of the Prisoners' Dilemma: Dawkins 1976/2016; Pinker 2011, 2021; Poundstone 1992.

6. Holzinger 2008; see table 6.5. DeScioli and Kurzban (2007) suggest that the seventy-eight games can be reduced to just four basic types.

7. Goldstein 2010; McAdams 2009; Skyrms 2004; Cronk & Leech 2013; see also Baumard, André, & Sperber 2013; Columbus, Molho, et al. 2021; Curry, Jones Chesters, & Van Lissa 2019; Thomas, DeScioli, et al. 2014.

8. Cheap talk: Aumann 1990; Farrell & Rabin 1996.

9. Dawkins 1976/2016; Simler & Hanson 2018; Spence 2002.

10. Simler & Hanson 2018, chap. 13.

11. Crawford 2016; Farrell & Rabin 1996.

12. Wariness: Mercier 2020. Maxim of honesty: Grice 1975; Pinker 2007, chap. 8.

13. Konnikova 2016.

14. Skyrms 2004, p. 68; Farrell & Rabin 1996, pp. 108–9; Cronk & Leech 2013, pp. 138–40; Massenkoff, DeScioli, et al. 2025.

15. Christiansen & Kirby 2003; Pinker & Bloom 1990.

16. Schelling 1960.

17. The example was subsequently used as the title of a book on coordination, Cronk & Leech 2013.

18. Schelling, 1960, pp. 57, 58.

19. Word order in conjunctions: Pinker & Birdsong 1979; Pinker 1994/2007, pp. 167–68, 170.

20. Cronk & Leech 2013, p. 136.

21. Lewis 1969.

22. Cronk & Leech 2013; Pinker 2002/2016, pp. 65–66.

23. Apparently named by my former teacher Duncan Luce in 1957 (Luce & Raiffa 1957). For clear explanations, see Binmore 2007; McAdams 2009. The gender-neutral replacement "Bach or Stravinsky" has not caught on.

24. Any similarity to actual persons, living or dead, is purely coincidental.

25. Frank 1988; Pinker 1997/2009, chap. 6, "Hotheads"; Schelling 1960.

26. Rousseau 1755/2022, my translation.

27. Stag Hunts: McAdams 2009; Skyrms 2004. Aumann (1990) failed to find an original source for the application of Rousseau's parable to game theory.

28. Aumann (1990) notes that if there was an advantage to the first hunter when the second one fruitlessly prepared for stag—say, less competition in a hare hunt—then cheap talk in the Stag Hunt would be worthless. In the version I've presented here, there is no such advantage. See Farrell & Rabin 1996 for discussion.

29. Alvard & Nolin 2002.

30. Black-or-white categories facilitate common knowledge: Hoffman & Yoeli 2022; Lee & Pinker 2010; Pinker, Nowak, & Lee 2008; Pinker & Prince 1996; Yoeli, Burum, et al. 2022.

31. N. Epstein, "See one reason why David Brooks is a fan of Steven Pinker—The Moment Magazine Great DNA Experiment," *Moment*, Sept.–Oct. 2012.

32. Stag hunts in different guises: McAdams 2009.

33. In the movie, the two characters drive their cars toward a cliff, and the first to bail out is the chicken.

34. Goldstein 2010. See also O'Neill 1999.

35. Dawkins 1976/2016; Maynard Smith 1988.

36. Equivalently, they wait until one bird, determined at random, gets impatient and leaves it to the other. The expected payoff also falls between gaining the territory and fighting over it, which is all that counts.

37. Johnson 2004; Lebow 2010; Pinker 2011, pp. 511–15.

38. Hume 1739/2000; DeScioli & Wilson 2011; McAdams 2009.

39. Goldstein 2010.

40. To be sure, if the Americans had had private knowledge of the Doomsday Machine via espionage, that would have been enough to deter them from an attack, but as Strangelove pointed out, the Soviets had no incentive to keep it a secret in the first place.

41. *Dr. Strangelove* (1964), directed by Stanley Kubrick, was based on *Red Alert* by Peter George, with a screenplay by Stanley Kubrick, Terry Southern, and Peter George.

42. Goldstein 2011, pp. 138–39.

43. Gat 2017; Goldstein 2011; Hathaway & Shapiro 2017; Mueller 2021; Pinker 2011.

44. Pinker 2011, pp. 257–61; Hathaway & Shapiro 2017; Zacher 2001; but see also Altman 2020.

45. Mediation as a focal point: Goldstein 2010.

46. Power of powerless courts: McAdams 2009; Ostrom 1990.

47. Ellickson 1991; Ostrom 1990.

48. Don't defund the police: Pinker 2011; Yglesias 2020, pp. 680–82.

Chapter 4: Reading the Mind of a Mind Reader

1. A version of this anonymous poem was excerpted by Robert Aumann (1996). According-ing to the Internet Archive (https://archive.org/search?query=go+to+father"), it was widely reproduced in school and trade publications from (at the latest) 1907 to the 1940s. One version included a verse which may resolve the suitor's interpretation of the lass's meaning: "We parted in anger my heart filled with woe/ For that was a place I cared not to go. / But the answer she gave I remember quite well / When I asked her to wed and she said, Go to Father." https://www.blogger.com/comment/fullpage/post/18806186/5861253957147742762.

2. Season 5, episode 14 (1999), "The One Where Everybody Finds Out," created by David Crane and Marta Kauffman, written by Alexa Junge. I have condensed the dialogue.

3. Representations of common knowledge: Barwise 1988; H. Clark 1996; H. Clark & Marshall 1981; Friedell 1969; Lederman 2018; Monderer & Samet 1989; Vanderschraaf & Sillari 2023.

4. We still have the problem of interpreting the three dots, that is, of knowing which rule to use in extrapolating the series, but in the case of recursive thoughts it seems obvious enough.

5. Self-referential representation of common knowledge: Barwise 1988; H. Clark 1996; Harman 1977. Skepticism: Robert Aumann, personal communication, Oct. 27– Nov. 19, 2020.

6. Aumann 1999; H. Clark 1996; Cubitt & Sugden 2003; Geanakoplos 1992; Mon-derer & Samet 1989.

7. H. Clark & Marshall 1981; Cubitt & Sugden 2003.

8. Dennett 1978.

9. Wimmer & Perner 1983.

10. Onishi & Baillargeon 2005.

11. Camerer, Lowenstein, & Weber 1989.

12. Perner & Wimmer 1985.

13. Piaget 1947/1972.

14. Rogoff, Sellers, et al. 1975.

15. Kinderman, Dunbar, & Bentall 1998.

16. Probably uttered by the US State Department spokesman Robert McCloskey during the Vietnam War; Keyes 2006.

17. Curry & Jones Chesters 2012; Valle, Massaro, et al. 2015.

18. The first sentence is from an English nursery rhyme. The second is from the verse "Chad Gadya" ("An Only Kid"), used in a game at the end of a Passover seder. Both are examples of a genre called cumulative tales or chain tales.

19. S. Clark & Gronlund 1996; McElree 2000. For a contrary theory, see Morton, Hammersley, & Bekerian 1985.

20. More accurately, a single circuit or neural ensemble; it needn't literally be a discrete location in the cortex. The intended contrast is with classical computer memory with its distinct addresses and contents.

21. Wegner 1989.

22. Hudson 1996; Miller & Chomsky 1963; see also Pinker 1994/2007, pp. 199–205.

23. Miller 1956.

24. Pinker 2021. The concept of ecological rationality comes from Tooby & Cosmides 1992 and Gigerenzer 1998.

25. H. Clark 1996; Stalnaker 1978, 2002; see also Grice 1989.

26. A mashup of many myths, quotes, and anecdotes; *Quote Investigator*, Aug. 22, 2021, https://quoteinvestigator.com/2021/08/22/turtles-down/.

27. "Footlights of consciousness" is from William James.

28. Aumann 1999; H. Clark 1996; Cubitt & Sugden 2003; Geanakoplos 1992; Monderer & Samet 1989.

29. Peacocke 2005; Tomasello, Carpenter, et al. 2005.

30. H. Clark 1996.

31. Schelling 1960; Sugden 1995.

32. H. Clark 1996; H. Clark & Marshall 1981.

33. H. Clark & Marshall 1981; Cubitt & Sugden 2003.

34. B. Crew, "The full moon just triggered one of the largest mass spawning events of 2016," *Science Alert*, Nov. 24, 2016.

35. Thomas, DeScioli, et al. 2014.

36. These percentages are from the first of our four experiments; the pattern was the same in the other three, though the exact percentages differed.

37. Bolander, Engelhardt, and Nicolet (2020) have suggested that people are vulnerable to a curse of higher-order knowledge, based on their participants' failure to desist from trying to coordinate in a counterintuitive coordination game they devised.

38. Why, then, did so many participants irrationally choose to coordinate when they had only second- and third-order knowledge? Based on the results of a personality test that we gave the participants, we conjectured that some of them were risk-takers who just enjoyed gambling for higher stakes, and some were altruists who got a bit of pleasure out of the prospect of cooperating with others.

39. De Freitas & Pinker 2020. See Lederman 2018 for skepticism that public knowledge leads to recursive knowledge.

40. About 72 percent of them agreed with #4, compared to 88 percent with #1.

41. Keynes 1936/2016. Sources differ on whether the newspapers of Keynes's day ever did run a beauty contest of the kind he described.

42. Mehta, Starmer, & Sugden 1994.

43. Favorite color: W. Jordan, "Why is blue the world's favorite color?" *YouGov*, May 12, 2015, https://today.yougov.com/international/articles/12335-why-blue -worlds-favorite-color. Most frequent color word: Francis & Kučera 1982 (not counting *black* and *white*).

44. Nagel 1995.

45. Bosch-Domènech, Montalvo, et al. 2002.

46. Thaler 2016.

47. A. Hayes, "What are meme stocks, and are they real investments?" *Investopedia*, May 14, 2024, https://www.investopedia.com/meme-stock-5206762.

48. Diamond & Dybvig 1983.

49. Bank runs as Stag Hunts: McAdams 2009. Bank runs as games with multiple equilibria: Diamond & Dybvig 1983; Morris & Shin 1998.

50. Hofstadter 1985.

51. Written around 1948 by Les Rice, president of the Ulster County, New York, chapter of the Farmers Union. Weavers' rendition: https://www.youtube.com /watch?v=ZzTT5fXquTo.

52. Fittingly, economic depressions were originally called "panics."

53. M. C. Klein, "Thoughts on the bank bailouts," *The Overshoot*, March 13, 2023, https://theovershoot.co/p/thoughts-on-the-bank-bailouts

54. Morris & Shin 1998; Summers 2000.

55. Speech to Congress, 1987, quoted in the *Wall Street Journal*, September 22, 1987.

56. "Business: Yes, we have no bananas." *Time*, Dec. 11, 1978. Kahn also got into trouble during the 1979 oil crisis for calling Arab oil producers "shnooks."

57. M. Fisher, "Flushing out the true cause of the global toilet paper shortage amid coronavirus pandemic," *Washington Post*, April 7, 2020.

58. J. Wolfers, "The economics of toilet paper shortages is the same as bank runs," *Twitter*, March 3, 2020, https://x.com/JustinWolfers/status/123499343137553 6128?s=20.

59. D. Eyon, "Did Johnny Carson cause a toilet paper shortage in 1973?" *Snopes*, Dec. 15, 2014, https://www.snopes.com/fact-check/johnny-carson-tp-shortage/.

60. From an interview in Winokur 1992.

61. J. D. Glater, "The nation; playing the election market," *New York Times*, Feb. 1, 2004; S. Arbesman, "Keynesian beauty contests and presidential primaries," *Wired*, Feb. 14, 2012.

62. A. Salvanto, F. Backus, J. De Pinto, & K. Khanna, "Increasing numbers of voters don't think Biden should be running after debate with Trump — CBS News poll," *CBS News*, July 1, 2024, https://www.cbsnews.com/news/poll-debate-should-biden-be-running-mental-abilities/. Biden's decline and common knowledge: B. Hunt, "Joe Biden and the common knowledge game," *Epsilon Theory*, July 1, 2024, https://www.epsilontheory.com/joe-biden-and-the-common-knowledge-game/.

63. Thomas, De Freitas, et al. 2016.

64. A scan of the original article may be found at https://timesmachine.nytimes.com/timesmachine/1964/03/27/97175042.html?pageNumber=1.

65. D. Dunlap, "1964 | How many witnessed the murder of Kitty Genovese?" *New York Times*, April 6, 2016; S. Roberts, "Sophia Farrar dies at 92; belied indifference to Kitty Genovese Attack," *New York Times*, Sept. 2, 2020. See also Gallo 2015.

66. Latané & Darley 1970.

67. Diekmann 1985.

68. Diekmann 1985; Pinker 2021, chap. 8; Thomas, De Freitas, et al. 2016.

Chapter 5: The Department of Social Relations

1. Manguel 2023; Nuland 2005.

2. His birth year is sometimes given as 1137 or 1138, and his articles of faith are sometimes counted as fifteen rather than thirteen.

3. Maimonides 1180/1993, chap. 10, "Gifts to the Poor," https://www.sefaria.org/Mishneh_Torah%2C_Gifts_to_the_Poor.9.19?lang=bi. Slightly condensed and paraphrased with the help of Rabbis Dani Passow, David Wolpe, and Hirschy Zarchi.

4. "Charity," *Halachipedia*, note 22; https://halachipedia.com/index.php?title=Charity#cite_note-22.

5. Season 6, episode 2 (2007), "The Anonymous Donor," written by Larry David.

6. D. W. Dunlap, "$3 million zoo gift revoked because plaque is too small," *New York Times*, May 15, 1997.

7. Pallotta 2009.

8. A. R. Sorkin, "The mystery of Steve Jobs's public giving," *New York Times*, Aug. 29, 2011.

9. P. Whoriskey, "Record thin on Steve Jobs's philanthropy," *Washington Post*, Oct. 6, 2011; C. C. Miller, "Laurene Powell Jobs and anonymous giving in Silicon Valley," *New York Times*, May 24, 2013; S. Farberov, "How Steve Jobs and his wife secretly gave away TENS OF MILLIONS of their own money to charity . . . even as critics accused him of not doing enough," *Daily Mail*, May 25, 2013.

10. Bono, "Bono praises Steve Jobs as generous and 'poetic'" (letter), *New York Times*, Sept. 1, 2011.

11. De Freitas, DeScioli, et al. 2019.

12. Baumard, André, & Sperber 2013; Noë & Hammerstein 1995. In his article introducing the theory of reciprocal altruism, the biologist Robert Trivers (1971) called the phenomenon "subtle cheating."

13. MacAskill 2015; Singer 2015.

14. Burum, Nowak, & Hoffman 2020.

15. Kurzban 2011; Valdesolo & DeSteno 2008.

16. *The Godfather* (1972), directed by Francis Ford Coppola was based on a novel by Mario Puzo, with a screenplay by Puzo and Coppola.

17. The title of this chapter refers to a renowned but defunct academic unit at Harvard (Allport & Boring 1946; Schmidt 2022; see also the Wikipedia entry "Harvard Department of Social Relations"). In 1946 the university created the Department of Social Relations by bringing together social and personality psychologists who felt alienated from the science-focused Department of Psychology with the sociologists and social anthropologists. It would come to house such luminaries as Gordon Allport, Daniel Bell, Roger Brown (my advisor), Jerome Bruner, Nathan Glazer, Seymour Martin Lipset, Eleanor Maccoby, Henry Murray, Talcott Parsons, and David Riesman. The experiment lasted until 1972, when the psychologists were reabsorbed into their original home, renamed the Department of Psychology and Social Relations. This is the department in which I earned my doctorate, got my first job, and now teach. During the twenty-two years I was away, the department voted to drop "Social Relations" from its name, to my chagrin.

18. Pinsof 2024; the list here is taken verbatim from his paper.

19. Feltovich, Harbaugh, & To 2002.

20. Feltovich, Harbaugh, & To 2002; Williams 2022.

21. Hoffman, Hilbe, & Nowak 2018.

22. Sznycer et al. 2017.

23. Hoffman, Hilbe, & Nowak 2018; De Freitas, DeScioli, et al. 2019.

24. Bellezza, Gino, & Keinan 2014; Williams 2022.

25. Pinker, Nowak, & Lee 2008; Powers & Altman 2023.

26. Barclay 2013; Benenson 2013.

27. De Freitas, DeScioli, et al. 2019; Newman & Cain 2014.

28. Smaldino, Flamson, & McElreath 2018.

29. Gkorezis & Bellou 2016.

30. Marie & Petersen 2024; Williams 2022.

31. Sznycer, Delton, et al. 2019.

32. Beer 2020.

33. Tooby & Cosmides 1996.

34. Fiske 1991, 1992, 2004a, 2004b.

35. Pinsof (2024) argues that such beliefs are necessary to reconcile the contradiction that values which promote the interests of the group, such as ruthless competitiveness against other groups, are at odds with the values cherished for individuals within the group.

36. Tooby 2017; Williams 2022.

37. *Pensées,* 319.

38. Goffman 1959, 1967.

39. The example is from Simler & Hanson 2018.

40. P. Brown & Levinson 1987a; see Pinker 2007, chap. 7.

41. Daly & Wilson 1988.

42. Nisbett & Cohen 1996.

43. Daly & Wilson 1988, p. 127.

44. Bolton & Zwick 1995; B. Brown 1968; Kim, Smith, & Brigham 1998.

45. Felson 1982; Baumeister 1997, pp. 155–56. See also McCullough 2008; McCullough, Kurzban, & Tabak 2011.

46. Anderson, Hildreth, & Howland 2015; Cheng 2020.

47. Van Vugt 2006.

48. Rapoport 1967; see also Van Vugt 2006.

49. In both Hawk–Dove and Leader–Follower, it's best to be the one who dominates while the other concedes, and worst for everyone when they both try to dominate. What makes the games different is that in Hawk–Dove, it's better to mutually concede (that is, both play Dove) than to be a Dove that loses to a Hawk. In Leader–Follower, it's better to follow a leader than for everyone to mill around following no one.

50. Hadfield 1999; McAdams 2009.

51. McAdams 2009.

52. McAdams's analysis omits other possibilities, such as the members of a dominant coalition coordinating among themselves to repel the challenging one, and individuals belonging to multiple, shifting, or overlapping coalitions; see Huang, DeScioli, & Murad 2021.

53. Skyrms 2004.

54. Schelling 1960, pp. 56–57. Ultimatum game: Binmore 2007, pp. 47–48; Reed, DeScioli, & Pinker 2014.

55. Skyrms 2004.

56. Fiske & Tetlock 1999; Tetlock 1999.

57. Fiske & Tetlock 1997.

58. Fiske 1991, pp. 47, 435; Fiske 2004b, p. 17.

59. The connection is made explicit in Fiske's book with Tage Rai, *Virtuous Violence,* which argues that human aggression at all scales largely consists of the morally motivated regulation of social relationships (Fiske & Rai 2015).

60. Schelling 1960, p. 90; Tooby 2020; Tooby & Cosmides 2010; Tooby, Cosmides, & Price 2006.

61. Horowitz 2001; Mueller 2006; Tooby 2020.

62. O'Neill 1999.

63. Kagan 1995.

64. Lebow 2010; from the summary of the book on p. i.

65. Strategic irrationality of nuclear arsenals: Mueller 2010; O'Neill 1999; Wilson 2007; F. Kaplan, "The illogic of nuclear escalation," *Asterisk*, 2022, https://asteriskmag .com/issues/01/the-illogic-of-nuclear-escalation.

66. Quoted in O'Neill 1999, p. 215.

67. Schelling 2005; Tannenwald 2005; see Pinker 2011, pp. 269–71.

Chapter 6: Laughing, Crying, Blushing, Staring, Glaring

1. Nine emotions are recognizable from a stationary head: Keltner & Cordaro 2017; personal communication with Dacher Keltner, 2024. Classic work by Ekman (2007) identified six universal emotional displays; subsequent studies by Keltner and others discovered twenty-two, but many are distinguished by head and body postures rather than just facial musculature (Keltner, Sauter, et al. 2019).

2. McCloud 2006.

3. Kret, Prochazkova, et al. 2020.

4. Darwin 1872/1998; for a review of a twentieth-century edition, see Pinker 1998b.

5. Joubert 1579/1980, quoted in Parvulescu 2010, pp. 28–30.

6. Ciston, Forster, et al. 2021; Qu, Yan, et al. 2017.

7. The problem with humor research: Greengross & Mankoff 2012; Provine 2001.

8. Provine 2001, 2012.

9. The story about counting horses' teeth is apocryphal; see Pinker 2021, pp. 94–95.

10. J. Stern, "The most hated sound on television," *The Atlantic*, April 15, 2024.

11. Provine 2012, p. 45.

12. Provine 2012, p. 56.

13. Liebenberg 2013.

14. To be fair to Yanomamö comedians, they had an even bigger laugh at his expense from a scatological and sexual practical joke they played on him, described in Chagnon 1992, pp. 24–25, and reproduced in Pinker 1997/2009, p. 548.

15. Milgram 1974.

16. Taddonio, P. "Watch: Inside the night President Obama took on Donald Trump," *PBS Frontline*, Sept. 22, 2016, https://www.pbs.org/wgbh/frontline/article/watch -inside-the-night-president-obama-took-on-donald-trump/.

17. Pinker 1994/2007, chap. 7; Pinker 2007, chap. 8.

18. Boehm 1999; Cheng 2020.

19. Tooby & Cosmides 1996.

20. Curry & Dunbar 2013.

21. *Quote Investigator*, Oct. 14, 2014, https://quoteinvestigator.com/2014/10/14/frog/.

22. Koestler 1964.

23. Also discussed repeatedly by Koestler 1964, starting on p. 33.

24. According to the Edinburgh Associative Thesaurus, and the University of South Florida Free Association Norms, http://rali.iro.umontreal.ca/word-associations /query/.

25. Deese 1962.

26. Overview of all aspects of weeping: Vingerhoets 2013.

27. Koestler 1964, p. 280.

28. Darwin 1872/1965; Vingerhoets 2013.

29. Fiske, Schubert, and Seibt (2025) describe a related emotion found in many cultures for which they suggest the Sanskrit word *kama muta*, "moved by love." It's also related to the emotion of "awe," analyzed by Dacher Keltner (2023).

30. https://www.pbs.org/video/lm-50-moment-ray-charles-sings-georgia-my-mind-1979-abhfr5/, 15:35–21:00.

31. Rozin 1996.

32. Darwin 1872/1965; Pinker 1998b.

33. Opponent processes in emotion: Solomon 1980.

34. Twain 1897/1989.

35. Stein & Bouwer 1997. For other reviews of blushing, see Castelfranchi & Poggi 1990; Leary, Britt, et al. 1992; Leary & Meadows 1991.

36. Kret, Prochazkova, et al. 2020.

37. Crozier 2023; Drummond & Lim 2000; Konotey-Ahulu 2004.

38. Darwin 1872/1965, p. 355.

39. Konotey-Ahulu 2004.

40. Keltner 1996; Keltner & Buswell 1997; Tracy & Robins 2004.

41. Robertson, Sznycer, et al. 2018.

42. Fridlund 1992.

43. Castelfranchi & Poggi 1990; Leary, Britt, et al. 1992; Stein & Bouwer 1997; Thomas, DeScioli, & Pinker 2018; Thorstenson, Pazda, & Lichterfeld 2020.

44. Dijk, Koenig, et al. 2011; Feinberg, Willer, & Keltner 2011; Stein & Bouwer 1997.

45. Leary & Meadows 1991.

46. Leary, Britt, et al. 1992; Leary & Meadows 1991; Stein & Bouwer 1997.

47. According to my Harvard Law School colleague Jeannie Suk Gersen, the man would have the subjective *mens rea* (guilty mind) of wanting to kiss her without her consent, and the objective circumstances offer no reason to think he believed she was consenting. (Note the importance of recursive mentalizing in law.) So he could be found guilty of the crime of sexual touching, or lose a tort of offensive sexual touching. But since she did want the kiss and presumably would say so, she would not be a good complaining witness; a prosecutor would not feel there was harm, so the case would probably not go forward. In contrast, at many American colleges an "affirmative consent" regime imposes strict liability (that is, irrelevance of intentions) for failure to request and receive an agreement to engage in a specific act, so the woman's accedence after the fact would not exculpate him.

48. Schelling 1996, p. 262.

49. Thomas, DeScioli, & Pinker 2018.

50. Drummond & Lim 2000.

51. Binmore 2007; Dalkiran, Hoffman, et al. 2012; Friedell 1969.

52. Kobayashi & Kohshima 2001.

53. Argyle 2004; Emery 2000.

54. Simler & Hanson 2018.

55. K. Timpf, "Netflix bans employees from looking at each other for more than five seconds," *National Review Online*, June 14, 2018, https://www.nationalreview.com/2018/06/netflix-five-second-staring-rule/.

56. Palmer, Bracken, et al. 2022.

57. Anstis 2021.

58. Friedell 1969.

59. Pinker 1998a.

60. "Tell me I'm fat," *This American Life*, 589, https://www.thisamericanlife.org/589/transcript.

61. K. Knibbs, "Apple Vision Pro isn't the future," *Wired*, June 8, 2023.

62. Bailenson 2021; Troje 2023.

63. Yi-Chia Chen, personal communication, Jan. 10, 2020, and Aug. 30, 2024; Doherty-Sneddon, Anderson, et al. 1997.

64. Krasnow, Delton, et al. 2013.

65. Binmore 2007, pp. 47–51.

66. According to standard game theory, you *can't* get there. The equitable/self-respecting equilibrium is off the table because the proposer knows that if a rational responder ever had to choose between scraps and nothing, he'd have to take the scraps, so the proposer, going first, always forces him into that "subgame." This means that even though the entire game has multiple Nash equilibria (which would make it a coordination dilemma), it has only one "subgame perfect" equilibrium which a pair of rational players could actually reach, namely greedy/pragmatic. And with a single equilibrium, it would not be a coordination dilemma. Binmore argues that the Ultimatum Game is a coordination dilemma after all, because human players use a broader rationality that evolved to deal with real social life with its repeated encounters. That rationality makes it possible for the responder to reject the lowball offer, which means that the proposer can't foreclose that possibility in making his offer, so the equitable/self-respecting equilibrium is back on the table. See Binmore 2007, pp. 44–56, and for another explanation of the concept of a subgame perfect equilibrium, Hoffman & Yoeli 2022, pp. 173–75.

67. Reed, DeScioli, & Pinker 2014.

Chapter 7: Weasel Words

1. *Schindler's List* (1993) was directed by Steven Spielberg, with a screenplay by Steven Zaillian, based on a novel by Thomas Keneally. James Lee deserves credit for drawing on its dialogue to begin and end our 2010 paper, from which parts of this chapter were adapted, together with another paper we coauthored with Martin Nowak; Lee & Pinker 2010; Pinker, Nowak, & Lee 2008.

2. P. Brown & Levinson 1987b; Clark 1996; Grice 1975; Grice 1989; Holtgraves 2002; Levinson 1983; see Pinker 2007, chap. 8, for an overview.

3. Season 5, episode 5 (2018), "Facial Recognition," written by Graham Wagner.

4. Season 4, episode 12 (2002), "Eloise," written by Terence Winter.

5. The attributions, mostly from the late nineteenth and early twentieth century, include Marcel Proust, Hjalmar Söderberg, Horatio Alger, and Alfred Hitchcock; see P. Tréguer, "History of 'come up and see my etchings,'" *Word Histories*, 2020, https://wordhistories.net/2020/01/11/come-see-my-etchings/, and the Wikipedia entry "Etchings."

6. "Netflix and chill," Wikipedia, https://en.wikipedia.org/wiki/Netflix_and_chill.

7. Indirect speech and the law: Solan & Tiersman 2010, part 4; J. Bohannon & E. Kintisch, "Biologist prevails in case of 'Fruit Bat Fellatio' harassment allegations," *Science*, Dec. 2, 2010, https://www.science.org/content/article/biologist-prevails-case-fruit-bat-fellatio-harassment-allegations.

8. Pinker 2019.

9. Maxims of conversation: Grice 1975.

10. Schelling 1960, pp. 139–42.

11. Pinker, Nowak, & Lee 2008. For a newer version, see Massenkoff, DeScioli, et al. 2025.

12. Lee & Pinker 2010.

13. Transparency International, Global Corruption Barometer, https://www.transparency.org/en/gcb/global/global-corruption-barometer-2017.

14. The correlation coefficient was 0.925, on a scale from −1 to 1. We did not report this goodness-of-fit test in Lee & Pinker 2010.

15. B. Feiler, "Pocketful of dough," *Gourmet*, Oct. 2000.

16. Fiske 1991, 1992, 2004b.

17. P. Brown & Levinson 1987b; Holtgraves 2002; Pinker 2007.

18. Season 2, episode 4 (1991), "The Phone Message," written by Larry David and Jerry Seinfeld.

19. Clark 1996; Stalnaker 1978.

20. Pinker 1994/2007, chap. 7, and Pinker 2014, chap. 5.

21. S. Alexander, "Lizardman's constant is 4%," *Slate Star Codex*, April 13, 2013, https://slatestarcodex.com/2013/04/12/noisy-poll-results-and-reptilian-muslim-climatologists-from-mars/.

22. On the psychological difference between certainty and very high probability, see Pinker 2021, pp. 188–96. Admittedly, our rating scale made it easy to select these options: it was delineated as 0%, 1%, 2–49%, 50%, 51–98%, 99%, 100%. In the threat and seduction scenarios, 100% was also the unanimous or near-unanimous choice for the direct proposition; 99% was not the top choice for most suggestive indirect one, but all the participants but one indicated that the intention was more likely than not. The likely reason for the discrepancy is that the degrees of indirectness of the indirect requests in the three scenarios were not directly commensurable.

23. For an argument that they are independent, see Lederman 2018.

24. Massenkoff, DeScioli, et al. 2025.

25. Orwell 1946/1970; see Bandura 1999; Pinker 2011, pp. 565–67.

Chapter 8: The Canceling Instinct

1. For reports on some of these incidents, see Dreger 2007, 2011; Hunt 1999; Kors & Silverglate 1998; Lukianoff 2012, 2014; Pinker 2002/2016; and the references in notes 26 and 28 below. For others, see the website *Canceled People*, https://canceledpeople.org/cancellations/, and the Foundation for Individual Rights and Expression's Scholars Under Fire database, https://www.thefire.org/research-learn/scholars-under-fire.

2. Frey & Stevens 2023; executive summary: https://www.thefire.org/research-learn/scholars-under-fire-attempts-sanction-scholars-2000-2022. The numbers have been updated through the first half of 2024 by Komi Frey, personal communication.

3. Frey & Stevens 2023; Jones & Arnold 2024.

4. Pinker 2023.

5. S. Stevens, "Harvard gets worst score ever in FIRE's College Free Speech Rankings," Foundation for Individual Rights and Expression, https://www.thefire.org/news/harvard-gets-worst-score-ever-fires-college-free-speech-rankings. Harvard replicated its last-place finish and grade of 0 in 2025: https://www.thefire.org/news/2025-college-free-speech-rankings-expose-threats-first-amendment-rights-campus.

6. C. Hooven, "Why I left Harvard," *The Free Press*, Jan. 16, 2044, https://www.thefp.com/p/carole-hooven-why-i-left-harvard; Hooven 2023; VanderWeele & Brooks 2023; M. Kelly, "Harvard disinvites feminist philosopher for opposing transgender ideology," *The College Fix*, April 25, 2022, https://www.thecollegefix.com/harvard-disinvites-feminist-philosopher-for-opposing-transgender-ideology/.

7. N. Honeycutt, "Confidence in colleges and universities hits new lows, per FIRE polls," Foundation for Individual Rights and Expression, https://www.thefire.org/news/confidence-colleges-and-universities-hits-new-lows-fire-polls. J. M. Jones, "Confidence in higher education down since 2015," *Gallup*, Oct. 9, 2018, https://news.gallup.com/opinion/gallup/242441/confidence-higher-education-down-2015.aspx. M. Brenan, "Americans' confidence in higher education down sharply," *Gallup*, July 11, 2023, https://news.gallup.com/poll/508352/americans-confidence-higher-education-down-sharply.aspx.

8. Pinker & Madras 2023. Website: https://sites.harvard.edu/cafh/.

9. Pinker 2021.

10. Obvious examples include the Catholic Church punishing Galileo for advocating heliocentrism, the 1925 "Monkey Trial" in Tennessee which convicted John Scopes for teaching evolution, and the Soviet Union killing and imprisoning biologists who dissented from Trofim Lysenko's Lamarckian biology. Recent histories of censorship: Berkowitz 2021; Mchangama 2022.

11. Tufekci, Z, "An object lesson from Covid on how to destroy public trust," *New York Times*, June 8, 2024.

12. Lukianoff 2012; Sunstein 2024.

13. Sunstein 2023, 2024.

14. C. Friedersdorf, "Is 'Ladies Lingerie' a harmless joke or harassment?" *The Atlantic*, May 9, 2018. The perpetrator was the political scientist Richard Ned Lebow, cited on p. 134.

15. L. Fadulu, "Columbia psychiatry chair suspended after tweet about dark-skinned model," *New York Times*, Feb. 23, 2022.

16. R. Soave, "USC suspended a communications professor for saying a Chinese word that sounds like a racial slur," *Reason*, Sept. 3, 2020.

17. History of censorship: Berkowitz 2021; Mchangama 2022

18. C. Clark, Jussim, et al. 2023.

19. For more discussion, see Pinker 2002/2016.

20. Mercier & Sperber 2011.

21. Liu & Ditto 2013.

22. Pinker 2021, pp. 298–303.

23. Finkel, Bail, et al. 2020.

24. Haidt 2016.

25. *Quote Investigator*, Feb. 9, 2011. https://quoteinvestigator.com/2011/02/09/darwinism-hope-pray/.

26. C. Clark, Fjeldmark, et al. 2024; C. Clark, Jussim, et al. 2023; Kaufmann 2021; for a recent review, see A. Krylov & J. Tanzman, "Spotlight on scientific censorship: A virtual collection," *Heterodox STEM*, Dec. 24, 2023, https://hxstem.substack.com/p/spotlight-on-scientific-censorship.

27. Editors of *Nature Human Behaviour* 2022.

28. Savolainen 2023; Teixeira da Silva 2021; J. Singal, "This is what a modern-day witch hunt looks like," *New York*, May 2, 2017; C. Flaherty, "Is retraction the new rebuttal?" *Inside Higher Ed*, Sept. 18, 2017; *Science* news staff, "Researchers retract controversial female mentorship paper," *Science*, Dec. 21, 2020, https://www.science.org/content/article/researchers-retract-controversial-female-mentorship-paper.

29. C. Clark, Fjeldmark, et al. 2024; Kaufmann 2021.

30. Honeycutt, Stevens, & Kaufmann 2023.

31. Kuran 1989; Noelle-Neumann 1974.

32. Noelle-Neumann 1974; Willer, Kuwabara, & Macy 2009; see also the Wikipedia entry "Abilene Paradox."

33. J. McCarthy, "Post-Affirmative action, views on admissions differ by race," *Gallup*, Jan. 16, 2004, https://news.gallup.com/poll/548528/post-affirmative-action-views -admissions-differ-race.aspx.

34. Van Boven 2000.

35. Raemon 2017.

36. C. Clark, Fjeldmark, et al. 2024.

37. Cofnas 2020; Fraser 1995; E. Turkheimer, K. P. Harden, & R. Nisbett, "There's still no good reason to believe black-white IQ differences are due to genes," *Vox*, June 17, 2017, https://www.vox.com/the-big-idea/2017/6/15/15797120 /race-black-white-iq-response-critics.

38. Chomsky 1973, pp. 361–62.

39. Lieberman 2001.

40. Cofnas 2020.

41. E. Turkheimer, K. P. Harden, & R. Nisbett, "There's still no good reason to believe black-white IQ differences are due to genes," *Vox*, June 17, 2017, https://www .vox.com/the-big-idea/2017/6/15/15797120/race-black-white-iq-response-critics.

42. Hughes 2024; C. Hughes, "Should the race and IQ discourse be brought into main- stream conversation?" (excerpt of an interview with Charles Murray), YouTube, July 4, 2021, https://www.youtube.com/watch?v=zWB5tfLbXcg.

43. Mill 1859.

Chapter 9: Radical Honesty, Rational Hypocrisy

1. Fiske & Tetlock 1997, p. 278, note 3. I have lumped market pricing with rational- legal organization, following a suggestion by Fiske himself; see Fiske 1991, pp. 47, 435; Fiske 2004b, p. 17.

2. Wouters 2007.

3. J. Carter, "Interview with *Playboy* magazine," reproduced in G. Peters & J. T. Wolley, *The American Presidency Project*, https://www.presidency.ucsb.edu/documents /interview-with-playboy-magazine.

4. Mueller 2018.

5. I. Teich, "The most embarrassing instances of famous people forgetting their mic was on," *Ranker*, April 22, 2024, https://www.ranker.com/list/embarrass ing-hot-mic-situations/isadora-teich.

6. A. Hamilton, "Amicus," Sept. 11, 1792, *Founder Online*, National Archives, https:// founders.archives.gov/documents/Hamilton/01-12-02-0272.

7. *Pensée* 101.

8. Gen-Z mental health crisis: Centers for Disease Control and Prevention 2021; Haidt 2024. Bias hotline: https://reportinghotline.harvard.edu/. Surveillance regime examples: In 2010 the dean of Harvard Law School pub icly shamed a student for a private email in which she suggested that both sides of a controversy be discussed (see W. Kaminer, "Who's bullying who?" *The Atlantic*, May 4, 2010). In 2019 it rescinded an offer of admission to a conservative student over trash talk with racial epithets he exchanged with some friends on social media when he was sixteen (S. Jaschik, "Harvard latest revoked admissions offer," *Inside Higher Ed*, June 23, 2019).

9. From *Tootsie* (1982), directed by Sydney Pollack; story by Don McGuire and Larry Gelbart; screenplay by Larry Gelbart and Murray Schisgal.

10. The most famous is the Jim Carrey movie *Liar Liar* (1997). Other examples include the *Twilight Zone* episode "The Whole Truth" (1961), two episodes of the situation comedy *Bewitched* ("Speak the Truth," 1965, and "The Truth, Nothing but the Truth, so Help Me Sam," 1972), James Halperin's science fiction novel *The Truth Machine* (1996), and Scott Westerfield's novel *Extras* (2007). The reverse scenario, with a single liar in a society of truth-tellers, is played out in the Ricky Gervais movie *The Invention of Lying* (2009).

11. "Core principles of Radical Honesty," *Radical Honesty*, https //www.radicalhonesty .com/core-principles-radical-honesty; Blanton 1994/2005.

12. S. Alexander, "Explicit honesty," *Astral Codex Ten*, April 5, 2024, https://www .astralcodexten.com/p/explicit-honesty.

13. Jacobs 2007.

14. A. Stevenson & M. Goldstein, "Bridgewater's Ray Dalio spreads his gospel of 'Radical Transparency,'" *New York Times*, Sept. 8, 2017.

15. M. Gimein, "Ever Had a Horrible Boss? 'The Fund' Is the Perfect Rage-Read," *New York Times*, Nov. 6, 2023.

16. L. Goss, "Bridgewater's new CEO says hedge fund must be 're-wired' following Ray Dalio's exit," *Morningstar*, May 9, 2024, https://www.morningstar.com/news /marketwatch/20240509189/bridgewaters-new-ceo-says-hedge-fund-must-be -rewired-following-ray-dalios-exit.

17. See chapters 3 and 5, and the references to the works of Alan Fiske.

18. Daly & Wilson 1988; Symons 1979; Trivers & Newton 1982; see the chapters "Family Values" in Pinker 1997/2009 and "The Many Roots of Our Suffering" in Pinker 2002/2016.

19. Symons 1979, 1980, 1992.

20. Hobbes 1651/1957, chap. 8.

21. Stephen 1883/2022.

22. Homicidal fantasies: Buss 2005; Crabb 2000; Kenrick & Sheets 1994. Sexual fantasies: Bivona & Critelli 2009; Byers, Purdon, & Clark 1998; Greendlinger & Byrne 1987; Kanin 1982; Leitenberg & Henning 1995; Malamuth 1981; Strassberg & Locker 1998.

23. Simler & Hanson 2018.

24. Fiske & Tetlock 1999; Tetlock 1999.

25. *The Language Instinct* and *Words and Rules*.

26. *How the Mind Works* and *The Stuff of Thought*.

27. *The Better Angels of Our Nature* and *Enlightenment Now*.

28. *Rationality*.

REFERENCES

Aaronson, S. 2015. Common knowledge and Aumann's Agreement Theorem. *Shtetl-Optimized*. https://scottaaronson.blog/?p=2410.

Allport, G. W., & Boring, E. G. 1946. Psychology and social relations at Harvard University. *American Psychologist, 1,* 119–22.

Altman, D. 2020. The evolution of territorial conquest after 1945 and the limits of the territorial integrity norm. *International Organization, 74,* 490–522.

Alvard, M., & Nolin, D. 2002. Rousseau's whale hunt? Coordination among big-game hunters. *Current Anthropology, 43,* 533–59.

Anderson, C., Hildreth, J. A. D., & Howland, L. 2015. Is the desire for status a fundamental human motive? A review of the empirical literature. *Psychological Bulletin, 141,* 574–601.

Anstis, S. 2021. The paradox of extreme close-up gaze. *Perception, 50,* 170–73.

Argyle, M. 2004. Eye contact (or "mutual gaze"). In R. L. Gregory, ed., *The Oxford Companion to the Mind*, 2nd ed. New York: Oxford University Press.

Aumann, R. 1976. Agreeing to disagree. *Annals of Statistics, 4,* 1236–39.

Aumann, R. 1990. Nash equilibria are not self-enforcing. In J. J. Gabszewicz, J.-F. Richard, & L. Wolsey, eds., *Economic decision making: Games, econometrics and optimisation.* Amsterdam: Elsevier.

Aumann, R. J. 1996. Reply to Binmore. *Games and Economic Behavior, 17,* 138–46.

Aumann, R. J. 1999. Interactive epistemology I: Knowledge. *International Journal of Game Theory, 28,* 263–300.

Bailenson, J. M. 2021. Nonverbal overload: A theoretical argument for the causes of Zoom fatigue. *Technology, Mind, and Behavior, 2.*

Bandura, A. 1999. Moral disengagement in the perpetration of inhumanities. *Personality and Social Psychology Review, 3,* 193–209.

Barclay, P. 2013. Strategies for cooperation in biological markets, especially for humans. *Evolution and Human Behavior, 34,* 164–75.

Barwise, J. 1988. Three views of common knowledge. In M. Y. Vardi, ed., *Proceedings of the 2nd Conference on Theoretical Aspects of Reasoning About Knowledge.* San Francisco: Morgan Kaufman.

Baumard, N., André, J.-B., & Sperber, D. 2013. A mutualistic approach to morality: The evolution of fairness by partner choice. *Behavioral and Brain Sciences, 36,* 59–122.

Baumeister, R. F. 1997. *Evil: Inside human violence and cruelty.* New York: Holt.

Beer, J. 2020. The inconvenient truth about your "authentic" self. *Scientific American* blog, https://www.scientificamerican.com/blog/observations/the-inconvenient-truth -about-your-authentic-self/.

Bellezza, S., Gino, F., & Keinan, A. 2014. The red sneakers effect: Inferring status and competence from signals of nonconformity. *Journal of Consumer Research, 41,* 35–54.

Benenson, J. F. 2013. The development of human female competition: Allies and adversaries. *Philosophical Transactions of the Royal Society of London, Series B, Biological Sciences, 368,* issue 1631.

Berkowitz, E. 2021. *Dangerous ideas: A brief history of censorship in the West, from the ancients to fake news.* Boston: Beacon Press.

Binmore, K. 1991. *Fun and games: A text on game theory.* Boston: Houghton Mifflin.

Binmore, K. 2007. *Game theory: A very short introduction.* New York: Oxford University Press.

Binmore, K., & Samuelson, L. 2001. Coordinated action in the Electronic Mail game. *Games and Economic Behavior, 35,* 6–30.

Bivona, J., & Critelli, J. 2009. The nature of women's rape fantasies: An analysis of prevalence, frequency, and contents. *Journal of Sex Research, 46,* 33–45.

Blanton, B. 1994/2005. *Radical honesty: How to transform your life by telling the truth.* Sparrowhawk Press.

Boehm, C. 1999. *Hierarchy in the forest: The evolution of egalitarian behavior.* Cambridge, MA: Harvard University Press.

Bolander, T., Engelhardt, R., & Nicolet, T. S. 2020. The curse of shared knowledge: Recursive belief reasoning in a coordination game with imperfect information. *arXiv.* http://arxiv.org/pdf/2008.08849v1.

Bolton, G. E., & Zwick, R. 1995. Anonymity versus punishment in ultimatum bargaining. *Games and Economic Behavior, 10,* 95–121.

Bosch-Domènech, A., Montalvo, J. G., Nagel, R., & Satorra, A. 2002. One, two, (three), infinity, . . . : Newspaper and lab beauty-contest experiments. *American Economic Review, 92,* 1687–1701.

Brown, B. R. 1968. The effects of need to maintain face on interpersonal bargaining. *Journal of Experimental Social Psychology, 4,* 107–22.

Brown, P., & Levinson, S. C. 1987a. Introduction to the reissue: A review of recent work. In *Politeness: Some universals in language usage.* New York: Cambridge University Press.

Brown, P., & Levinson, S. C. 1987b. *Politeness: Some universals in language usage.* New York: Cambridge University Press.

Buckels, E. E., Trapnell, P. D., & Paulhus, D. L. 2014. Trolls just want to have fun. *Personality and Individual Differences*, 67, 97–102.

Burum, B., Nowak, M. A., & Hoffman, M. 2020. An evolutionary explanation for ineffective altruism. *Nature Human Behaviour*, 4, 1245–57.

Buss, D. M. 2005. *The murderer next door: Why the mind is designed to kill.* New York: Penguin.

Byers, E. S., Purdon, C., & Clark, D. A. 1998. Sexual intrusive thoughts of college students. *Journal of Sex Research*, 35, 359–69.

Camerer, C., Lowenstein, G., & Weber, M. 1989. The curse of knowledge in economic settings: An experimental analysis. *Journal of Political Economy*, 97, 1232–54.

Castelfranchi, C., & Poggi, I. 1990. Blushing as a discourse: Was Darwin wrong? In R. Crozier, ed., *Shyness and embarrassment: Perspectives from social psychology.* New York: Cambridge University Press.

Cathcart, T., & Klein, D. 2007. *Plato and a platypus walk into a bar: Understanding philosophy through jokes.* New York: Harry Abrams.

Centers for Disease Control and Prevention. 2021. *Youth risk behavior survey 2011–2021.* https://www.cdc.gov/healthyyouth/data/yrbs/pdf/YRBS_Data-Summary-Trends_Report2023_508.pdf.

Centola, D., Willer, R., & Macy, M. 2005. The emperor's dilemma: A computational model of self-enforcing norms. *American Journal of Sociology*, 110 1009–40.

Chagnon, N. A. 1992. *Yanomamö: The last days of Eden.* New York: Harcourt Brace.

Cheng, J. T. 2020. Dominance, prestige, and the role of leveling in human social hierarchy and equality. *Current Opinion in Psychology*, 33, 238–44.

Chenoweth, E. 2020. The future of nonviolent resistance. *Journal of Democracy*, 31, 69–84.

Chenoweth, E., & Stephan, M. J. 2011. *Why civil resistance works: The strategic logic of nonviolent conflict.* New York: Columbia University Press.

Chomsky, N. 1972/2006. *Language and mind*, extended ed. New York: Cambridge University Press.

Chomsky, N. 1973. Psychology and ideology. In N. Chomsky, ed., *For reasons of state.* New York: Vintage.

Christiansen, M., & Kirby, S., eds. 2003. *Language evolution: States of the art.* New York: Oxford University Press.

Chwe, M. S.-Y. 2001. *Rational ritual: Culture, coordination, and common knowledge.* Princeton, NJ: Princeton University Press.

Ciston, A. B., Forster, C., Brick, T. R., Kühn, S., Verrel, J., et al. 2021. Limited metacognitive access to one's own facial expressions. *bioRxiv*, 2021.2003.2008.434069.

Clark, C. J., Fjeldmark, M., Lu, L., Baumeister, R. F., Ceci, S., et al. 2024. Taboos and self-censorship among us psychology professors. *Perspectives on Psychological Science*, 1–17.

Clark, C. J., Jussim, L., Frey, K., Stevens, S. T., Al-Gharbi, M., et al. 2023. Prosocial motives underlie scientific censorship by scientists: A perspective and research agenda. *Proceedings of the National Academy of Sciences, 120*, e2301642120.

Clark, E. V. 1993. *The lexicon in acquisition.* New York: Cambridge University Press.

Clark, H. H. 1996. *Using language.* New York: Cambridge University Press.

Clark, H. H., & Carlson, T. B. 1981. Speech acts and hearers' beliefs. In N. V. Smith, ed., *Mutual knowledge.* New York: Academic Press.

Clark, H. H., & Marshall, C. R. 1981. Definite reference and mutual knowledge. In A. K. Joshi, B. L. Webber, & I. A. Sag, eds., *Elements of discourse understanding.* New York: Cambridge University Press.

Clark, S. E., & Gronlund, S. D. 1996. Global matching models of recognition memory: How the models match the data. *Psychonomic Bulletin & Review, 3*, 37–60.

Cofnas, N. 2020. Research on group differences in intelligence: A defense of free inquiry. *Philosophical Psychology, 33*, 125–47.

Columbus, S., Molho, C., Righetti, F., & Balliet, D. 2021. Interdependence and cooperation in daily life. *Journal of Personality and Social Psychology, 120*, 626–50.

Cowen, T., & Hanson, R. 2004. Are disagreements honest? George Mason University. https://mason.gmu.edu/~rhanson/deceive.pdf.

Crabb, P. B. 2000. The material culture of homicidal fantasies. *Aggressive Behavior, 26*, 225–34.

Crawford, V. P. 2016. New directions for modeling strategic behavior: Game-theoretic models of communication, coordination, and cooperation in economic relationships. *Journal of Economic Perspectives, 30*, 131–50.

Cronk, L., & Leech, B. L. 2013. *Meeting at Grand Central: Understanding the social and evolutionary roots of cooperation.* Princeton, NJ: Princeton University Press.

Crozier, W. R. 2023. Skin complexion and the blush. *Emotion Review, 15*, 118–26.

Crystal, D., & Crystal, H. 2000. *Words on words: Quotations about language and languages.* Chicago: University of Chicago Press.

Cubitt, R. C., & Sugden, R. 2003. Common knowledge, salience and convention: A reconstruction of David Lewis' game theory. *Economics and Philosophy, 19*, 175–210.

Curry, O. S., & Dunbar, R. I. M. 2013. Sharing a joke: The effects of a similar sense of humor on affiliation and altruism. *Evolution and Human Behavior, 34*, 125–29.

Curry, O. S., & Jones Chesters, M. 2012. "Putting ourselves in the other fellow's shoes": The role of "theory of mind" in solving coordination problems. *Journal of Cognition and Culture, 12*, 147–59.

Curry, O. S., Jones Chesters, M., & Van Lissa, C. J. 2019. Mapping morality with a compass: Testing the theory of "morality-as-cooperation" with a new questionnaire. *Journal of Research in Personality, 78*, 106–24.

Cushman, F., Sheketoff, R., Wharton, S., & Carey, S. 2013. The development of intent-based moral judgment. *Cognition, 127*, 6–21.

Dalkiran, N. A., Hoffman, M., Paturi, R., Ricketts, D., Vattani, A. 2012. Common Knowledge and state-dependent equilibria. In Serna, M., ed., *Algorithmic Game Theory*. Berlin: Springer. https://doi.org/10.1007/978-3-642-33996-7_8.

Daly, M., & Wilson, M. 1988. *Homicide*. New York: Aldine De Gruyter.

Darwin, C. R. 1872/1965. *The expression of the emotions in man and animals*. Chicago: University of Chicago Press.

Darwin, C. R. 1872/1998. *The expression of the emotions in man and animals: Definitive edition*. London: HarperCollins.

Dawkins, R. 1976/2016. *The selfish gene*, 40th anniv. ed. New York: Oxford University Press.

De Freitas, J., DeScioli, P., Thomas, K. A., & Pinker, S. 2019. Maimonides' Ladder: States of mutual knowledge and the perception of charitability. *Journal of Experimental Psychology: General, 148*, 158–73.

De Freitas, J., & Pinker, S. 2020. The psychological representation of common knowledge. Unpublished manuscript.

De Freitas, J., Thomas, K., DeScioli, P., & Pinker, S. 2019. Common knowledge, coordination, and strategic mentalizing in human social life. *Proceedings of the National Academy of Sciences, 116*, 13751–58.

Deese, J. 1962. On the structure of associative meaning. *Psychological Review, 69*, 161–75.

Dennett, D. C. 1978. Beliefs about beliefs (commentary on Premack & Woodruff's "Does a chimpanzee have a theory of mind?"). *Behavioral and Brain Sciences, 1*, 568–70.

DeScioli, P., & Kurzban, R. 2007. The games people play. In S. Gangestad & J. A. Simpson, eds., *The evolution of mind: Fundamental questions and controversies*. New York: Guilford.

DeScioli, P., & Kurzban, R. 2009. Mysteries of morality. *Cognition, 112*, 281–99.

DeScioli, P., & Kurzban, R. 2018. Morality is for choosing sides. In *Atlas of Moral Psychology*. New York: Guilford.

DeScioli, P., & Wilson, B. J. 2011. The territorial foundations of human property. *Evolution and Human Behavior, 32*, 297–304.

Diamond, D. W., & Dybvig, P. H. 1983. Bank runs, deposit insurance, and liquidity. *Journal of Political Economy, 91*, 401–19.

Diekmann, A. 1985. Volunteer's dilemma. *Journal of Conflict Resolution, 29*, 605–10.

Diesendruck, G., & Markson, L. 2001. Children's avoidance of lexical overlap: A pragmatic account. *Developmental Psychology, 37*, 630–44.

Dijk, C., Koenig, B., Ketelaar, T., & de Jong, P. J. 2011. Saved by the blush: Being trusted despite defecting. *Emotion, 11*, 313–19.

Dobson, W. J. 2012. *The dictator's learning curve: Inside the global battle for democracy.* New York: Anchor.

Doherty-Sneddon, G., Anderson, A., O'Malley, C., Langton, S., Garrod, S., et al. 1997. Face-to-face and video-mediated communication: A comparison of dialogue structure and task performance. *Journal of Experimental Psychology: Applied, 3,* 105.

Dreger, A. D. 2007. The controversy surrounding "The Man Who Would Be Queen": A case history of the politics of science, identity, and sex in the internet age. *Archives of Sexual Behavior, 37,* 366–421.

Dreger, A. D. 2011. Darkness's descent on the American Anthropological Association: A cautionary tale. *Human Nature, 22,* 225–46.

Drummond, P. D., & Lim, H. K. 2000. The significance of blushing for fair- and dark-skinned people. *Personality and Individual Differences, 29,* 1123–32.

Dulleck, U. 1997. *A note on the e-mail game: Bounded rationality and induction.* Berlin: Humboldt University of Berlin.

Editors of *Nature Human Behaviour.* 2022. Science must respect the dignity and rights of all humans. *Nature Human Behaviour, 6,* 1029–31.

Ekman, P. 2007. *Emotions revealed, second edition: Recognizing faces and feelings to improve communication and emotional life.* New York: Holt.

Ellickson, R. C. 1991. *Order without law: How neighbors settle disputes.* Cambridge, MA: Harvard University Press.

Emery, N. J. 2000. The eyes have it: The neuroethology, function and evolution of social gaze. *Neuroscience & Biobehavioral Reviews, 24,* 581–604.

Farrell, J., & Rabin, M. 1996. Cheap talk. *Journal of Economic Perspectives, 10,* 103–18.

Feinberg, M., Willer, M., & Keltner, D. 2011. Flustered and faithful: Embarrassment as a signal of prosociality. *Journal of Personality and Social Psychology, 102,* 81–97.

Felson, R. B. 1982. Impression management and the escalation of aggression and violence. *Social Psychology Quarterly, 45,* 245–54.

Feltovich, N., Harbaugh, R., & To, T. 2002. Too cool for school? Signalling and countersignalling. *The RAND Journal of Economics, 33,* 630–49.

Finkel, E. J., Bail, C. A., Cikara, M., Ditto, P. H., Iyengar, S., et al. 2020. Political sectarianism in America. *Science, 370,* 533–36.

Fiske, A. P. 1991. *Structures of social life: The four elementary forms of human relations.* New York: Free Press.

Fiske, A. P. 1992. The four elementary forms of sociality: Framework for a unified theory of social relations. *Psychological Review, 99,* 689–723.

Fiske, A. P. 2004a. Four modes of constituting relationships: Consubstantial assimilation; space, magnitude, time, and force; concrete procedures; abstract symbolism. In N. Haslam, ed., *Relational models theory: A contemporary overview.* Mahwah, NJ: Erlbaum Associates.

Fiske, A. P. 2004b. Relational models theory 2.0. In N. Haslam, ed., *Relational models theory: A contemporary overview*. Mahwah, NJ: Erlbaum Associates.

Fiske, A. P., & Rai, T. 2015. *Virtuous violence: Hurting and killing to create, sustain, end, and honor social relationships*. New York: Cambridge University Press.

Fiske, A. P., Schubert, T. W., & Seibt, B. 2025. Seeking communal emotions in social practices that culturally evolved to evoke the emotions: Worship, kitten videos, memorials, narratives of love, and more. *Annual Review of Psychology, 76*.

Fiske, A. P., & Tetlock, P. E. 1997. Taboo trade-offs: Reactions to transactions that transgress the spheres of justice. *Political Psychology, 18*, 255–97.

Fiske, A. P., & Tetlock, P. E. 1999. Taboo tradeoffs: Constitutive prerequisites for social life. In S. A. Renshon & J. Duckitt, eds., *Political psychology: Cultural and cross-cultural perspectives*. London: MacMillan.

Francis, N., & Kučera, H. 1982. *Frequency analysis of English usage: Lexicon and grammar*. Boston: Houghton Mifflin.

Frank, R. H. 1988. *Passions within reason: The strategic role of the emotions*. New York: W. W. Norton.

Fraser, S., ed. 1995. *The Bell Curve wars: Race, intelligence, and the future of America*. New York: Basic Books.

Frey, K., & Stevens, S. T. 2023. *Scholars under fire: Attempts to sanction scholars from 2000 to 2022*. Philadelphia: Foundation for Individual Rights and Expression. https://www.thefire.org/research-learn/scholars-under-fire-attempts-sanctionscholars-2000-2022.

Fridlund, A. 1992. Darwin's anti-Darwinism in "The expression of the emotions in man and animals." In K. T. Strongman, ed., *International review of studies of emotion*, vol. 2. New York: Wiley.

Friedell, M. F. 1969. On the structure of shared awareness. *Behavioral Science, 14*, 28–39.

Galef, J. 2021. *The scout mindset: Why some people see things clearly and others don't*. New York: Penguin.

Gallo, M. M. 2015. *"No one helped": Kitty Genovese, New York City, and the myth of urban apathy*. Ithaca, NY: Cornell Unversity Press.

Gamow, G., & Stern, M. 1958. Forty unfaithful wives. In *Puzzle-math*. New York: Viking.

Gardner, M. 1984. The castrati of Womensa. In *Puzzles from other worlds*. New York: Vintage.

Gat, A. 2017. *The causes of war and the spread of peace*. New York: Oxford University Press.

Geanakoplos, J. 1992. Common knowledge. *Journal of Economic Perspectives, 6*, 53–82.

Geanakoplos, J., & Polemarchakis, H. M. 1982. We can't disagree forever. *Journal of Economic Theory, 28*, 192–200.

Geddes, P. 2022. *Transparent investing: How to play the stock market without getting played*. Mill Valley, CA: Perspicuum Press.

Gigerenzer, G. 1998. Ecological intelligence: An adaptation for frequencies. In D. D. Cummins & C. Allen, eds., *The evolution of mind*. New York: Oxford University Press.

Gkorezis, P., & Bellou, V. 2016. The relationship between leader self-deprecating humor and perceived effectiveness: Trust in leader as a mediator. *Leadership & Organization Development Journal*, 37, 882–98.

Goffman, E. 1959. *The presentation of self in everyday life*. New York: Doubleday.

Goffman, E. 1967. On face-work: An analysis of ritual elements in social interaction. In *Interaction ritual: Essays on face-to-face behavior*. New York: Random House.

Goldstein, J. S. 2010. Chicken dilemmas: Crossing the road to cooperation. In I. W. Zartman & S. Touval, eds., *International cooperation: The extents and limits of multilateralism*. New York: Cambridge University Press.

Goldstein, J. S. 2011. *Winning the war on war: The decline of armed conflict worldwide*. New York: Penguin.

Greendlinger, V., & Byrne, D. 1987. Coercive sexual fantasies of college men as predictors of self-reported likelihood to rape and overt sexual aggression. *Journal of Sex Research*, 23, 1–11.

Greengross, G., & Mankoff, R. 2012. Inside "Inside Jokes": The hidden side of humor (review of M. Hurley, D. Dennett, and R. Adams Jr.'s "Inside jokes: Using humor to reverse-engineer the mind"). *Evolutionary Psychology, 10,* 443–56.

Grice, H. P. 1975. Logic and conversation. In P. Cole & J. L. Morgan, eds., *Syntax & semantics*, vol. 3, *Speech acts*. New York: Academic Press.

Grice, H. P. 1989. *Studies in the way of words*. Cambridge, MA: Harvard University Press.

Hadfield, G. K. 1999. A coordination model of the sexual division of labor. *Journal of Economic Behavior & Organization*, 40, 125–53.

Haidt, J. 2016. Why universities must choose one telos: Truth or social justice. *Heterodox Academy*, Oct. 16. https://heterodoxacademy.org/blog/one-telos-truth-or-social-justice-2/.

Haidt, J. 2024. *The anxious generation: How the great rewiring of childhood is causing an epidemic of mental illness*. New York: Penguin Random House.

Halpern, J. Y., & Moses, Y. 1990. Knowledge and common knowledge in a distributed environment. *Journal of the Association for Computing Machinery*, 37, 549–87.

Hanson, R. 2002. Disagreement is unpredictable. *Economics Letters*, 77, 365–69.

Hanson, R. 2006. Uncommon priors require origin disputes. *Theory and Decision*, 61, 319–28.

Harman, G. 1977. Review of J. Bennett's "Linguistic behavior." *Language*, 53, 417–24.

Harsanyi, J. C. 1983. Bayesian decision theory, subjective and objective probabilities, and acceptance of empirical hypotheses. *Synthese*, 57, 341–65.

Hathaway, O., & Shapiro, C. 2017. *The internationalists: How a radical plan to outlaw war remade our world*. New York: Simon & Schuster.

Henrich, J. 2006. Costly punishment across human societies. *Science, 312,* 1767–70.

Henrich, J. 2020. *The WEIRDest people in the world: How the West became psychologically peculiar and particularly prosperous.* New York: Farrar, Straus & Giroux.

Hobbes, T. 1651/1957. *Leviathan.* New York: Oxford University Press.

Hoffman, M., Hilbe, C., & Nowak, M. A. 2018. The signal-burying game can explain why we obscure positive traits and good deeds. *Nature Human Behaviour, 2,* 397–404.

Hoffman, M., & Yoeli, E. 2022. *Hidden games: The surprising power of game theory to explain irrational human behavior.* New York: Basic Books.

Hofstadter, D. R. 1985. Dilemmas for superrational thinkers, leading up to a luring lottery. In *Metamagical themas: Questing for the essence of mind and pattern.* New York: Basic Books.

Holtgraves, T. M. 2002. *Language as social action: Social psychology and language use.* Mahwah, NJ: Erlbaum Associates.

Holzinger, K. 2008. *Transnational common goods: Strategic constellations, collective action problems, and multi-level provision.* New York: Palgrave MacMillan.

Honeycutt, N., Stevens, S. T., & Kaufmann, E. 2023. *The academic mind in 2022: What faculty think about free expression and academic freedom on campus.* Foundation for Individual Rights and Expression. https://www.thefire.org/research-learn/academic-mind-2022-what-faculty-think-about-free-expression-and-academic-freedom.

Hooven, C. K. 2023. Academic freedom is social justice: Sex, gender, and cancel culture on campus. *Archives of Sexual Behavior, 52,* 35–41.

Horowitz, D. L. 2001. *The deadly ethnic riot.* Berkeley: University of California Press.

Huang, L., DeScioli, P., & Murad, Z. 2021. Pulling for the team: Competition between political partisans. *Evolutionary Psychological Science, 7,* 97–105.

Hudson, R. 1996. The difficulty of (so-called) self-embedded structures. *UCS Working Papers in Linguistics, 8,* 1–33.

Hughes, C. 2024. *The end of race politics: Arguments for a colorblind America.* New York: Penguin Random House.

Hume, D. 1739/2000. *A treatise of human nature.* New York: Oxford University Press.

Hunt, M. 1999. *The new know-nothings: The political foes of the scientific study of human nature.* New Brunswick, NJ: Transaction Publishers.

Ichikawa, J. J., & Steup, M. 2018. The analysis of knowledge. In E. N. Zalta, ed., *The Stanford Encyclopedia of Philosophy* (summer 2018 ed.).

Jacobs, A. J. 2007. I think you're fat. *Esquire, 148,* 120.

Johnson, D. D. P. 2004. *Overconfidence and war: The havoc and glory of positive illusions.* Cambridge, MA: Harvard University Press.

Jones, P., & Arnold, A. 2024. *Reluctance to discuss controversial issues on campus: Raw numbers from the 2023 campus expression survey.* New York: Heterodox Academy.

Joubert, L. 1579/1980. *Treatise on laughter*, trans. G. D. de Rocher. Birmingham: University of Alabama Press.

Kagan, D. 1995. *On the origins of war and the preservation of peace*. New York: Doubleday.

Kanin, E. J. 1982. Female rape fantasies: A victimization study. *Victimology*, 7, 114.

Kaufmann, E. 2021. *Academic freedom in crisis: Punishment, political discrimination, and self-censorship*. https://cspicenter.org/reports/academicfreedom/.

Keltner, D. 1996. Evidence for the distinctness of embarrassment, shame, and guilt: A study of recalled antecedents and facial expressions of emotion. *Cognition & Emotion*, 10, 155–72.

Keltner, D. 2023. *Awe: The new science of everyday wonder and how it can transform your life*. New York: Penguin.

Keltner, D., & Buswell, B. N. 1997. Embarrassment: Its distinct form and appeasement functions. *Psychological Bulletin*, 122, 250–70.

Keltner, D., & Cordaro, D. T. 2017. Understanding multimodal emotional expressions: Recent advances in basic emotion theory. In J.-M. Fernández-Dols & J. A. Russell, eds., *The science of facial expressions*. New York: Oxford University Press.

Keltner, D., Sauter, D., Tracy, J., & Cowen, A. 2019. Emotional expression: Advances in basic emotion theory. *Journal of Nonverbal Behavior*, 43, 133–60.

Kenrick, D. T., & Sheets, V. 1994. Homicidal fantasies. *Ethology and Sociobiology*, 14, 231–46.

Keyes, R. 2006. *The Quote Verifier—Who said what, where and when*. New York: St. Martin's.

Keynes, J. M. 1936/2016. *The general theory of employment, interest, and money*. Houghton Mifflin Harcourt.

Kim, S. H., Smith, R. H., & Brigham, N. L. 1998. Effects of power imbalance and the presence of third parties on reactions to harm: Upward and downward revenge. *Personality and Social Psychology Bulletin*, 24, 353–61.

Kinderman, P., Dunbar, R., & Bentall, R. P. 1998. Theory-of-mind deficits and causal attributions. *British Journal of Psychology*, 89, 191–204.

King, G., Pan, J., & Roberts, M. E. 2014. Reverse-engineering censorship in China: Randomized experimentation and participant observation. *Science*, 345, 1251722.

Kobayashi, H., & Kohshima, S. 2001. Unique morphology of the human eye and its adaptive meaning: Comparative studies on external morphology of the primate eye. *Journal of Human Evolution*, 40, 419–35.

Koestler, A. 1964. *The act of creation*. New York: Dell.

Konnikova, M. 2016. *The confidence game: Why we fall for it . . . every time*. New York: Viking.

Konotey-Ahulu, F. I. D. 2004. Blushing in black skin. *Journal of Cosmetic Dermatology*, 2, 59–60.

Kors, A. C., & Silverglate, H. A. 1998. *The shadow university: The betrayal of liberty on America's campuses*. New York: Free Press.

Krasnow, M. M., Cosmides, L., Pedersen, E. J., & Tooby, J. 2012. What are punishment and reputation for? *PLoS ONE*, 7, e45662.

Krasnow, M. M., Delton, A. W., Tooby, J., & Cosmides, L. 2013. Meeting now suggests we will meet again: Implications for debates on the evolution of cooperation. *Scientific Reports*, 3.

Kret, M. E., Prochazkova, E., Sterck, E. H. M., & Clay, Z. 2020. Emotional expressions in human and non-human great apes. *Neuroscience & Biobehavioral Reviews*, 115, 378–95.

Kuran, T. 1989. Sparks and prairie fires: A theory of unanticipated political revolution. *Public Choice*, 61, 41–74.

Kurzban, R. 2011. *Why everyone (else) is a hypocrite*. Princeton, NJ: Princeton University Press.

Lakoff, G., & Johnson, M. 1980. *Metaphors we live by*. Chicago: University of Chicago Press.

Latané, B., & Darley, J. M. 1970. *The unresponsive bystander: Why doesn't he help?* New York: Appleton-Century-Crofts.

Leary, M. R., Britt, T. W., Cutlip, W. D., & Templeton, J. L. 1992. Social blushing. *Psychological Bulletin*, 112, 446–60.

Leary, M. R., & Meadows, S. 1991. Predictors, elicitors, and concomitants of social blushing. *Journal of Personality and Social Psychology*, 60, 254–62.

Lebow, R. N. 2010. *Why nations fight: Past and future motives for war*. New York: Cambridge University Press.

Lederman, H. 2018. Uncommon knowledge. *Mind*, 127, 1069–1105.

Lee, J. J., & Pinker, S. 2010. Rationales for indirect speech: The theory of the strategic speaker. *Psychological Review*, 117, 785–807.

Leitenberg, H., & Henning, K. 1995. Sexual fantasy. *Psychological Bulletin*, 117, 469–96.

Levinson, S. C. 1983. *Pragmatics*. New York: Cambridge University Press.

Lewis, D. K. 1969. *Convention: A philosophical study*. Cambridge, MA: Harvard University Press.

Liebenberg, L. 2013. *The origin of science: The evolutionary roots of scientific reasoning and its implications for tracking science*, 2nd ed. https://www.cybertracker.org /downloads/tracking/Liebenberg-2013-The-Origin-of-Science.pdf.

Lieberman, R. 2001. A tale of two countries: The politics of color blindness in France and the United States. *French Politics, Culture and Society*, 19, 32–59.

Liu, B. S., & Ditto, P. H. 2013. What dilemma? Moral evaluation shapes factual belief. *Social Psychological and Personality Science*, 4, 316–23.

Lohmann, S. 1994. The dynamics of informational cascades: The Monday demonstrations in Leipzig, East Germany, 1989–91. *World Politics*, 47, 42–101.

Luce, R. D., & Raiffa, H. 1957. *Games and decisions: Introduction and critical survey*. New York: Dover.

Lukianoff, G. 2012. *Unlearning liberty: Campus censorship and the end of American debate*. New York: Encounter Books.

Lukianoff, G. 2014. *Freedom from speech*. New York: Encounter Books.

MacAskill, W. 2015. *Doing good better: Effective altruism and how you can make a difference*. New York: Penguin.

Maimonides. 1180/1993. *Mishneh Torah: The book of mitzvoth*, trans. E. Touger. New York: Moznaim.

Malamuth, N. M. 1981. Rape proclivity among males. *Journal of Social Issues*, 37, 138–57.

Manguel, A. 2023. *Maimonides: Faith in reason*. New Haven: Yale University Press.

Marie, A., & Petersen, M. B. 2024. Moralization of rationality can stimulate sharing of hostile and false news on social media, but intellectual humility inhibits it. *Political Communication*, 1–28.

Massenkoff, M., DeScioli, P., Thomas, K. A., & Pinker, S. 2025. What happens in vagueness. Naval Postgraduate School.

Maynard Smith, J. 1988. *Games, sex, and evolution*. New York: Harvester Wheatsheaf.

McAdams, R. H. 2009. Beyond the Prisoners' Dilemma: Coordination, game theory, and law. *Southern California Law Review*, 82, 209–58.

McCloud, S. 2006. *Making comics: Storytelling secrets of comics, manga, and graphic novels*. New York: William Morrow.

McCullough, M. E. 2008. *Beyond revenge: The evolution of the forgiveness instinct*. San Francisco: Jossey-Bass.

McCullough, M. E., Kurzban, R. O., & Tabak, B. A. 2011. Cognitive systems for revenge and forgiveness. *Behavioral and Brain Sciences*, 36, 1–15.

McElree, B. 2000. Sentence comprehension is mediated by content-addressable memory structures. *Journal of Psycholinguistic Research*, 29, 111–23.

Mchangama, J. 2022. *Free speech: A history from Socrates to social media*. New York: Basic Books.

Mehta, J., Starmer, C., & Sugden, R. 1994. Focal points in pure coordination games: An experimental investigation. *Theory and Decision*, 36, 163–85.

Mercier, H. 2020. *Not born yesterday: The science of who we trust and what we believe*. Princeton, NJ: Princeton University Press.

Mercier, H., & Sperber, D. 2011. Why do humans reason? Arguments for an argumentative theory. *Behavioral and Brain Sciences, 34,* 57–111.

Michel, J.-B., Shen, Y. K., Aiden, A. P., Veres, A., Gray, M. K., et al. 2010. Quantitative analysis of culture using millions of digitized books. *Science, 331,* 167–82.

Milgram, S. 1974. *Obedience to authority: An experimental view.* New York: Harper & Row.

Milgrom, P., & Stokey, N. 1982. Information, trade, and common knowledge. *Journal of Economic Theory, 26,* 17–27.

Mill, J. S. 1859. On liberty. https://www.econlib.org/library/Mill/mlLbty.html.

Miller, G. A. 1956. The magical number seven, plus or minus two: Some limits on our capacity for processing information. *Psychological Review, 63,* 81–96.

Miller, G. A., & Chomsky, N. 1963. Finitary models of language users. In R. D. Luce, R. R. Bush, and E. Galanter, eds., *Handbook of mathematical psychology,* vol. 2. New York: Wiley.

Monderer, D., & Samet, D. 1989. Approximating common knowledge with common belief. *Games and Economic Behavior, 1,* 170–90.

Morris, S. 2002. Coordination, communication, and common knowledge: A retrospective on the electronic-mail game. *Oxford Review of Economic Policy, 18,* 433–45.

Morris, S., & Shin, H. S. 1998. Unique equilibrium in a model of self-fulfilling currency attacks. *American Economic Review, 88,* 587–97.

Morton, J., Hammersley, R. H., & Bekerian, D. A. 1985. Headed records: A model for memory and its failures. *Cognition, 20,* 1–23.

Mueller, J. 2006. *Overblown: How politicians and the terrorism industry inflate national security threats, and why we believe them.* New York: Free Press.

Mueller, J. 2010. *Atomic obsession: Nuclear alarmism from Hiroshima to al-Qaeda.* New York: Oxford University Press.

Mueller, J. 2018. *Embracing threatlessness: US military spending, Newt Gingrich, and the Costa Rica option.* Abingdon, UK: Routledge.

Mueller, J. 2021. *The stupidity of war: American foreign policy and the case for complacency.* New York: Cambridge University Press.

Munroe, R. P. N.d. Blue eyes: The hardest logic puzzle in the world. *XKCD.* https://xkcd.com/blue_eyes.html.

Nagel, R. 1995. Unraveling in guessing games: An experimental study. *American Economic Review, 85,* 1313–26.

Newman, G. E., & Cain, D. M. 2014. Tainted altruism: When doing some good is evaluated as worse than doing no good at all. *Psychological Science, 25,* 648–55.

Nisbett, R. E., & Cohen, D. 1996. *Culture of honor: The psychology of violence in the South.* New York: HarperCollins.

Noë, R., & Hammerstein, P. 1995. Biological markets. *Trends in Ecology & Evolution (Amsterdam)*, *10*, 336–39.

Noelle-Neumann, E. 1974. The spiral of silence: A theory of public opinion. *Journal of Communication*, *24*, 43–51.

Nozick, R. 1963. *The normative theory of individual choice*. PhD diss., Princeton University.

Nuland, S. B. 2005. *Maimonides*. New York: Schocken.

O'Neill, B. 1999. *Honor symbols and war*. Ann Arbor: University of Michigan Press.

Onishi, K. H., & Baillargeon, R. 2005. Do 15-month-old infants understand false beliefs? *Science*, *308*, 255–58.

Orwell, G. 1946/1970. Politics and the English language, In *A collection of essays*. Boston: Mariner Books.

Ostrom, E. 1990. *Governing the commons: The evolution of institutions for collective action*. New York: Cambridge University Press.

Palmer, C. J., Bracken, S. G., Otsuka, Y., & Clifford, C. W. G. 2022. Is there a "zone of eye contact" within the borders of the face? *Cognition*, *220*, 104981.

Pallotta, D. 2009. *Uncharitable: How restraints on nonprofits undermine their potential*. Lebanon, NH: University Press of New England.

Parvulescu, A. 2010. *Laughter: Notes on a passion*. Cambridge, MA: MIT Press.

Peacocke, C. 2005. Joint attention: Its nature, reflexivity, and relation to common knowledge. In N. Eilan, C. Hoerl, T. McCormack, & J. Roessler, eds., *Joint attention: Communication and other minds*. New York: Oxford University Press.

Perner, J., & Wimmer, H. 1985. "John thinks that Mary thinks that . . . ": Attribution of second-order beliefs by five- to 10-year-old children. *Journal of Experimental Child Psychology*, *39*, 437–71.

Piaget, J. 1947/1972. *The psychology of intelligence*. Totowa, NJ: Littlefield, Adams.

Pinker, S. 1994/2007. *The language instinct*. New York: HarperCollins.

Pinker, S. 1997/2009. *How the mind works*. New York: W. W. Norton.

Pinker, S. 1998a. Obituary: Roger Brown. *Cognition*, *66*, 199–213.

Pinker, S. 1998b. Still relevant after all these years (review of Charles Darwin's "The expression of the emotions in man and animals," 3rd ed.). *Science*, *281*, 522–23.

Pinker, S. 1999/2011. *Words and rules: The ingredients of language*. New York: HarperCollins.

Pinker, S. 2002/2016. *The blank slate: The modern denial of human nature*. New York: Penguin.

Pinker, S. 2006. Block that metaphor! (review of George Lakoff's "Whose freedom?"). *New Republic*, Oct. 9.

Pinker, S. 2007. *The stuff of thought: Language as a window into human nature.* New York: Viking.

Pinker, S. 2011. *The better angels of our nature: Why violence has declined.* New York: Viking.

Pinker, S. 2014. *The sense of style: The thinking person's guide to writing in the 21st century.* New York: Penguin.

Pinker, S. 2019. A linguist's guide to quid pro quo. *New York Times*, Oct. 7.

Pinker, S. 2021. *Rationality: What it is, why it seems scarce, why it matters.* New York: Penguin.

Pinker, S. 2023. A five-point plan to save Harvard from itself. *Boston Globe*, Dec. 11.

Pinker, S., & Birdsong, D. 1979. Speakers' sensitivity to rules of frozen word order. *Journal of Verbal Learning and Verbal Behavior, 18,* 497–508.

Pinker, S., & Bloom, P. 1990. Natural language and natural selection. *Behavioral and Brain Sciences, 13,* 707–84.

Pinker, S., & Madras, B. 2023. New faculty-led organization at Harvard will defend academic freedom. *Boston Globe,* Apr. 12.

Pinker, S., Nowak, M. A., & Lee, J. J. 2008. The logic of indirect speech. *Proceedings of the National Academy of Sciences, 105,* 833–38.

Pinker, S., & Prince, A. 1996. The nature of human concepts: Evidence from an unusual source. *Communication and Cognition, 29,* 307–61.

Pinsof, D. 2024. The evolution of social paradoxes. Unpublished manuscript.

Posner, R. A. 1980. A theory of primitive society, with special reference to law. *Journal of Law & Economics, 23,* 1–53.

Poundstone, W. 1992. *Prisoner's dilemma: John von Neumann, game theory, and the puzzle of the bomb.* New York: Anchor.

Powers, K. E., & Altman, D. 2023. The psychology of coercion failure: How reactance explains resistance to threats. *American Journal of Political Science, 67,* 221–38.

Provine, R. R. 2001. *Laughter: A scientific investigation.* New York: Penguin.

Provine, R. R. 2012. *Curious behavior: Yawning, laughing, hiccupping, and beyond.* Cambridge, MA: Harvard University Press.

Qu, F., Yan, W. J., Chen, Y. H., Li, K., Zhang, H., et al. 2017. "You should have seen the look on your face . . . ": Self-awareness of facial expressions. *Frontiers in Psychology, 8,* 832.

Raemon. 2017. What exactly is the "Rationality Community"? *LessWrong,* Apr. 9. https://www.lesswrong.com/posts/s8yvtCbbZW2S4WnhE/what-exactly-is-the-rationality-community.

Rapoport, A. 1967. Exploiter, leader, hero, and martyr: The four archetypes of the 2x2 game. *Behavioral Science, 12,* 81–84.

Reed, L. I., DeScioli, P., & Pinker, S. 2014. The commitment function of angry facial expressions. *Psychological Science*, *25*, 1511–17.

Roberts, M. E. 2018. *Censored: Distraction and diversion inside China's great firewall.* Princeton, NJ: Princeton University Press.

Robertson, T. E., Sznycer, D., Delton, A. W., Tooby, J., & Cosmides, L. 2018. The true trigger of shame: Social devaluation is sufficient, wrongdoing is unnecessary. *Evolution and Human Behavior*, *39*, 566–73.

Rogoff, B., Sellers, M. J., Pirrotta, S., Fox, N., & White, S. H. 1975. Age of assignment of roles and responsibilities to children: A cross-cultural survey. *Human Development*, *18*, 353–69.

Rosenthal, E. C. 2011. *The Complete Idiot's Guide to Game Theory.* New York: Penguin.

Rousseau, J.-J. 1755/2022. *Discours sur l'origine et les fondements de l'inégalité parmi les hommes.* Paris: J'ai lu.

Rozin, P. 1996. Towards a psychology of food and eating: From motivation to module to model to marker, morality, meaning, and metaphor. *Current Directions in Psychological Science*, *5*, 18–24.

Rubinstein, A. 1989. The electronic mail game: Strategic behavior under "almost common knowledge." *American Economic Review*, *79*, 385–91.

Savolainen, J. 2023. Unequal treatment under the flaw: Race, crime and retractions. *Current Psychology*, *43*, 16002–14.

Schelling, T. C. 1960. *The strategy of conflict.* Cambridge, MA: Harvard University Press.

Schelling, T. C. 1996. Coping rationally with lapses from rationality. *Eastern Economic Journal*, *22*, 251–69.

Schelling, T. C. 2005. An astonishing sixty years: The legacy of Hiroshima. In K. Grandin, ed., *Les Prix Nobel.* Stockholm: Nobel Foundation.

Schiffer, S. R. 1972. *Meaning.* New York: Oxford University Press.

Schmidt, P. L. 2022. *Harvard's quixotic pursuit of a new science: The rise and fall of the Department of Social Relations.* Lanham, MD: Rowman & Littlefield.

Simler, K., & Hanson, R. 2018. *The elephant in the brain: Hidden motives in everyday life.* New York: Oxford University Press.

Singer, P. 2015. *The most good you can do: How effective altruism is changing ideas about living ethically.* New Haven, CT: Yale University Press.

Skyrms, B. 2004. *The Stag Hunt and the evolution of social structure.* New York: Cambridge University Press.

Smaldino, P. E., Flamson, T. J., & McElreath, R. 2018. The evolution of covert signaling. *Scientific Reports*, *8*, 4905–10.

Smith, N. V., ed. 1982. *Mutual knowledge.* New York: Academic Press.

Solan, L. M., & Tiersman, P. M. 2010. *Speaking of crime: The language of criminal justice.* Chicago: University of Chicago Press.

Solomon, R. L. 1980. The opponent-process theory of acquired motivation. *American Psychologist, 35,* 691–712.

Spence, A. M. 2001. Signaling in retrospect and the informational structure of markets. Nobel Lecture. https://www.nobelprize.org/uploads/2018/06/spence-lecture.pdf.

Stalnaker, R. C. 1978. Assertion. In P. Cole, ed., *Syntax and semantics 9: Pragmatics.* New York: Academic Press.

Stalnaker, R. C. 2002. Common ground. *Linguistics and Philosophy, 25,* 701–21.

Stein, D. J., & Bouwer, C. 1997. Blushing and social phobia: A neuroethological speculation. *Medical Hypotheses, 49,* 101–8.

Stephen, J. F. 1883/2022. *A history of the criminal law of England,* vol.1. New York: Cambridge University Press.

Strassberg, D. S., & Locker, L. K. 1998. Force in women's sexual fantasies. *Archives of Sexual Behavior, 27,* 403–14.

Sugden, R. 1995. A theory of focal points. *Economic Journal, 105,* 533–50.

Suler, J. 2004. The online disinhibition effect. *CyberPsychology & Behavior, 7,* 321–26.

Summers, L. H. 2000. International financial crises: Causes, prevention, and cures. *American Economic Review, 90,* 1–16.

Sunstein, C. R. 2023. Free speech on campus? Thirty-seven questions (and almost as many answers). https://papers.ssrn.com/sol3/papers.cfm?abstract_id=4674320.

Sunstein, C. R. 2024. *Campus free speech: A pocket guide.* Cambridge, MA: Harvard University Press.

Symons, D. 1979. *The evolution of human sexuality.* New York: Oxford University Press.

Symons, D. 1980. Précis and multiple book review of "The evolution of human sexuality." *Behavioral and Brain Sciences, 3,* 171–214.

Symons, D. 1992. On the use and misuse of Darwinism in the study of human behavior. In J. H. Barkow, L. Cosmides, & J. Tooby, eds., *The adapted mind: Evolutionary psychology and the generation of culture.* New York: Oxford University Press.

Sznycer, D., Al-Shawaf, L., Bereby-Meyer, Y., Curry, O. S., De Smet, D., et al. 2017. Cross-cultural regularities in the cognitive architecture of pride. *Proceedings of the National Academy of Sciences, 114,* 1874–79.

Sznycer, D., Delton, A. W., Robertson, T. E., Cosmides, L., & Tooby, J. 2019. The ecological rationality of helping others: Potential helpers integrate cues of recipients' need and willingness to sacrifice. *Evolution and Human Behavior, 40,* 34–45.

Tannenwald, N. 2005. Stigmatizing the bomb: Origins of the nuclear taboo. *International Security, 29,* 5–49.

Teixeira da Silva, J. 2021. How to shape academic freedom in the digital age? Are the retractions of opinionated papers a prelude to "cancel culture" in academia? *Current Research in Behavioral Sciences*, 2, 100035.

Tetlock, P. E. 1999. Coping with tradeoffs: Psychological constraints and political implications. In A. Lupia, M. McCubbins, & S. Popkin, eds., *Political reasoning and choice*. Berkeley: University of California Press.

Tetlock, P. E., & Gardner, D. 2015. *Superforecasting: The art and science of prediction*. New York: Crown.

Thaler, R. H. 2016. Behavioral economics: Past, present, and future. *American Economic Review*, 106, 1577–1600.

Thomas, K. A., De Freitas, J., DeScioli, P., & Pinker, S. 2016. Recursive mentalizing and common knowledge in the bystander effect. *Journal of Experimental Psychology: General*, 145, 621–29.

Thomas, K. A., DeScioli, P., Haque, O. S., & Pinker, S. 2014. The psychology of coordination and common knowledge. *Journal of Personality and Social Psychology*, 107, 657–76.

Thomas, K. A., DeScioli, P., & Pinker, S. 2018. Common knowledge, coordination, and the logic of self-conscious emotions. *Evolution and Human Behavior*, 39, 179–90.

Thorstenson, C. A., Pazda, A. D., & Lichtenfeld, S. 2020. Facial blushing influences perceived embarrassment and related social functional evaluations. *Cognition and Emotion*, 34, 413–26.

Tomasello, M., Carpenter, M., Call, J., Behne, T., & Moll, H. 2005. Understanding and sharing intentions: The origins of cultural cognition. *Behavioral and Brain Sciences*, 28, 675–91.

Tooby, J. 2017. Coalitional instincts. *Edge*. https://www.edge.org/response-detail/27168.

Tooby, J. 2020. Evolutionary psychology as the crystalizing core of a unified modern social science. *Evolutionary Behavioral Sciences*, 14, 390–403.

Tooby, J., & Cosmides, L. 1992. Ecological rationality and the multimodular mind: Grounding normative theories in adaptive problems. Center for Evolutionary Psychology, University of California, Santa Barbara, https://www.cep.ucsb.edu/papers/1992ToobyCosmides_EcologicalRationality.pdf.

Tooby, J., & Cosmides, L. 1996. Friendship and the banker's paradox: Other pathways to the evolution of adaptations for altruism. *Proceedings of the British Academy*, 88, 119–43.

Tooby, J., & Cosmides, L. 2010. Groups in mind: The coalitional roots of war and morality. In H. Høgh-Olesen, ed., *Human morality and sociality: Evolutionary and comparative perspectives*. New York: Palgrave MacMillan.

Tooby, J., Cosmides, L., & Price, M. E. 2006. Cognitive adaptations for *n*-person exchange: The evolutionary roots of organizational behavior. *Managerial and Decision Economics*, 27, 103–29.

Tracy, J. L., & Robins, R. W. 2004. Putting the self into self-conscious emotions: A theoretical model. *Psychological Inquiry, 15*, 103–25.

Trivers, R. L. 1971. The evolution of reciprocal altruism. *Quarterly Review of Biology, 46*, 35–57.

Trivers, R. L. 2011. *Deceit and self-deception*. New York: Penguin.

Trivers, R. L., & Newton, H. P. 1982. The crash of Flight 90: Doomed by self-deception? *Science Digest*, 66–68.

Troje, N. F. 2023. Depth from motion parallax: Deictic consistency, eye contact, and a serious problem with Zoom. *Journal of Vision, 23*.

Tversky, A., & Kahneman, D. 1974. Judgment under uncertainty: Heuristics and biases. *Science, 185*, 1124–31.

Twain, M. 1897/1989. *Following the equator*. New York: Dover.

Valdesolo, P., & DeSteno, D. 2008. The duality of virtue: Deconstructing the moral hypocrite. *Journal of Experimental Social Psychology, 44*, 1334–38.

Valle, A., Massaro, D., Castelli, I., & Marchetti, A. 2015. Theory of mind development in adolescence and early adulthood: The growing complexity of recursive thinking ability. *Europe's Journal of Psychology, 11*, 112–24.

Van Boven, L. 2000. Pluralistic ignorance and political correctness: The case of affirmative action. *Political Psychology, 21*, 267–76.

Van Vugt, M. 2006. Evolutionary origins of leadership and followership. *Personality and Social Psychology Review, 10*, 354–71.

Vanderschraaf, P., & Sillari, G. 2023. Common knowledge. In E. N. Zalta, ed., *The Stanford Encyclopedia of Philosophy* (winter 2023 ed.).

VanderWeele, T. J., & Brooks, A. C. 2023. A public health approach to negative news media: The 3-to-1 solution. *American Journal of Health Promotion, 37*, 447–49.

Vingerhoets, A. 2013. *Why only humans weep: Unravelling the mysteries of tears*. New York: Oxford University Press.

Wegner, D. 1989. *White bears and other unwanted thoughts: Suppression, obsession, and the psychology of mental control*. New York: Guilford.

Willer, R., Kuwabara, K., & Macy, M. 2009. The false enforcement of unpopular norms. *American Journal of Sociology, 115*, 451–90.

Williams, D. 2022. Signalling, commitment, and strategic absurdities. *Mind & Language, 37*, 1011–29.

Wilson, W. 2007. The winning weapon? Rethinking nuclear weapons in light of Hiroshima. *International Security, 31*, 162–79.

Wimmer, H., & Perner, J. 1983. Beliefs about beliefs: Representation and constraining function of wrong beliefs in young children's understanding of deception. *Cognition, 13*, 103–28.

Winokur, J. 1992. *The portable curmudgeon.* New York: Plume.

Wouters, C. 2007. *Informalization: Manners and emotions since 1890.* Los Angeles: Sage.

Yglesias, M. 2020. Defund police is a bad idea, not a bad slogan. *Slow Boring*, Dec. 7. https://www.slowboring.com/p/defund-police-is-a-bad-idea-not-a.

Yoeli, E., Burum, B., Dalkiran, N. A., Nowak, M., & Hoffman, M. 2022. The emergence of categorical norms. https://www.researchsquare.com/article/rs-2050019/v1.

Zacher, M. W. 2001. The territorial integrity norm: International boundaries and the use of force. *International Organization*, 55, 215–50.

INDEX

NOTE: Page references in *italics* refer to figures.

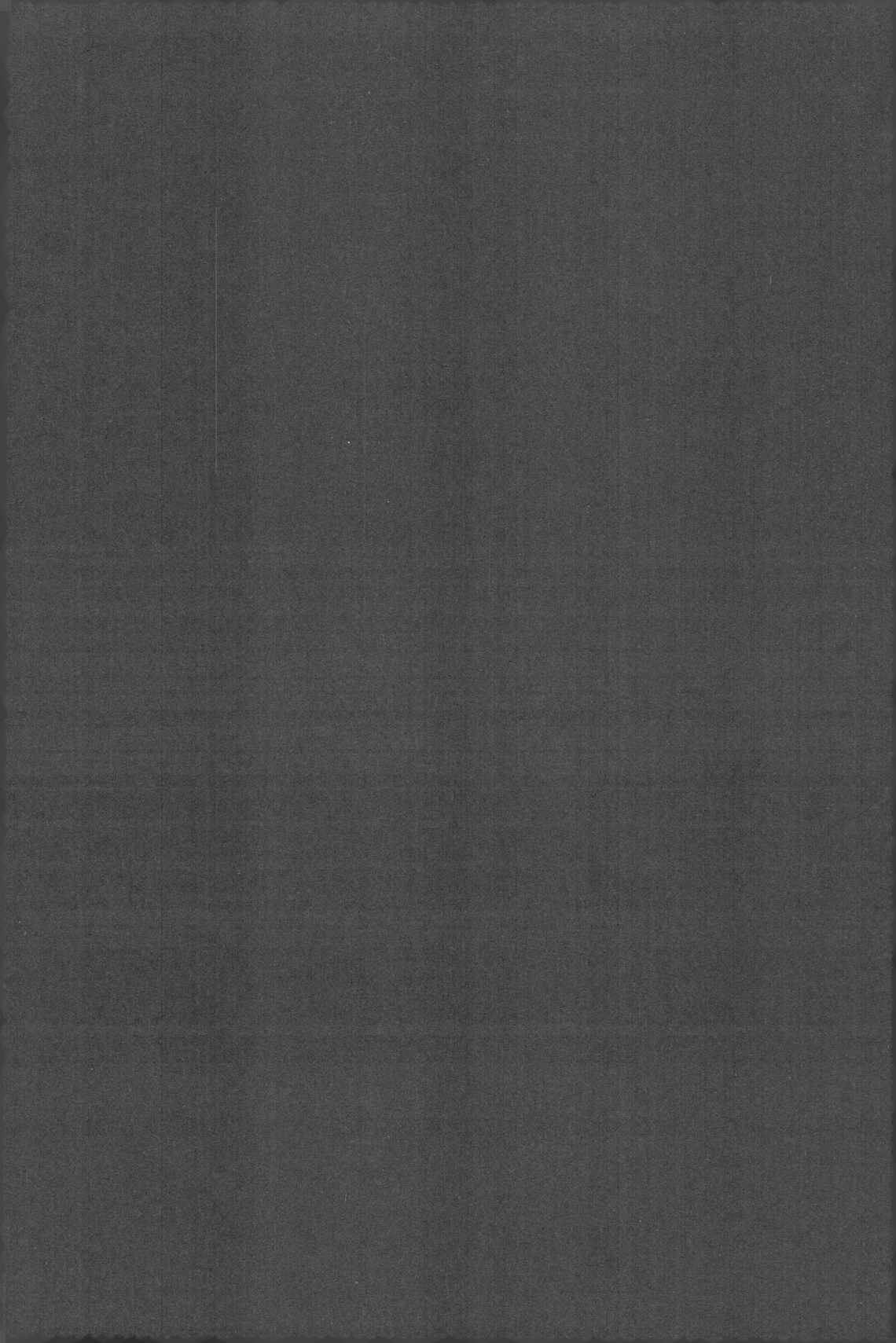